STOLEN IMAGES

Pagan Symbolism and Christianity

Peter Knight

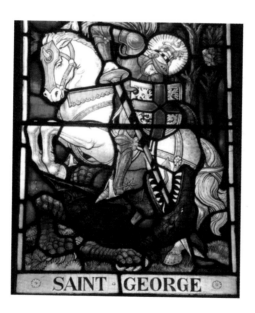

SAINT · GEORGE

Best wishes
Pete K

Stone Seeker Publishing
Wiltshire UK
Honouring ancient wisdom and the Earth

Published Beltaine 2015

Stone Seeker Publishing,
Calne, Wiltshire, SN11 9AT, UK
www.stoneseeker.net
email: stoneseeker@waitrose.com

ISBN: 978-0-9560342-4-3

Cover images:
Front cover: left – St John the Divine, Shillingstone, Dorset; centre – The Eye of Horus
(Egyptian); right – Green Man, Cattistock, Dorset. **Back cover:** top left – Isis & Horus,
Walters Museum, Baltimore; top centre – St George and the dragon, Broadclyst, Devon;
top right: Jesus and Mary Magdalene, Kilmore, Mull; centre – triple spiral at Newgrange,
Ireland; bottom – Sheela-na-gig, Kilpeck, Herefordshire.

Title page: George and the Dragon, Broadclyst, Devon.

Cover design: Peter Knight ©

 Printed and bound by CPI Antony Rowe, Chippenham, on FSC paper.

Also by Peter Knight

Ancient Stones of Dorset - 1996
Sacred Dorset: On the Path of the Dragon - 1998
Dorset Pilgrimages: A Millennium Handbook (with Mike Power) - 2000
Earth Mysteries: An Illustrated Encyclopaedia of Britain (CD-ROM) - 2004
Thirteen Moons: Conversations with the Goddess - 2007 (& 2012 ed.)
The Wessex Astrum: Sacred Geometry in a Mystical Landscape (with Toni Perrott) – 2008
West Kennet Long Barrow: Landscape, Shamans and the Cosmos – 2011
The Cerne Giant: Landscape, Gods and the Stargate – 2013
Calne – Gateway to Ancient Wiltshire (with Sue Wallace) - 2014

Signed and dedicated copies of most of these are available from the author.

Website: www.stoneseeker.net
Follow Peter Knight on FaceBook

Blue dragon, Golden Mile, Edinburgh

3

Contents

Mary Magdalene, RC Church, Edinburgh

'The great thing about myths is that they are always pregnant with new meanings'

(Tim Freke and Peter Gandy, *Jesus and the Goddess*)

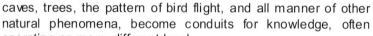

1. The Nature of Symbols

The Birth of Symbolism

The story of symbolism takes us on a journey back to observations made by early Man that the cosmos was full of natural objects and processes that were seen as having spiritual meaning, to the extent that they were endowed with supernatural attributes. These may have been such things as rocks that resembled animals, stalagmites that mimicked the human phallus, or faces that peered out of the bark of trees. Today, science interprets these as mere co-incidences, inevitable instances of pure chance. A non-scientific, more shamanic, mindset suggests that *everything that exists or is observed may hold a message.* The mystics and shamans of old would not have regarded simulacra as coincidences, for the concept of *'chance'* cannot exist in a world that is the consequence of the *divine* processes of cause and effect. Hills, stones,

caves, trees, the pattern of bird flight, and all manner of other natural phenomena, become conduits for knowledge, often operating on many different levels.

A natural 'omen' can be multifaceted, meaning different things to different people, as interpretations of what was actually observed varies, such as unexplained light phenomena in the sky; one man's UFO is another man's angel. Cultural diversity also ensures that a light seen as a fairy in one part of the world may be interpreted as a dragon in another culture. And none of these interpretations would necessarily be 'wrong'; for the beauty of symbols is that they really are in the eye of the beholder. Symbols can be used to articulate love, joy, artistic expression, or, conversely, to control entire nations. Symbolism has enabled Man to pass down his ideals, histories, mythologies and experiences, in both art and science.

During prehistory, concepts gradually developed to embrace and develop imagery as tools to potentially reveal and explain cosmologies, to evolve creation myths, and to interpret the workings of the everyday world; Man was indeed both creating and attuning to collective archetypes (Jung 1964). Myths could be birthed by symbols, and, conversely, mythologies were constructed to amazingly complex degrees through symbolism. Yet a motif in itself carries no intrinsic meaning, for it is human *interaction* that gives it significance. Every culture has developed symbolism, to the extent that Confucius said, *'Signs and symbols rule the world, not words or laws'.* For example, few can deny the *'pulling power'* of the altruistic Jesus hung on the cross.

From the onset, we must make a clear distinction between a symbol and a sign. A sign holds no mystery and has but one meaning (except perhaps for a learner driver seeking to absorb road signs in the Highway code!). They are designed to be appreciated and understood in a split second, regardless of language or belief system. Symbols, on the other hand, may be embellished with endless meanings, interpretations and mystery, often beyond the grasp of the rational, logical mind. They can connect the ethereal and material worlds, and could be described as *visual shorthand,* acting as a conduit to unite our outer sensory and inner subconscious worlds. Joseph Campbell regarded symbols as, *'... an energy-evoking and directing agent'.* Carl Jung affirmed that, *'... an image is symbolic when it implies something more than its obvious and immediate meaning... as a mind explores a symbol, it is led to ideas that lie beyond the grasp of reason'* (Jung 1964). A symbol may make a concept less complicated and easier to embrace than pages of dialogue – a picture really does have the capacity to tell a thousand words. When symbols and myths are combined, the potential to comprehend the irrational and spiritual is greatly heightened, and can help navigate the psycho-spiritual landscapes beyond which we normally tread. To literalists, symbols and myths have but one meaning; to Gnostics, they are tools for self-knowing. For myths should not be regarded as trivial stories for spiritual novices, but rather pathways to deeper understandings; whenever we think we have 'decoded' a myth, we have not actually deprived it of its meaning, but rather have found a doorway that may take it to a whole new level.

Ultimately, I believe that our capacity to imagine is one of the qualities that separates us from all other creatures on this amazing planet. Although intelligence is often cited as the attribute that differentiates Man from other life forms, I think a close run second is the gift of imagination, with symbolism very much at its heart.

Of course it must be acknowledged, as I have said, that the meaning of any particular symbol may lie in the eye of the beholder. One man's religious sigil is another man's decoration, and someone else's icon of terror and oppression. The swastika, for instance, has been used by both Nazis and Buddhists alike. Symbols have the power to divide a community, or to unite it under a common banner, such as a national flag. When it comes to the meanings of symbols, it is all about association, perception, and a large sprinkling of imagination.

Today, corporations employ logos and symbols to enable their brands to be instantly recognizable. A picture, nowadays, sells a thousand products.

2. Symbols of Nature

I t was perhaps inevitable that a great deal of cultural symbolism was birthed from processes observed and experienced in Nature. And the natural world is full of symbolism, which you may, if you believe in a God or Goddess, or indeed sign up to another spiritual belief system, interpret as

Man has long noted that Nature exhibits sacred geometry.

manifestations of Divinity. After all, if God/Goddess comprises all that exists (as it has to by definition!) then everything is an expression of that God/Goddess. There is nothing 'New Age' about this way of looking at the universe, for we would have trouble finding a more ancient concept.

Sacred geometry is the perception that Nature is an expression of mathematics, or rather mathematics is the means by which the God/Goddess manifests in this physical dimension (see French 2012, Gibson-Forty 2012, Stewart 2011). Man has sought to bring Divine proportion and measure into sacred sites and rituals the world over, and sacred geometry is a global tradition recognized and employed by Roman and Greek, Egyptian and Inca, Aborigine and African Bushman. By watching and recording natural events, people have been able to understand the world around them, and the symbols used were often replicated from those seen in the natural world. This included their observations of birds, animals, simulacra in rocks, trees, stalactites, flowers, the shape of cave entrances, rainbows, snowflakes, thunder and lightning, the Sun and Moon, and the stars – the list is indeed infinite.

Take Bees for instance; their honeycombs comprise of hexagons, six-sided figures which are strong and stable **(top image, previous page).** The Greeks suspected that the Bees possessed, *"... a certain geometrical forethought",* as one philosopher put it. Charles Darwin marveled at the engineering skills of bees, declaring that honeybee dwellings were, *"...absolutely perfect in economising labour and wax".*

Although snowflakes exhibit a variety of beautiful designs, the basic template is always six-pointed, a phenomenon recorded as early as 135 BC by Chinese philosopher Han Yang. Many flowers show the hexagram/hexagon, such as the daffodil and varieties of the lily family. There is even a lily named Solomon's Seal (*Polygonatum multiflorum*), after the six-pointed symbol of the Biblical king. The Giant's Causeway, in Ireland, and the patterns of turtle and tortoise shells, also exhibit hexagons.

Spirals in nature include tornados, rams horns, unfurling ferns, sea shells, galaxies, spiralling cyclonic cloud formations, and a host of others. The Fibonacci Series demonstrates the self-replicating growth in Nature, as shown here in the Nautilus shell and a flower **(centre & lower images, previous page).** The Phi Ratio, or the Golden Mean, is a double spiral, seen in the growth of sunflowers, cauliflowers, pineapples and strawberries.

Larger manifestations were also implicit in the birthing of symbolism, as Nature was seen to express forms that were reminiscent of something else. Simulacra are natural objects that lend themselves to be fodder for our imagination; rocks that look like faces, stalactites and clouds that resemble human or animal features, perforated rocks replicating the vulva/yoni (see Krőnig 2001). To a shaman, natural features symbolise the cosmos, and allow interaction with other realms; to a shaman there is never one landscape, but rather many. In 2007, I visited the Domus dell 'elefante, at Castelsardo, Sardinia **(top image, previous page)**. It is a natural outcrop resembling an elephant that was used as a tomb in prehistory.

Whilst in Sardinia, I also visited Roccia Il Fungo (Mushroom Rock), at Arzachena **(second image, previous page)**. This huge, natural mushroom-shaped outcrop was later used for Bronze Age burial and ritual. Another huge natural rock pillar I visited in Portugal, known as Rocha dos Enamoradus, is said to represent a donkey's penis and is associated with Easter fertility ceremonies. Also shown here **(third image, previous page)** is a simulacrum that was revealed to me on Vixen Tor, Dartmoor. This huge head, over 12ft high, looks eastwards towards the Merrivale Stone Rows, suggesting a possible ritual link between the two sites. The bottom image, previous page, is from Bodmin Moor, and demonstrates some of the wind-eroded anthropomorphs that can be perceived across the moor. Bowerman's Nose is another stunning simulacrum on Dartmoor **(right),** and also shown here **(bottom)** is another simulacrum perceived in the cliffs at Tintagel, Cornwall.

More examples abound across the ancient world (Devereux 2000); Mount Hymettos appears as the breasts of the Earth Goddess when viewed from the Acropolis at Athens, as do the Paps of Anu in Killarney in Ireland (see Knight 1998 for images). From Poros in Greece, a nearby mountain resembles a reclining woman, and Glastonbury Tor is often said to be the ripe pregnant tummy of the Earth Mother.

Many tribal cultures, ancient and contemporary, have seen such forms as evidence that nature spirits, gods and

Examples of simulacra.

Top: yonic cave entrance, Brockley. Second: Bowerman's Nose, Dartmoor. Third: stalagmites. Right: Tolmen Stone, Dartmoor. Far right: Tintagel, Cornwall.

goddesses, or mythical creatures, are in residence; for instance, a huge simulacrum head on the summit of Carn Brae in Cornwall is associated with a giant. Many of the stones of Avebury stone circle may have been brought into the monument because of their anthropomorphic features **(image p. 13)**.

Many caves around the world have been seen as the womb of the Earth Mother, their entrances being her yoni or vulva **(top, previous page)**. These are places where Man had transcendental experiences, where access to the Underworld was achieved, and many have been found to contain countless ritual objects. To go into a cave is a liminal experience, where normal senses are replaced by a world of darkness and mystery – we are beckoned into the unknown. Once inside a cave people encountered stalactites and stalagmites, which were reminiscent of the phallus; I found the examples shown here in the Binigaus Ravine Caves on Minorca **(third image, previous page)**. Much later, our Neolithic ancestors sought to replicate such conditions by building chambered tombs, such as at Newgrange, Ireland, and West Kennet Long Barrow, Wiltshire (Knight 2011).

It was not just caves where the imaginations of our distant ancestor's were let loose. The huge Tolmen Stone on Dartmoor nestles in the young River Teign, whose waters lash around its base The stone is perforated by a one metre wide hole **(bottom left, previous page** – with my daughter Leela passing through); legend has it that Druids met here for rituals, and today's Pagans still gather here for ceremony and initiation. I have told previously how on one full moon night I passed through the hole (Knight 2007). This association with perforated rocks and rebirth led to the erection of holed stones at several Neolithic and Bronze Age sites, famously at Men-an-Tol in Cornwall **(image p. 199)**.

Today it is not unusual to walk through a wood and perceive Ent-like faces in trees **(top)**, or see branches that resemble limbs or antlers. Man has had a close practical connection with trees for many thousands of years, and yet the bond has also been spiritual. It is known that Iron Age Druids gathered in sacred groves rather than manmade sites, and spent time alone with trees. Christianity later brought tree spirits and the *Lord of the Forest* into churches in the form of the Green Man.

The Sun and Moon **(centre)** have been major influences on Mankind, being responsible as they are for the revolving days, nights and seasons, the ripening of the crops, and the changing tides. The disc or circle they form in the sky is also the symbol of wholeness, completion, oneness, and is a key mathematical shape, which can be of infinite proportions, as well as both 'full' or 'empty'. The

10

resulting solid of a circle, the sphere, is seen everywhere in Nature, from berries to water droplets, from bubbles to frogspawn. The circle was later used extensively in prehistoric sacred site design, and later still employed with great effect in the holy places of several religions.

A holon is a circle filled with concentric circles, as seen, for instance, in a sliced onion, an agate, the orbits of the planets, tree rings or spiders webs **(bottom, previous page)**. Here there is an expression of time, of the consecutive cycles inherent in Nature. Many prehistoric sites incorporated concentric stone or timber circles, and sometimes a combination of the two, and Neolithic chambered tombs in Ireland and Brittany display carved concentric circles **(image p. 13)**.

Observations of, and interaction with Nature was at the very genesis of Man's preoccupation with symbols. Our religious beliefs have their roots firmly rooted within the concepts of animism and the sacredness of the natural world. Prehistoric peoples had great sensitivity to their environment and this is reflected in the huge amount of imagery inspired by the natural world. Gods and Goddesses were seen to be omnipresent and eternal, and whilst contact with deities was sought to harness their power for positive outcomes, what was equally acknowledged was that these divinities also had the capacity to unleash forces of destruction. In later religions, it was this *'fear factor'* that was pushed centre stage, as Nature became something to be conquered, feared and ultimately subdued. Man had isolated himself from the magic of the Universe and Nature, from the very energies he once sought to live in harmony with and understand. As scientific discovery has developed, so our world has become dehumanised, and with the rise in rationality has gone the profound, emotional and spiritual connection that the symbolism of the natural world once gifted us.

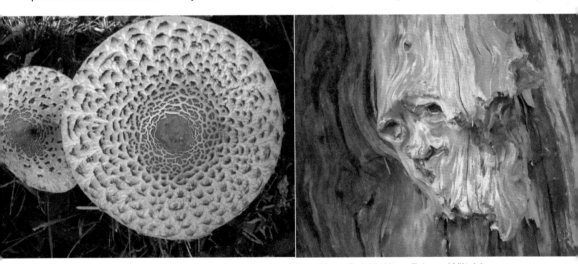

Left: large mushrooms, Isle of Wight. Right: Yew *'Tree Spirit'*, Alton Priors, Wiltshire.

3. Ancient Symbolism

Freud once called symbols *'archaic remnants'* that originated way back in prehistory and have been inherited ever since through each generation, passed on collectively from one to the next; Jung called these *archetypes*. From the earliest times Man has expressed the world around him in symbols; Neanderthal burials have revealed symbolic objects that suggest ritual activity was present. Over 30,000 years ago, elaborate carvings were etched into animal bones, including those of Mammoth, and amazing art painted in Palaeolithic (Ice Age) caves across Europe (Devereux 2000, Bahn and Vertut 1997). Much of this imagery is of animals, and may have been the result of shamanic rites to connect with the spirits of potential prey, to illicit them to sacrifice themselves to the hunt **(top)**. To the shaman, perhaps cave walls were not even seen as solid, but rather as veils through which the Otherworld could be accessed.

It was noticed by researchers that concentrations of cave art were often where the acoustics did weird things when chants or other sounds were projected into the darkness; at such places were found the best echoes, or where sound was distorted or amplified. This would suggest some shamanic *interaction* with the environment. The next image **(left)** is from Lascaux, France, and is around 17,000 years old. It appears to show a shaman with exposed phallus facing up to a bison, whilst his head shape-shifts into that of a bird. The *'Sorcerer of Les Trois Freres'* appears to be a shaman who has donned antlers in a sympathetic magic ritual **(image p. 92)**. Cave art has been an almost continuous and universal practice, which is perpetuated by aboriginal cultures today **(header, top of page)**.

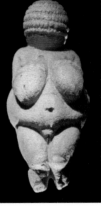

As well as expressing art in caves and on rock faces, hundreds of portable artifacts have been found across Europe, many dating to over 35,000 years old. The famous 'Venus' figurines are, typically, handheld objects, and are usually, but not exclusively, depicting a female. The breasts, buttocks and hips are often large, symbolic of the fecundity of the Earth Goddess, and may have been connected with fertility and reproduction rituals. Shown here **(far left)** is the Venus of Lespugue, from France (age

c. 20,000BC), carved on mammoth ivory, whilst next to it is the iconic Venus of Willendorf, from Austria, which is made of limestone and dated at around 20,000-18,000BC. They both display pendulous breasts, large hips and thighs, and genitalia, but both lack facial features. Do they represent all women, or the faceless Earth Goddess? Whatever their meanings (which were probably varied and multilayered), these ancient figurines clearly express a very sophisticated belief system, and an ever-expanding world view.

By the Neolithic (c. 4200-3000BC), Man had developed a vast array of sigils, long before the advent of the written word. Spirals, circles, triangles, ziz-zags and other geometric forms all conspired to weave complex webs of visual narrative, which are still impressive and awe-inspiring today. Many escape interpretation, and perhaps the messages were always intended to be 'in the eye of the beholder'. It has been suggested that the abstract patterns in Neolithic tombs are entopics, images seen by shamans whilst in a trance state, as they journeyed to the realms of the Ancestors; I have observed such circular patterns at Gavrinis, Brittany **(top)**, and zigzags at the Fourknocks chambered tomb in Ireland **(right)**.

Figurines and votive objects continued to be a part of ritual ceremonies, and hundreds have been found dating from the Neolithic and Bronze Age. The third image here is *The Sleeping Lady*, found in the underground chambers of the Hal Saflieni Hypogeum in Malta **(right)**. It is over 5,000 years old, and I stood mesmerized as I gazed upon its form in the Museum at Veletta. I also observed that in some of the walls of the goddess temples on Malta there was often a solitary phallic-shaped stone – the yang principle midst the yin **(below centre)**. Another figurine from Malta is shown

Examples of prehistoric symbolism using the shapes of megaliths and imagery on them, and the fabric of the landscape itself.

at the end of this chapter.

One of the stones of the Avenue at Avebury is shown here **(bottom left, previous page)**. It clearly resembles a shark and the stone may have been selected because of its appearance. Many other megaliths at Avebury, some of which are astronomically aligned, reveal more creatures.

Chalk hill figures are further examples of ancient people utilising the natural landscape to express their spiritual beliefs. The Uffington White Horse **(bottom right, previous page)** has been dated as Bronze Age; the Long Man of Wilmington, Sussex, may be pre-Roman, and I have demonstrated that the Cerne Giant in Dorset **(image p. 35)** is around 2000 years old (Knight 2013).

When I travelled around the temples and tombs of Egypt, I was struck how almost every square inch of stone and wall was adorned with figures, motifs and glyphs. More than this, each Egyptian symbol was imbued with power, as if it took on the very essence of that which it represented. This may have been the case in most ancient cultures. The Egyptians, especially, made imagery into a fine art, using symbols to paint a picture of every aspect of their culture. These could be events such as farming and warfare, death and rebirth, Gods and Goddesses, and the inevitable epic victories of the Pharaohs; PR is an ancient concept! Egyptian symbolic art arguably reached a crescendo with the death mask of Tutankhamun **(top)**.

Throughout the Iron Age, symbolism was employed extensively by the Greeks, Romans and other cultures across Europe, such as the Vikings and the Gauls. The Greeks and Romans had many symbols and motifs to represent their deities, which ranged from huge statues of the Gods in temple settings, down to small statuettes on home altars. At sacred sites across the Roman Empire thousands of tons of votive offerings were left for the gods, such as at the hot springs in Bath; here is a bust of the Goddess Sulis-Minerva **(second image)**. The classical superhero Orion is also shown here, featured in a Roman statue on a column in Messina, Sicily, in Italy **(left)**.

Arguably the greatest expression of non-Imperial Iron Age symbolism is to be seen on the famous *Gunderstrup Cauldron,* a gilt silver bowl found in Denmark, dated 4th – 2nd century BC. It displays beautifully crafted images of gods and animals, and a Cernunnos/shaman figure **(left, and p. 49)**.

It must also be said that a particular image placed in a temple or shrine may have a different purpose to that of its placement in a domestic setting. In some cases a god or goddess was considered to physically inhabit an object which it represented, such as in a huge temple statue, whereby in others it was just a 'good luck' charm.

We shall return to prehistoric and early historical times

later, when we deal in turn with specific categories of symbols and how they were brought into the Church. But it is worth noting now how the Romans assimilated and absorbed local deities of newly conquered lands, often reassigning them to Roman equivalents. Later, as the Church spread through Pagan lands it sought to convert, it was to pursue a similar practice regarding ancient imagery and myths. More than this, the early Gnostic Christians based their symbols on archetypes that they knew possessed energetic properties, as well as associating themselves with myths that lead them to self-knowledge. Later still, the Church used adopted symbols and myths to stamp its authority, ensuring the buildings, and ultimately the parishioners, were in tune with God's design and purpose. The difference between early Gnostic Christian beginnings and later Christianity was that with the Gnostics it was all about self-knowledge, to *Know Thy Self,* whereas what developed latterly was the concept of a *God Almighty*, whom you feared and worshipped (see Freke and Gandy 2002, for an excellent overview on the subject).

It is with great irony that the symbols and myths of the Goddess were ultimately used *against* the very cultures that revered her, due to the Church's fervor of male chauvinism. It is equally ironic that the adoption of Pagan imagery into Christian (as well Islamic) architecture has ensured their survival.

To recap, according to Carl Jung, symbols are archetypal expressions of Man's collective consciousness (Jung 1964). The concept of archetypes dates back to Plato, who believed that they are imprinted into the soul prior to birth, what Jung later called, '*primordial images*'. So, as successive cultures and religions came and went, each new one arrival 'tuned in' to appropriate images and myths; Christianity was to be no exception - nothing, it seems, is new.

Neolithic Goddess figurine, Malta.   Isis and Osiris in tomb of Rameses III, Egypt.

15

4. Cometh the Cross

The premise of this book is that the majority of Christian myths and symbols can be traced back to an earlier origin. It is no heresy or mystery how many ancient myths and symbols came to be incorporated into the Old Testament of the Bible. In 597BC, Jerusalem fell to Nebuchadnezzar II, and many Judeans were taken and kept in bondage and servitude in Babylonia. Daniel (of Lion taming fame) taught in schools in Babylon, and would have been forced to teach Babylonian myths as part of the syllabus. Scholars believe that, following the fall of Babylon to the Persian King Cyrus in 539BC, exiled Jews began to return to their homeland, bringing with them myths, parables and fables from their time in captivity.

The close proximity of Egypt also led to exchanges of trade and philosophies, and with these came a cross-fertilization of cultural symbols. When the Romans conquered much of the Middle East, yet more influences were heaped upon the Hebrew homelands. Amidst this melting pot of myths, ideals and symbolism, a certain man called Jesus was allegedly born. Christianity's subsequent spread across Europe following the death of Constantine was achieved in no small measure by the fact that potential convertees would recognize many of the myths and symbols touted by the new religion. The myth of the annual life and death cycle of Osiris/Dionysus was reflected in the story of Jesus, whilst Mary the Mother filled the void left by a vanquished Earth Goddess.

In the art of the Romans, Vikings, Picts and other cultures around this time we see an interesting overlap and blending of the old with the new. Old standing stones were remodelled, or else had the addition of a cross or other Christian symbolism **(image p. 20)**. The earliest surviving Christian art comes from walls of the tombs and catacombs of Rome. This is dated 2nd to early 4th century, a time when the followers of Jesus were being persecuted. Symbols such as the fish and the lamb were then already in use, and later the cross and the Dove came to represent Jesus. Scenes of Noah, the Good Shepherd and Moses are also amongst the earliest Christian depictions; the scene shown here **(top)** is the Adoration of the Magi, from the 3rd century AD.

16

The Roman Empire became Christian following the conversion of Constantine in 312AD. By 380AD, public expression of ancient cults was made illegal, although it wasn't until late in the 5th century that anyone practicing Pagan rites on their premises was penalised. One of the earliest signs of Christianity amongst Romans was the Chi-Rho cross, which is formed superimposing the first two letters of the Greek for Christ, Chi (X) and Rho (P). Constantine himself had the symbol put on the shields of his soldiers. Early versions of the cross show the lines crossing at angles that represent those of the celestial equator and the path of the Sun, the ecliptic. Later versions show these lines crossing at 90°. This Roman mosaic found at Hinton St Mary, Dorset, shows a fine Chi-Rho cross, and also shows what is thought to be the oldest depiction of Jesus in Britain. It is dated as early 4th century AD **(centre, previous page, & p. 217)**.

The Christianisation of Scandinavia took place between the 8th and 12th centuries. Prior to that the Vikings had wreaked havoc on Christian missionaries, relieving them of gold and other relics. I have had the pleasure of viewing the Gosforth Cross, in the grounds of St Mary's, Gosforth, Cumbria **(bottom, previous page)**; this wonderful blend of Pagan and Christian imagery tells of a time in the 10th century when Viking conversions were taking place. The cross depicts scenes from the Norse *Prose Edda,* including Loki and his wife, the god Heimdallr with his horn, and Thor's attempt to catch the giant serpent Jormungandr. A fine Viking pendant of the Crucifixion is also shown here **(top)**, which comes from Sweden.

The Picts were the 'fly in the ointment' of Roman ambitions to bring the whole of Britain into the Empire. Pictish carvings are particularly good examples of the synthesis of the old with the new. 'Pictish Art' vaguely refers to artistic objects found north of the River Forth in Scotland, and are dated 400 – 1000AD. Ancient symbols such as circles, spirals, concentric circles, birds and animals, crescents, mirrors, dragons, the salmon of wisdom and so on, all sit alongside Christian saints and the cross. These Pagan and Christian symbols may be accompanied by Celtic knot work of fine quality and artistic merit.

On a recent visit to the National Museum of Scotland, in Edinburgh, I was in awe of their large collection of beautiful carved Pictish stones, two of which are illustrated here. Many images are carved on crosses, others on memorials to Christian dead. The first example **(centre)** shows a cross at the top with four monks below, whilst at the foot are two figures with bird's beaks – clearly depicting the shamanic ritual of shape-shifting or sympathetic magic. The second image **(right)** shows a cross with intricate knot work, accompanied by a spiral on the left face; the spiral is one of Man's most enduring images, examples of which go back many thousands of years, and which we shall look at in more detail later (Chapter 21).

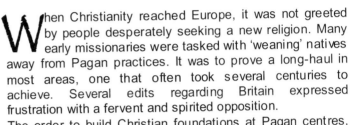

5. There's a New God in Town

When Christianity reached Europe, it was not greeted by people desperately seeking a new religion. Many early missionaries were tasked with 'weaning' natives away from Pagan practices. It was to prove a long-haul in most areas, one that often took several centuries to achieve. Several edits regarding Britain expressed frustration with a fervent and spirited opposition.

The order to build Christian foundations at Pagan centres, rather than destroy them, came right from the top, from Pope Gregory himself. Gregory's edict of 595AD was directed at Britain in particular, as the Venerable Bede recounts: *'The temples of the idols in that nation ought not be destroyed, but only the idols in them. Let holy water be made and sprinkled in said temples, and let altars be erected, and relics placed'*. There are many examples of the takeover of Pagan sites by Christianity across Europe, good examples being Knowlton, Dorset **(bottom)**, Tara (Ireland), Glastonbury **(left)**, Chartres Cathedral, and London. Countless Roman Catholic cathedrals were built to replace major Pagan temples, and chapels erected on hilltops to takeover these ancient Sun hills, and to replace centres held by the Celtic Church; *'These 'centres of light' often stood over old Druid sanctuaries long before the Saxons and Romans came to Britain'* (Biltcliffe and Hoare 2012).

The St Michael Line and the Belinus Line are two long-distance landscape alignments that cross Britain, and both have numerous examples of ancient centres that were later usurped by the Church, such as St Michael's Mount, Glastonbury and Winchester. The Romans, you may remember, did similar practices when they came to Britain, taking over existing sacred sites and renaming the native gods and goddesses.

On the St Michael Line in Cornwall, a chapel was built on Roche Rock **(top)**; note the superb simulacrum inherent in the rock face. I have also visited La Hougue Bie on Jersey, where a church was constructed over a Neolithic chambered passage grave (**right**). Similarly, a chapel was built on top of the mound of a Neolithic tomb at Tumulus St Michel in Brittany, France, and there are many more examples.

Sometimes a prehistoric site can become an integral component of a Christian structure. On a recent trip to Portugal, I visited two Neolithic dolmens that had been incorporated into the fabric of chapels, at the Chapel Anta do San Brissos, and Chapel Anta de Pavia; the latter is shown here (**centre**). At Cerne Abbas, in Dorset, an entire abbey complex was built around an ancient sacred spring (Knight 2013). At Stanton Drew, in Somerset, a church was built next to prehistoric stone circles and a megalithic cove (**bottom**). All of these examples serve to demonstrate what is sometimes known as site evolution, where there is evidence of a continuity of usage by successive religions or cultures, sometimes spanning millennia.

At Knowlton, Dorset, a Norman Church was built within a Neolithic Henge (**bottom image, previous page**), one of several monuments in a complex of sites. Some stones have recently been found at the site, suggesting evidence of a former stone circle. Some large stones can be seen in the fabric of the church, which may have been part of the destroyed megalithic site (**top image, next page**).

Many ancient megaliths were also given the Christian treatment across Europe. If not pulled down and replaced by crosses, many were carved with crosses and even more elaborate decoration, such as some of the large megaliths in Brittany (**centre image, next page**). In ancient times such large, and often phallic, stones represented the Axis Mundi, the World Tree, or the Cosmic Pillar, and Christianity had its own version with the Cross and its shaft. Ironically, the Christian cross itself is a variation of the much earlier Egyptian ankh (**images p. 33, 99 & 215**).

The reason the Church wished to replace Pagan places with their own structures was twofold in nature. Firstly, by not destroying the old sites and putting Christian buildings on them, the local populace could still attend their sacred sites, but now there was a new God in town, so to speak, making the task of conversion that much easier. It also legitimized the Church as the prime spiritual focus. Secondly, it was the very

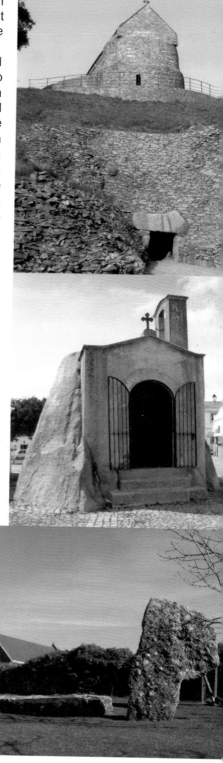

power of the places that was sought, where palpable earth energies could be utilized by means of employing sacred geometry into the architecture, just as Pagan temples and stone circles had for thousands of years. As I have said, certain places around the world have been regarded as sacred by successive cultures.

Sometimes places are sacred to different religions at the *same time*, such centres seemingly able to convey to all-comers whatever it is they seek. Jerusalem, Glastonbury, and Rome itself are prime examples. Adam's Peak in Sri Lanka is sacred to Buddhists, Taoists, Muslims and Christians alike. At Jerusalem, the Dome on the Rock was built on Temple Mount by Muslims in 691AD **(bottom)**, and whose golden dome dominates the modern skyline. Prior to that the Mount was sacred to Jews, and still is by Christian pilgrims seeking to walk in the footsteps of Jesus.

This would imply that in many cases it is the *locality* itself that possesses the sanctity, holding the energies and connections to the 'Divine' in whatever form one believes that to be. Such places were often regarded as an omphalos, the World Navel or Cosmic Egg. Delphi and Crete were omphalos localities, as too was Jerusalem, which Hebrews regarded as the centre of the Holy Land; Muslims believe that the rock on which Jerusalem is built is the place where Mohammed ascended to Heaven. Chartres Cathedral was built by the Knights Templar on a site once deemed sacred by the Druids.

Furthermore, it was not just ancient sites that were Christianised, but the Pagan festivals and annual celebrations too, as we shall now see.

6. Festivals and the Turning Year

It is well proven that astronomical alignments were integral to the design of countless prehistoric sites. These configurations were primarily concerned with the two solstices, the two equinoxes and the four so-called *'Celtic Fire Festivals'* of Samhain, Imbolc, Beltaine and Lugnassad. These eight divisions of the year were also augmented by lunar events, notably the major and minor standstills, which are involved in a complicated 18½-year cycle. Although alignments can be associated with places of the dead, and many may therefore have been places of ancestral ceremonies, most would have existed to enable the *living* to celebrate and honour the turning of the year. In particular, they marked the close relationship and interaction between the Sun, Moon and the Earth. The *Calendar Stone* at Knowth, Ireland, is a Neolithic megalith carved with various symbols and configurations **(top)** that have been interpreted as having astronomical significance (Brennan 1994).

The midsummer/midwinter alignment at Stonehenge, and the midwinter equivalent at Newgrange, are two notable examples. Many Christian buildings were to be orientated with these 'Pagan' alignments, and it can be commonly observed that churches are frequently *not* aligned with true east, which is opposed to the general consensus. These demonstrate vestiges of Pagan alignments at such sites; Knights Templar chapels and churches show a propensity for astronomical alignment, as well as being lined up with local topographical features, such as holy hills or ancient sites. Shown here is St Catherine's Hill, Winchester, **(centre)**; the axis of the Knight's Hospitaller church of St Cross is aligned with this sacred solar hill (Biltcliffe and Hoare 2012). I observed many years ago that the axis of Knowlton church, Dorset **(right)**, which is set midst a Neolithic henge, is aligned with the Beltaine (May Day) sunrise.

There are, of course, plenty of churches that *are* indeed aligned to the east, like Rosslyn Chapel for instance. Such places align with the equinox sunrise twice a year, in March and September, when day and night are equal – times of balance. This general sunrise direction is taken as symbolic of the Resurrection of Jesus.

Annual festivals are well attested across the ancient world, and the Romans, Greeks and Egyptians developed a cavalcade of calendrical festivals. With the coming of Christianity, these celebrations were assimilated into a Church which was forging a new version of a religious calendar. And it was not just seasonal festivals that were absorbed, for Saints' days would also be placed on notable dates of the pre-Christian year.

Long before a certain prophet was born in Bethlehem, people knew that survival meant acknowledging the seasons and working with them. Springtime was about mating, summer the season of growing crops and herds, and autumn was the busy harvest time. Winter was a period in which to rest, a time of storytelling and introspection. Pagan religions celebrated every season, each of which had its own myths, rituals and celebrations. Many of these ancient rites and observances were still alive and kicking 2000 yrs ago, at the onset of Christianity; they needed to be supplanted.

Christmas/Midwinter Solstice

In the Christian calendar, Christmas celebrates the birth of Jesus, but this time was celebrated long before his birth around 2000 yrs ago. I have already commented on the

fact that prehistoric sites had been aligned with the midwinter sunrise and sunset since at least the Neolithic. These were times when the shortest day and longest night was recognized, and the Sun was urged to return, and with it life to return to the Earth as a new annual cycle commenced. The Earth Mother was in her Crone stage, seen as the Hag of Winter, as Kali in India, or celebrated as Saturnalia by the Romans. Although it occurs before midwinter, Diwali, or *'Festival of Lights'*, is a celebration shared by Hindus, Sikhs and Jainists, and signifies the victory of light over darkness. This is echoed in the West by countless lantern parades held today. The *Twelve Days of Christmas* may have its origin in the ancient Babylonian *Twelve Days of Anarchy,* a mythological struggle with the Goddess of Chaos. Following the solstice, December 25th is the first day when the Sun can be detected to set slightly later, and weeklong festivals were carried out to celebrate this rebirth of the solar god. As will be discussed in more detail later in Chapter 38, Jesus took over the role of sacrificed Sun gods such as Osiris, Dionysus, Mithras, Attis, Horus and Krishna, who were all born on December 25th. Unwittingly, the West has fallen into the symbolism of solar rebirth. The renewal of the year was celebrated on December 25th in later Roman times as the *Dies Natalis* of the *Sol Invictus,* the *'Birthday of the Unconquerable Sun'.* Shown here **(top)** is a 3/4th century AD image that was found under the Vatican. It shows Jesus as the *Sol Invictus.* Celebrations to these old dying/rebirth gods needed to be replaced by a major Christian festival, and the birth of Jesus was suitably significant and appropriate to fit the bill (see p. 204 for more on this subject).

The concept of giving gifts at Christmas has subverted the real meaning of this time; the real gift is the prospect of the return of the Sun. In decorating a tree (in itself an ancient symbol of the Earth Goddess) with glowing lights, we mark the return of the sun's light. We find much comfort in this very ancient festival.

Wassailing probably goes back to at least Anglo-Saxon times, and is often carried out around midwinter, whereby apple orchards are approached by locals who make an offering to the trees, tapping them with sticks, echoing former tree worship **(lower image, previous page)**. Mumming Plays, such as on January 1st at Padstow, Cornwall, depict the battle between light and dark around midwinter, with St George playing the hero, and which may be genuine survivals from the Pre-Christian epoch (Whitlock 1979). A Medicine Man and a Beelzebub are also involved, and a character named Jack, reminding us of Jack-of-the-Green and the Green Man. The Yule Log was dragged indoors and placed on the hearth, mirroring the ancient act of midwinter fire ceremonies. In Shetland, the Up-Helly-Aa Festival, soon after midwinter, involves the community burning a full scale replica of a Viking long ship **(top)**, signaling the end of the old year and a return to the light. In former times this was followed by doors being flung open and demons chased out of the home.

In many areas of Britain the Hunting of the Wren took place on December 26th, St Stephen's Day. Wren's had become associated with the Underworld because of their habit of disappearing into crevices and caves, and killing wren's around this time (and ONLY around this time) represented the slaying of the darkness (Whitlock 1979).

Candlemas/Imbolc

The Christian festival of Candlemas celebrates when the newborn Jesus was taken to the Temple in Jerusalem, and is generally held 40 days after Christmas. Importantly, this is one of the ancient 'cross quarter days', called Imbolc, which occurs between midwinter and spring equinox. Its ancient origin is proven by the alignment of several megalithic sites with the sunrise of that date, such as at the Mound of Hostages at Tara, at other Irish sites (Brennan 1994), and across Europe. Imbolc means *'in the belly'*, and refers to the pregnancy of ewes at this time, and the lighting of candles represents the return of the warmth of the Sun. It was traditionally the Pagan festival to the Gaelic goddess Brighid or Bride, the original Divine Virgin and daughter of the Dagda; she was later metamorphosed into St Brighid or Brigid **(right)**. At Imbolc, Brighid's crosses **(centre)** are made from dried stems of wheat or barley

23

from the previous year's harvest, and doll-like effigies would be made to bless the hearth, for it was thought the Goddess visited homes at this time. She is associated with serpents, which emerge from their hibernation holes at this time. Imbolc is also the time of Groundhog Day in the USA, when clues are sought for the coming weather and outcome of crops; it is interesting therefore that Brighid is associated with divination. The Feast of Mary the Virgin's Purification was fixed on February 2, to further the absorption of Imbolc.

Easter/Spring Equinox

The Spring Equinox occurs around March 21-23, when days and nights are of equal length, and the Sun is halfway along its passage from midwinter to midsummer. Many ancient sites are aligned with the equinox sunrise and sunset, such as West Kennet Long Barrow (Knight 2011), as indeed are many churches. It is not coincidence that St Patrick's Day (March 17) was fixed just days before this event.

Easter, whose name comes from the ancient Goddess Eostre or Eoestra, moves around the calendar in a seemingly illogical way, not fixed to a particular date. This is because it is held on the first Sunday following the first full Moon after spring equinox; this major Christian event is fixed by the movements of the Moon! The Resurrection of Jesus, like that of the Sun gods before him, marks the passage from winter to summer.

However, the spring equinox, which once represented a point in the *annual* cycle of the turning year, has now metamorphosed into a celebration of a once-only, unique event where Jesus ascends **(top)** to be at the right hand of God. It is the finality of this that differentiates the Christian story from other resurrected God myths; the myths of gods and heroes being reborn, like Jesus, include Dionysus, Adonis, Orpheus, Osiris, Tammuz, and Balder, and many others are embedded into the myths of the ancient world. At least the annual Easter celebration ensures some memory of the meaning of ancient celebrations at this time of year.

Regarding the Easter Bunny, the story goes that a goddess saved a bird from freezing to death by turning it into a Rabbit, which was subsequently still able to lay eggs. Rabbits often appear in folklore, as the trickster archetype, and the Aztecs had many rabbit gods. Rabbits and Hares are key characters of several pre-Christian myths, and Moon-gazing Hares are a popular icon of today's Pagans. The earliest record of a rabbit's foot being carried for good fortune is from 600BC. The Christian Holy Trinity is often expressed today as three Rabbits or Hares running in a circle **(left)**. Lambs are also associated with this time of the year; Jesus is known as the Lamb of God **(image p. 91)**. Lambs were a popular sacrificial animal in many ancient cultures, and this practice features in the Old Testament. Even the humble hot cross bun (the bread at the Last Supper) is an ancient solar motif – a cross within a circle **(images p. 216)**.

24

The egg is a primeval symbol of creation, fertility and potentiality, which we shall look at in more detail in Chapter 17. Egg images were important right back in the Palaeolithic, and engraved ostrich eggs dating to 60,000 years old have been found in Africa; later Neolithic depictions are associated with the Bird Goddess. Gold and silver eggs were placed in Egyptian tombs as early as 5,000 years ago, thought to represent the rebirth of the departed soul. The Egyptian ankh is a cross with an egg mounted on the top, a potent symbol of rebirth **(image p. 215)**. The Omphalos, or Cosmic Egg, is a stone sometimes found at ancient sites, such as at Delphi, which marked the centre or navel of the world, and used in oracle rituals **(image p. 68)**.

Some scholars say the egg also represents the empty tomb of the resurrected Jesus, or the round stone that covered the entrance. Early Christians in Mesopotamia painted eggs red to represent the blood of Christ, and there is a legend that Mary Magdalene turned an egg red in front of Tiberius in Rome (see Chapter 17).

May Day/Beltaine

Beltaine is an extremely ancient festival which traditionally marked the first day of summer, and has today been reassigned as the early May bank holiday. It is thought to have been named after the solar god Bel, Belinus or Baal, whose name meant *bright fire,* and huge Beltaine Fires were lit at this time. It is a time when rites are undertaken to ensure a plentiful harvest in the succeeding months of summer, and a time when people noted that mating amongst animals and birds was at its most frenetic. Beltaine is thus a time for romance and lovers, when sensual scents filled the air and apple blossom signalled the erection of maypoles **(right)**. The maypole itself is an ancient symbol, which in ancient Rome represented the phallus of the fertility gods Attis and Priapus. Beltaine is the time of the goddesses of love, of Venus, Rhiannon and Aphrodite, of Cernunnos, the antlered *Lord of the Forest*, and Gwyn ap Nudd, the Lord of Annwn (the Underworld), and of the rising energies of the Green Man. Many ancient sites are aligned with the Beltaine sunrise, such as one I found associated with the Cerne Giant in Dorset (Knight 2013), and it is the sunrise axis of the famous St Michael Line (Miller and Broadhurst 1989).

It was vital for this major Pagan festival to be Christianised, and there are numerous records of locals continuing to carry out practices which the Church regarded as sinful, such as courting couples sloping off into the woods, girls wearing garlands, leaving offerings on trees, feasting, and general merriment, and of seeking out fairies, which could be communed with at this time as the veil between worlds opened.

Some vestiges of ancient rites are still carried out to this day. At Padstow, Cornwall, I have witnessed the amazing 'Obby 'Oss celebrations **(top),** where the whole village parades behind two round figures, accompanied by gestures and songs that leave little to the imagination regarding fertility rites; St George is also celebrated during the day at Padstow (whose festival is on April 23, but used to be May 4). In Helston, also in Cornwall, the annual May 'Flurry Day' or 'Flora Day' tells of the battle between light and dark, which is played out with the defeat of a dragon by both St George and St Michael, and the performance of a ritual drama called *Hal-an-Tow*. A *Jack-in-the-Green* festival is held in early May at Deptford, London, and at Hastings, whilst Morris dancing is traditionally carried out on May Day **(bottom image, previous page)**, as well as the

dressing of wells around Europe. The latter is the relic of ancient practices thanking the spirits of springs for their life-giving waters. Although we now have to read between the lines at many modern May Day celebrations, Pagans the world over still regard Beltaine as one of the main festivals, and gather at sacred sites such as Avebury and Glastonbury.

Midsummer/Summer Solstice

Cultures around the ancient world celebrated midsummer, and aligned their sacred sites with the sunrise on this day, most famously at Stonehenge **(left)**. The word *solstice* comes from the Latin *solstitium,* meaning *'sun stands still'.* In most prehistoric cultures, the longest day of the year, around June 21-22 in the northern hemisphere, was celebrated, as it still is in many parts of the world today; the Muslim fasting time of Ramadan straddles the summer solstice. In Egypt, many temples dedicated to the sun god Amon-re/Ra were aligned with this sunrise, as well as Aztec and Mayan sacred sites. Angkor Wat, the amazing temple complex in Cambodia, likewise has midsummer alignments.

Countless villages and towns around Britain would build huge midsummer bonfires to celebrate the culmination of the Sun's path in the sky. The Christianisation of midsummer comes in the form of bonfires on St John's Eve, June 23, before the feast day of John the Baptist **(centre)**, which is one of the few feast days that honours the birth of a saint, rather than their death. It is celebrated across the world in Catholic countries, and in some cultures people leap over fires, symbolising a cleansing of the soul and protection from evil spirits. Up and down Britain midsummer celebrations still take place; the Golowan Festival is held at midsummer in Penzance, Cornwall; the name comes from *Gol-Jowan,* the Cornish for the *'Feast of St John'.* Activities include the rolling of flaming wheels (symbolising the Sun), an 'obby 'oss called Penglaz **(left)**, and a wild *serpent dance.* Although this festival does not have a long history, it demonstrates the impetus to celebrate the longest day of the year.

Fairies are also said to abound at midsummer, as famously portrayed in the story of the Fairy King,

Oberon, and the Fairy Queen, Titania, in Shakespeare's *'A Midsummer Night's Dream'*. It is a time for dreams and divination, for seeing into the future; there are tales of young girls looking into the waters of holy wells on midsummer night in the hope they would see an image of the man they would marry.

Lammas/Lugnassad

In early August, Celtic countries have long celebrated the festival of Lammas or Lammastide, which derived from the Anglo-Saxon word for *Loaf Mass*. It marked the time when the first small loaves were made following the harvest and which were ritually consumed, and there were processions around farmland and pastures. Lammas fairs are still held all over Europe, particularly in Ireland, and are traditionally times of dancing, games and storytelling, a celebration of the abundance of wild berries, apples and grain.

However, in more ancient times, we can clearly identify this festival with Lughnassad or Lughnasadh, named after the ancient god Lugh or Lud **(right)**. He is a solar deity, the *'Light Bearer'*, also known variously as Llew, Lug, Lugus, or Lludd. He first appears in Portugal around 700BC and was later replaced by Mercury or Nodens as the Romans spread across Europe, and later still was metamorphosed into archangel St Michael. Root words concerning his name suggest *lightning* and *raven,* an association we shall see with other deities. Lugh is the god of the harvest, metalwork and blacksmiths, and is known as *'Lugh of the Long Arm'* or *'long-handed'* and in Wales as *'Llew of the skilled hand'*. He was skilled with a slingshot and possessed a magical spear. The River Lea in London is Lugh's River, and it rises from springs at Waulid's Bank, a Neolithic site where tradition says Lugh took the waters to receive his divine powers. It is interesting, and perhaps not coincidental, that the 2012 London Olympics were held alongside this river, and at Lammas! (Thorley 2012). This links back to ancient Greece, where the birthday of Athena was celebrated with huge festivals around this time.

It is interesting that the St Michael Line, the great Cornwall to East Anglia alignment, is usually described as lining up with sunrise on Beltaine. However, the annual cycle of the Sun ensures that it also aligns with sunrise in early August, at Lughnassad (Thorley 2012).

Autumn Equinox/Harvest Festival/Michaelmas

Today, Churches traditionally hold Harvest Festival on the nearest Sunday to the Harvest Moon, the full moon closest the autumn equinox, a time when days and nights are again equal. A selection of wheat, barley and other produce is displayed in churches **(centre)** and appropriate hymns sung. These practices reflect similar ones that have been held for

thousands of years in other cultures, to honour the ancient deities that had blessed the crops. Shown here **(bottom image, previous page)** is a display during a Hindu agricultural festival sacred to Vishnu, celebrated throughout India.

Corn dollies **(left)** are traditionally made from the very last stalks of grain when a field is harvested. This has been carried out since ancient times as it was believed that the Grain Mother was homeless following the harvest. The dolly was ploughed back into the field the following spring. The goddess in question is Ceres, the Roman goddess of the grain, from which the word cereal is derived **(centre)**. Osiris was the 'green man' and god of the fields in ancient Egypt **(images p. 59 & 207)**. John Barleycorn was a harvest god, whose body was sacrificed by ploughing it into the earth, to be harvested later and made into bread and ale. Cornish people still celebrate *Crying the Neck* in early September, which involves the ceremonial cutting of the very last sheaves of wheat, which are then taken into the church, and followed by a special harvest thanksgiving service. (In the USA, *Thanksgiving* is a major celebration and public holiday, although this event is held in November.)

In Abbots Bromley, Staffordshire, a Horn Dance is performed on the first Sunday after September 4 **(bottom)**. Real antlers are mounted on replica deer heads, six painted white and six black, symbolising the conflict between the light and the dark. Dancing ensues, and includes characters such as Maiden Marian, a bowman and an 'Obby 'Oss. Carbon-dating suggests that the antlers date back to the 11th century, and it is possible that the festival goes back to at least Anglo-Saxon times. There may also be links to the worship of Cernunnos, the antlered *'Lord of the Forest'* **(image p. 93)**, who the Church was later to tar with the same brush as the Devil. Prehistoric cave art has been found depicting shamans wearing antler headdresses and carrying bows **(image p. 92)**. These probably depict the act of sympathetic magic, rites to attract herds for hunting, and many antlers were ceremonially deposited in Neolithic and Bronze Age burials.

In the Christian calendar, Michaelmas is celebrated on September 29, just after the equinox, and generally marks the end of the harvest. Fairs were often held on this day, which commemorates the much celebrated defeat of Lucifer by St Michael the Archangel, although the latter is probably a replacement for Lugh and Mercury. The scales he holds in some images remind us of this balancing/ tipping point between highest and lowest Sun.

Waldorf schools celebrate this day as the *Festival of Strong Will,* and Steiner considered it second in importance only to Easter. Traditionally a Goose is eaten, as well as nuts and a special *Michael Cake,* made using the grains of all the cereal crops. Modern Druids perform an annual ceremony, first recorded in 1792, on Primrose Hill, London, at this time.

All Hallows Eve/Samhain

Samhain is the quarter-day which falls on Oct 31/Nov 1, and which used to mark the Celtic new year; this time was also known as Summer End, or Winter's Eve. Excess cattle were slaughtered prior to winter, and ewes were mated for lambing in the spring. Great fires were lit and some of the animals were offered as sacrifices to the gods. It was the time when the Grain Mother became the Crone, the Hag or Cailleach, the *Dark Mother of Winter,* seen as a time when the veil between this world and the ancestral Otherworld was the thinnest; the Druids regarded it as a fortuitous time for divination. In the Neolithic, it was at this time that people may have entered the dark chambers of places such as Newgrange and West Kennet Long Barrow, to commune with their own ancestors (Knight 2011).

This association of Samhain with the ancestors and the dead had to be turned around by a Church, who found the idea of communing with the dead to be abhorrent. So all manner of negatives were attached, such as ghosts and the living dead, all the cohorts of the Devil and Hell; Hellenes was in fact the Norse Queen of the Underworld. This important Pagan festival was supplanted with All Saints' Day and, the day after, All Souls' Day. The slaughter of animals now became associated with Martinmas (Nov 11) and, in some areas, St Andrew's Day (Nov 30). The Samhain bonfires were transferred to November 5, with Guy Fawkes becoming the new sacrificial victim; children dressed as ghouls and zombies doing their *trick or treat* have replaced a once-sacred festival. When I attend private bonfires at this time I take a dragon kite, which flies unencumbered from the old year into the new **(right)**.

Carved and illuminated pumpkins, swedes and turnips used to represent the cauldron of the Hag Goddess, her light seeing us through the dark nights ahead, warding off evil **(top)**. I run a Samhain gathering at West Kennet Long Barrow, in which we drum and then have a quiet time to connect with the ancestors. We usually take a carved pumpkin, which is placed in the west chamber **(centre)**; our pumpkin always wears a big friendly smile.

7. High Places

Since the dawn of Man's spirituality, mountains and hills have been regarded as special, holy places, and in many cases lie at the very heart of cultural cosmologies. As well as places of inspiration and aspiration, mountains are symbolic of transcendence, spiritual ascension, and the home of the immortals, nature spirits and the gods. They are places where we look not only to the land below, but also into our heart and soul. Perhaps their significance is that they are close to the heavens – closest to deity. Mount Fuji **(image p. 166)** is Japan's highest mountain and is sacred to both Shintoism and Buddhism, whose followers believe it to be a physical manifestation of God. Australian Aborigines revere Uluru **(top)** as the site of the Dreamtime. The Potala Palace at Lhasa is a place of pilgrimage for Tibetan Buddhists and is perched on one of the highest parts of the Himalayas. Mount Kailash, also in the Himalayas, has four sides which have been compared to a diamond by Buddhists, and the mountain is also sacred to Hindus. As well as being a volcano, Mount Olympus **(centre)** is famously the home of the Greek gods. The Greeks also believed that the gods chained the multi-headed Typhon within Mount Etna, and that the creature was responsible for its volcanic activity. The Greek oracle centre at Delphi also nestles within a mountainous setting.

Devil's Tower (made famous by the movie *Close Encounters of the Third Kind*), is a mountain that is sacred to several of the Great Plains Indian tribes, and Machu Picchu, the sacred Inca site, is perched nearly 8,000ft (2400m) up in the Peruvian Andes.

Around Europe, hills and mountains were the abode of dragons, trolls, goblins, dwarves and elves, places where magical weapons and rings were forged (Knight 1998); *Hall of the Mountain King* by Greig, for instance, tells the story of a Troll King. King Arthur rests inside both Glastonbury Tor **(bottom)** and Cadbury Castle, depending on the myth; the King of the Otherworld, Gwyn ap Nudd, also holds court beneath the Tor. Merlin is said to lie beneath the mound at Marlborough College, in Wiltshire, and in the same county, King Sil is said to be sitting upright on his horse deep within Silbury Hill. Tower Hill, on which the Tower of London stands, is where the oracular head of Bran was buried, as well as the grave of Brutus, the founder of London. The Hill of Tara, Ireland, was the seat of the ancient Irish kings, and has monuments dating back to the Neolithic, demonstrating that it has been a holy hill for millennia **(right)**.

Sometimes the very topography of the land was perceived as the body of the Earth Goddess, such as twinned hills that resembled breasts, or rounded hills seen as her pregnant tummy. The Cerne Giant, the ithyphallic chalk figure in Dorset, is appropriately positioned on a elongated, phallic-shaped hill (Knight 2013).

When Christianity spread across Europe, it was met at every turn with people celebrating on sacred hills and mountains, even making pilgrimage to them. Hundreds of churches and chapels were erected on these lofty Pagan *Sun Hills,* many of which were rededicated to St Michael, like at St Michael's Mount in Cornwall **(centre image, next page)** and Mont St Michel in Brittany **(image p. 168)**. Many of these are on solar alignments, such as the St Michael Line and the Apollo/Athena Line, where, having replaced the old gods, it was now St Michael and St George who were standing guard, as these two dragon-slayers took over many of the attributes of the vanquished gods. In Chinese geomancy, it is believed that the male (yang) energies flow across mountaintops, whereas the feminine (yin) energies occupy lower ground such as valleys (Biltcliffe and Hoare 2012). It is appropriate, therefore, that two *male* saints should have been chosen to Christianise the Pagan hilltop shrines. St Anne is associated with hills due to her replacing the Celtic god Tan and the Earth Mother Anu. Sports were formerly held on Tan Hill in Wiltshire on St Anne's Day, August 6, close to the festival of Lammas/Lughnassad. Many Christian saints are recorded having had mystical experiences at these elevated pre-Christian sacred places.

Sometimes there is a dynamic inter-relationship between hills and the Sun. The solar disc climbs up the north side of Glastonbury Tor at the midwinter solstice when viewed from a nearby hill (Mann and Glasson 2007). I have witnessed the Sun rolling down Silbury Hill, Wiltshire, at midsummer solstice sunset **(images bottom of next page)**.

It is hardly surprising that mountains crop up at fairly regular intervals in the Bible. By taking themselves up isolated mountains, away from their own people, Moses **(centre)** and other Biblical heroes are carrying out a very ancient and shamanic practice. Biblical stories also demonstrated how it was now God (singular) that resided in high places, and no longer the banished gods, demons or trolls. Moses felt compelled to trek up Mount Sinai **(right)**, a huge granite mountain in Egypt, on his shamanic vision quest (perhaps to *Moses' Cave),* where

31

he 'visioned' the Ten Commandments, most probably during a dream sleep, a well known practice amongst shamans. The hill is sacred to Jews, Christians and Muslims. St Catherine, the 4th century martyr, is also associated with high places due to the legend that she was carried to Mount Sinai by angels following her martyrdom. Mount Sinai is now home to two chapels, which further Christianise this ancient sacred mountain. Moses later saw the Promised Land from another high place, Mount Pisgah.

Mount Carmel is where Elijah defeated the priests of the god Baal. Legend has it he challenged 450 Pagan priests/prophets to light a sacrificial fire on the altar in his cave. After they failed to achieve this, Elijah succeeded, despite saturating the altar with water, proclaiming the power of God.

Mountains are featured elsewhere in the Bible; the Ark of Noah came to rest on Mount Ararat following the great flood **(image p. 156)**; Mount Gilead was the scene of a covenant between Laban and Jacob; Mount Lebanon was the source of wood for Solomon's Temple; Mount Moriah was the site of Abraham's intended sacrifice; the *Sermon on the Mount* took place on a high point in Galilee and was Jesus' longest discourse **(top),** which included *The Lord's Prayer.* He was later crucified on Mount Olivet, or the Mount of Olives, which also featured in David's flight from Absalom.

In so many ways, the wise men of the Bible replicated the heroes and shamans of the pre-Christian era, going on shamanic vision quests to attain divine intervention, wisdom, and a purification of their souls. It must be remembered that most of the Biblical events unfolded in the Bronze and Iron Age, times when shamanism as a vehicle for enlightenment and contact with the gods and the ancestors was at its peak.

The *Silbury Roll,* observed by the author at the 2011 summer solstice sunset.

8. Gods and Thunderbolts

Most Pagan cultures, be they pre-Christian or even from the historical era, have believed in the existence of a host of gods and goddesses, who control all aspects of their lives and of all life on this planet. This has been cited as the main difference between Pagan religions and Christianity, where the latter has just one Supreme Being, the *One God*. But the more we look at ancient cultures, the more we see that even in Pagan belief systems there is usually one supreme and omnipotent god, one that may be the father to all the others, or at least sits atop the hierarchical tree.

Christianity stemmed from Judaic origins, which similarly only has one God – they both embrace monotheism. Jews can trace their ancestry back to the Hebrews, whose story is told in the Old Testament. Even the God of Christianity has three aspects, the Father, the Son and the Holy Spirit – a triple deity, like so many before. The more we look at the omnipotent and omnipresent Judaic-Islamic-Christian God, the more we see similarities with the ancient alpha male deities such as Zeus **(second)** and Jupiter **(right)**.

Hinduism is one of the world's oldest surviving religions. The chief deity is Brahman, the God of Creation, said to have been self-born from a lotus flower. He is split into three aspects (as in the Christian Trinity) called Brahma, the creator, Vishnu, the preserver, and Shiva, the destroyer and re-creator. These reign supreme over a whole pantheon of other deities that oversee all aspects of Hindu life. Brahman is frequently depicted with three heads, again reminiscent of the Holy Trinity. Although Buddhism had its origins in the 5rd century BC, the major difference in Hindu and Buddhist belief is the non-adherence by the latter to the concept of a supreme God. However, later we shall see how some aspects of Buddhist imagery were indeed drawn into Christian symbolism.

Although there were many gods and goddesses in ancient Egypt, the chief male deity was Ra or Ra-Atum **(top image)**, later to be known as Amon-Ra, the solar god and creator of all that exists and ruler of the world; the Pharaohs called themselves the *Sons of Ra*. In his daily journey across the sky, Ra is shown in a boat. In many other images he is seated on a throne, similar to how God is depicted by the Church **(right)**; Ra

was the consort of both Hathor and Isis. The sacrifice of bulls was a central theme in the worship of Ra, and this was repeated by cultures across the ancient world, including Jewish and Christian. Sekhmet was a violent lioness goddess who was created from the fire in Ra's eye; lions were later to feature in Christian myths and symbolism. The *'Eye of Horus'*, like the eye of God, sees all and is a frequently depicted icon **(image, front cover)**

The Greeks, like the Egyptians, had many gods and deities that ruled over the affairs of the world of men and Nature, and yet the greatest of these was undoubtedly Zeus, who ruled a pantheon of 12 great gods on Mount Olympus. Zeus is different from other supreme gods in respect that other gods preceded him, so, in effect, he was *not* the *creator* of all things. He is characterised by hurling lightning and thunderbolts when enraged, and he bore the goddess Athena through his own forehead, as if she were a product of his own creative mind. Again, Zeus is often depicted seated on a throne **(second image, previous page)**, master of all he surveys.

The supreme Roman god was Jupiter **(third image, previous page)**, who was the god of light, and who was also capable of hurling thunderbolts and lightning across the sky **(top)**, like Zeus, the Norse god Thor, and the Christian God. Jupiter was the great protector of cities and the State, guardian of public morality, oaths and treaties. His name was also Jove, and this invites comparison with the Judaic-Christian name for God – Jehovah.

The Christian-Hebrew God of both Biblical Testaments can be seen to embrace many of the attributes of earlier supreme beings, such as wrath, mercy, the use of thunder and lightning **(second image)**, and can be seated on a throne somewhere 'on high', such as in the sky or on top of a mountain; he is physically unobtainable and his lofty position means he sees all. The similarities are hardly surprising when we consider the roots of Christianity and Judaism have a common origin, which, ironically, can be found midst the polytheist religions that heavily influenced them.

The *Eye of God* or the *All Seeing Eye* is a well known Christian icon for God, but, as mentioned above, the Egyptians used their own *Eye of God* way back in prehistory. Egyptian boats had eyes painted on their prows for divine protection. Most Buddhist stupas, or shrines, display four eyes **(third image)**, known as the *Eyes of Wisdom,* facing the four directions, symbolising the all-seeing omniscience of the Buddha. Sometimes eyes are set into the palms of the Buddha's hands, and similar hands with inset eyes were used as amulets to Ishtar and Inanna in prehistoric Mesopotamia, which were said to offer protection against evil. The Phoenicians had a similar hand that represented Tanit, again used to ward off evil. Muslims have a similar symbol, known as the *Hand of Fatima,* after Mohammed's wife.

One is reminded of the eye of Sauron, the all-seeing eye of Tolkien's *Lord of the Rings*.

The eye is featured on the American one dollar bill, rising in a triangle at the apex of a pyramid **(bottom left, previous page)**, and this image was adopted as part of the Great Seal of the USA. This is known by Freemasons as the 'Eye of Providence', first illustrated in Freemasonry literature in 1797, serving as a reminder that the Great Architect of the Universe observes their actions. An eye inside a triangle is a frequent depiction in secular and Christian art.

Doves are a common Christian representation for the Holy Spirit aspect of the Holy Trinity, seen here as hovering over the Madonna and Child **(bottom right, previous page)**. But, once again, there is an older origin for these birds representing divinity. In the Middle East, doves symbolised the Goddess; Iron Age shrines dedicated to Astarte and Asherah had doves perched on the top, and some Roman votive offerings depicting pilgrims holding doves were found at a shrine in Gaul, brought as gifts for Apollo. In churches, sometimes the *Eye of God* and a dove descending from Heaven are shown together, as shown here from a church in County Down, Northern Ireland **(top)**.

Sometimes it is the *Hand of God* that reveals itself, such as when the Ten Commandments were carved for Moses, or the *Hand of God* that created Adam, so beautifully depicted by Michelangelo in the Sistine Chapel **(below right).** Yet again, ancient gods are frequently shown gesturing to mere mortals, or bestowing blessings or warnings to them. Zeus is shown here **(second image),** and the next image shows the extended hand of the Cerne Giant, Dorset **(right)**, whose empty hand gestures to the local sacred spring, as well as south to the culminating Sun (Knight 2013). Sumerian gods also extended their hands to indicate help or friendship, or as a display of chastisement **(below left)**.

One difference between Christianity and Pagan religions is that in the latter there were also a host of goddesses, female deities who were venerated in equal measure to that of the gods, and sometimes even more so. However, the creatrix Goddess *did* survive the patriarchal dogma of the Church, if subliminally, as we shall see later.

It must be reiterated that the Church did not invent the concept of Monotheism - *One God.* The radical Egyptian pharaoh Akhenaten had championed that concept before 1336BC, which was met with horror and rebuttal by the Egyptian priesthood as it rejected all the ideals and mythologies that had gone before.

William Blake shows many components of the ancient mythos of an Almighty God in two of his dramatic paintings illustrated here **(images p. 53 and 58)**.

9. Heavenly Hosts

The '*Heavenly Hosts'* refers to a group of holy angels mentioned in both the Hebrew and Christian Bibles (e.g. Luke 2:13), as well as other texts (*'host'* comes from the Hebrew *Sabaoth,* meaning *'armies'*). They participate in wars, particularly against the Devil/Satan, and can also be purveyors of morality, punishers of wrong doings, and messengers; the word *angel* in fact derives from the Greek word for *'messenger'*. There is a whole cluster of angelic beings, which theologians have layered into several hierarchies. This is so reminiscent of the pantheons of ancient cultures, whereby supreme deities had lesser, subservient beings at their behest.

Angels
Nowadays, angels are usually thought of as purely Christian or Hebrew characters, immortal beings living outside time, who appear at important junctures in the Bible. Angels ascending Jacob's ladder **(top)** is one popular parable involving these winged allies of God. An angel is often shown passing a Grail to Jesus prior to his arrest **(images p. 187)**, and it is an angel who announces to Mary Magdalene at the empty tomb that, *'He is risen'.* But God's winged allies are much older than Christianity. The Egyptians often depicted a winged Sun disc, and had winged deities such as Maat **(centre)**. Winged beings are a common image of Assyro-Babylonian cultures of the Middle East **(left)**. In Sumerian and Hebrew mythology, the demonic sexually dynamic Lilith is shown as a female winged figure, who derived from a Babylonian being called Lilitu, meaning *spirit*. She is shown on the iconic *Burney Relief* from Babylonia, now in the British Museum,

and is dated 1800-1750BC; she is naked and curvaceous, and was known as the *Lady of the Night* **(right)**.

In Mesopotamia, an 8th century BC Hebrew seal shows a winged solar disc and winged lions, and a statue of a benevolent winged male figure stood at the gates of the palace of Sargon II at Khorsabad, and is also dated 8th century BC. An Assyrian bas-relief from 885BC depicts an eagle-headed winged male figure. Clearly, Hebrews were well aware of winged creatures before their departure from Babylon and the return to their homeland in 539BC, and it is easy to see that they would be worked into Christian mythology.

Eros of the Greeks **(centre)**, and his Roman equivalent Cupid, was the winged god of love, who still features in romantic ballads today; he is spoken of by Hesiod as early as 700BC. In ancient Greece, the Anemoi or *wind gods* were often personified as winged men; the Greek myths of winged Icarus **(bottom image)** flying too close to the Sun is another winged man who clearly aspires to join angelic realms; an Etruscan myth tells of a winged man named Tailate, who is shown on a mug dated 630BC. Pegasus, Chimera, and the Sirens are yet more winged mythological beasts, whilst the Aztecs worshipped Huitzilopochtli, another winged god. Buddhism's equivalent of angels are devas, beings occupying non-earthly planes but which can be contacted by more enlightened humans. The Hindu equivalents are the Dakini, or *Sky Walkers,* who are immortal, ethereal beings who carry the souls of the dead up into the sky; the winged Valkyries of Norse myths do likewise **(image p. 171)**.

Archangels

There are four Archangels in Christian mythology, and they are some of the most commonly depicted icons to be found in churches. It may be worth looking at their qualities and attributes before we look for their ancient counterparts.

St Raphael is often shown with a pilgrim's staff or a fish, for he stirred the healing waters of the Pool of Bethesda, where Jesus healed a paralytic **(image p. 210)**.

St Gabriel has a Lily and a trumpet amongst his symbols. He appeared to the Virgin Mary at the Annunciation (hence the Lily – Mary's symbol), and he also announced the birth of John the Baptist; it is also said that it is Gabriel who appeared to Mary Magdalene and others after the Resurrection **(top left, next page)**. It will be he who will proclaim the Last Judgment by the blowing of his horn.

St Uriel often holds a scroll or book, and is first described in the Book of Enoch, from the Hebrew *Apocrypha*. He came down to Earth and bred with human women, fathering a race of giants, which some researchers allude to aliens seeding the Earth. It was St Uriel who appeared to Noah,

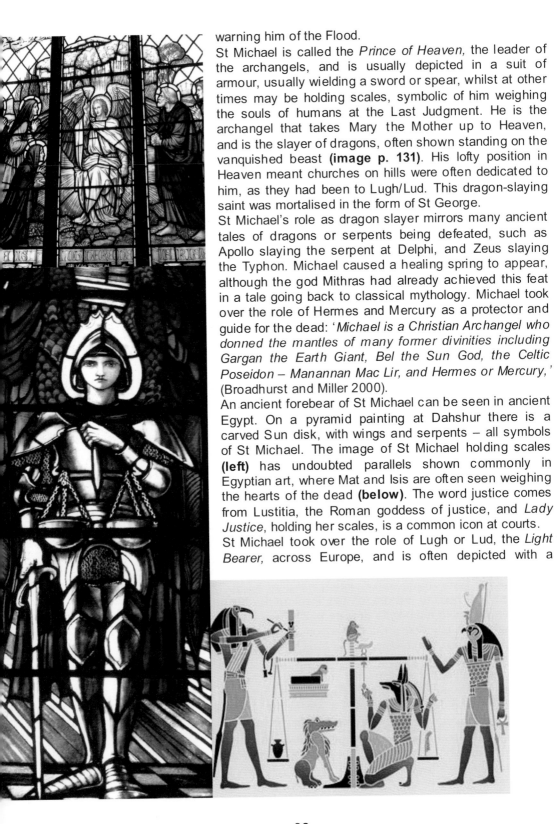

warning him of the Flood.

St Michael is called the *Prince of Heaven,* the leader of the archangels, and is usually depicted in a suit of armour, usually wielding a sword or spear, whilst at other times may be holding scales, symbolic of him weighing the souls of humans at the Last Judgment. He is the archangel that takes Mary the Mother up to Heaven, and is the slayer of dragons, often shown standing on the vanquished beast **(image p. 131)**. His lofty position in Heaven meant churches on hills were often dedicated to him, as they had been to Lugh/Lud. This dragon-slaying saint was mortalised in the form of St George.

St Michael's role as dragon slayer mirrors many ancient tales of dragons or serpents being defeated, such as Apollo slaying the serpent at Delphi, and Zeus slaying the Typhon. Michael caused a healing spring to appear, although the god Mithras had already achieved this feat in a tale going back to classical mythology. Michael took over the role of Hermes and Mercury as a protector and guide for the dead: '*Michael is a Christian Archangel who donned the mantles of many former divinities including Gargan the Earth Giant, Bel the Sun God, the Celtic Poseidon – Manannan Mac Lir, and Hermes or Mercury,*' (Broadhurst and Miller 2000).

An ancient forebear of St Michael can be seen in ancient Egypt. On a pyramid painting at Dahshur there is a carved Sun disk, with wings and serpents – all symbols of St Michael. The image of St Michael holding scales **(left)** has undoubted parallels shown commonly in Egyptian art, where Mat and Isis are often seen weighing the hearts of the dead **(below)**. The word justice comes from Lustitia, the Roman goddess of justice, and *Lady Justice*, holding her scales, is a common icon at courts.

St Michael took over the role of Lugh or Lud, the *Light Bearer,* across Europe, and is often depicted with a flaming sword, which has its origins in several ancient myths. In Norse myth, for instance, the leader of the giants, Surtur, wields a flaming sword. Magical swords abound in ancient mythology, and one is reminded of Excalibur of Arthurian legend, and, in modern sagas, the light sabers of the Star Wars movies. We shall return to St Michael regarding his dragon-slaying exploits later. In many aspects St Michael took on the mantle of Nike, the Greek winged goddess, who later became Victoria to the Romans.

Like the archangel, she is the winged goddess of strength and triumphant victory, and often carries a spear; she is depicted on the original World Cup Jules Rimet trophy, and the example here **(right)** stands at the top of the Victory Column in Berlin.

It is interesting that there are **four** Archangels, each assigned with both a particular element and a compass direction (e.g. St Michael is associated with fire and the east). This is very much in keeping with many ancient gods and goddesses. In Norse mythology, four dwarves are described in the *Prose Edda,* each of whom support a pillar of the heavenly dome at each cardinal point; four stags guarded the world ash Yggdrasil; in Egypt, Horus had four sons, whilst the Anemoi or *wind gods* of the Greeks were each ascribed a direction of the compass. In Buddhism, *Four Heavenly Kings* watch the cardinal points.

The concept of angels was also adopted by Islam. To Muslims, angels are beings of light who praise Allah and carry out his will. The chief angel, Jibril, was Mohammed's constant helper and purified the prophet's heart in preparation for his ascension. He is sometimes equated with St Gabriel, but his role as recorder of a person's deeds on the *Last Day* invites comparison with St Michael.

Seraphim and Cherubim

These lesser angelic beings perform more menial roles at God's behest. Seraphim appeared in visions to both Isaiah and St Francis. It is interesting that in Christian Gnostic texts Seraphim are described as *'dragon-shaped angels',* suggesting a link to older myths. Cherubim accompany God's chariot-throne, guard the Tree of Life, and stand at the gates of Eden, or Paradise, with flaming swords (Genesis 3:24); yet two more were installed on top of the Ark of the Covenant **(two images, right)**. Cherubim are often depicted directing winds, echoing the wind gods of ancient myths. In the Jewish Kabbalah, Cherubim are said to have mystical roles, whereas later art relegated them to appear as chubby children with wings **(image p. 221)**.

In this chapter, I have illustrated images from the Mesopotamians, Egyptians, Greeks, Hebrews, and some from Christianity. I hope I have demonstrated how old the concept of the angels really is, and how it was adopted, like so many other elements, by the Church.

10. Starry Starry Night

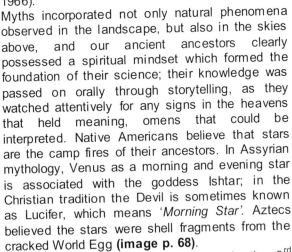

The nursery rhyme *'Twinkle Twinkle Little Star'* is one that millions of children have known and grown to love for generations. Man has always watched the heavens, wondering at the attributes of the twinkles overhead. Like music, stars speak to us in a universal language, enabling them to be mythologised and interpreted regardless of millennia, religion, culture and geographical location. Way back in prehistory, once the stars and planets had been named and myths attached to them, they were promoted in status, possessing the very energies and supernatural powers of the gods they represented; George Scott observed: *'It was but a small step from the personification of an object or force to the deification of that same object or force. Thus the moon, the sun, the stars, the heavens, became deities'* (Scott 1966).

Myths incorporated not only natural phenomena observed in the landscape, but also in the skies above, and our ancient ancestors clearly possessed a spiritual mindset which formed the foundation of their science; their knowledge was passed on orally through storytelling, as they watched attentively for any signs in the heavens that held meaning, omens that could be interpreted. Native Americans believe that stars are the camp fires of their ancestors. In Assyrian mythology, Venus as a morning and evening star is associated with the goddess Ishtar; in the Christian tradition the Devil is sometimes known as Lucifer, which means *'Morning Star'*. Aztecs believed the stars were shell fragments from the cracked World Egg **(image p. 68)**.

Ancient Egyptians and Babylonians, in the 3rd millennium BC, were studying the motions of their sky gods, relating them to issues such as the Creation, as they strove to find Mankind's place in their cosmology; for all natural forces were seen as products of the will and actions of the gods. In ancient Egypt, deities were often represented by stars; Isis was seen as Sothis, or Sirius, whilst Osiris was Orion **(top)**. The sky goddess Nut is often shown with a body covered in stars **(left)**, and *The Book of Nut* is a series of in-depth Egyptian astronomical texts.

The constellations and familiar zodiac signs are an

inheritance passed down to us from cultures such as the Sumerians in the Indus Valley, some 5,500 years ago; the zodiac circle was known as the *Furrow of Heaven,* ploughed by the heavenly bull, Taurus, in records dating from 3880BC. The stars not only influenced people's lives, but political and social order was celestially governed. The belief that the Sun, the Moon, and the planets influence our lives is ancient (and one of course that persists to this day); the Babylonians, Hebrews, Greeks, Romans and Hindus all had their own version of the zodiac. The Dendera Zodiac is a complex map of the heavens seen through Egyptian eyes in the 1st millennium BC (Knight 2013, p. 113). It was found in 1799 on the ceiling of the Ptolemaic temple of Hathor at Dendera, and shows constellations, stars and planets portrayed as mythic gods, goddesses and animals; the Greek word for *zodiac* simply means, *'house of the animals',* and we shall look further into animal mythology later.

Zodiac signs have designated elements and rulers, and have been an important part of alchemical practices. Pliny, writing in 270BC, listed 45 constellations, whilst Ptolemy mentions 48; Aristotle stated that the gods were originally stars, and that all the forces that control Man's destiny resided in the starry vaults. Today we make a clear distinction between mythology and science, and perhaps our world is the poorer for it. Even in ancient times, this state of affairs was already rearing its head, as Aristotle observed: *'We tend to think of the stars as mere bodies or items arranged in order, without soul or Life. We ought rather to regard them as possessed of Life and activity.'*

Neolithic sites across the world are aligned with stars (Knight 2011 & 2013). Recent research at Gőbekli Tepe, the ancient temple complex in Turkey, has revealed stellar alignments (Collins 2014), and the pyramids at Giza are famously aligned with Sirius and Orion. Much later, the lives of Iron Age people were controlled as much by the stars as they were by the Sun. Sometimes the heavens were mirrored on Earth, as in the Glastonbury Zodiac (Leitch 2014). The Cerne Giant in Dorset has been dated as Iron Age by means of my work on its stellar alignments; and I discuss this and more stellar lore in my work on the Giant (Knight 2013).

In light of the ancient tradition that stars can be portents and affect humans, it is hardly surprising that they turn up at key moments in the Hebrew-Christian tradition. To the Greeks, many stars had been placed in the night sky by the god Zeus; but it now had to be shown that it was the God of Abraham who was orchestrating the heavens. In the Old Testament, at the very moment of the Creation in Genesis, God creates the stars in the firmament. Later, Job 38: 21-32 states, *'Can you bind the chains of the Pleiades, or loose the cords of Orion?' Can you lead forth Mazzaroth in their season, and can you guide the Bear [Ursa Major] and it's children'.* There are many more references to stars throughout the Bible, and even near the end, in Revelations 8:10, we find the passage, *'The third angel blew his trumpet, and a great star fell from Heaven'.* A Hebrew zodiac from a synagogue is shown here **(top)**, dated 6th century AD. The Romans brought the solar god Mithras to Britain, and here he sacrifices Taurus the bull, encircled by zodiac symbols **(bottom).** One of the riches of Chartres Cathedral is the amazing *Zodiac Window* **(images p. 103 & 108).**

41

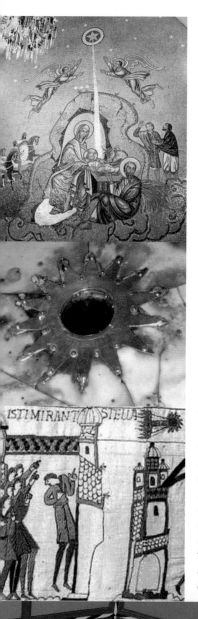

The Star of Bethlehem **(left)**, as told of in Matthew's Gospel, is a perennial favourite, sung about and re-created every year as an adornment of countless Christmas trees. The site believed to be the birthplace of Jesus in Bethlehem is, in fact, marked by a star or sun set into the floor **(second image)**. The star was followed by the Three Magi (Chapter 32), who saw it as the *Star of Prophecy,* heralding the coming of the Messiah. In the Eastern Orthodox Church, it is believed that the star was an angel sent to lead the Magi, whilst Jehovah's Witness adherents believe this star was a product of the Devil, as it led the Magi to Herod. Debate has raged as to whether this bright star was a planetary conjunction, or Venus, or an exploding supernova, and even Christians thought such unusual or temporary stars were portents. Famously, Halley's Comet is depicted on the Bayeux Tapestry **(third image)**, seen by the Normans as an assurance from God that victory over the English was guaranteed. Note also the stars around the Madonna and Child in the image on p. 34.

Although its use as a magical symbol goes way back into prehistory, in Christian tradition the five-pointed pentagram represents the five wounds of Jesus. The Greeks used five-pointed stars to represent the seeds that the god Cronos placed within Earth, and alchemists have used five-pointed star sigil for millennia; it is used today as a symbol of the Goddess by Pagans (it is, after all, an ancient sign for Venus). The roof of Rosslyn Chapel is adorned with dozens of five-pointed stars **(below right)**. The six-pointed Star of David is the classic political-religious symbol recognized universally as a symbol of Judaism and Israel, but which is equally ancient, as I will demonstrate later.

Stars have been used extensively in heraldry over the centuries, and even today are corporate and nationalist icons; 56 nations around the globe have stars on their flags.

So when you go into a church today and see stars adorning the ceiling **(below left)**, pause to think that over 2000 years ago temples were similarly decorated as an acknowledgment of the importance of stars; nothing is new.

11. Moments in Time – What's in a Name?

Man has perpetually used symbolism and ritual to mark the cycles and rhythms of life. Countless ancient sites, including Stonehenge and Avebury, marked out the positions of the Sun, Moon and the stars as they changed throughout the year, and through much longer cycles. The Aztecs and Maya carved huge *calendar stones* to mark the passage of time, sometimes covering many millennia, and we also know the Egyptians used sundials. The concept that zodiacal stars divided up the turning year is very ancient, as I described in the previous chapter. The Moon's cycles, especially, regulated the calendars of the Celtics, and to this day Chinese, Muslim and Jewish calendars are lunar based (see Chapter 35). Chronos **(right)** was the Greek god of time, who is often shown entwined with a serpent representing eternity. The words *chronology* and *chronicle* both derive from his name, and in Greek mosaics he is sometimes shown turning the zodiacal wheel. Father Time is the anthropomorphism of the relentless march of time, who is depicted as carrying a scythe or hourglass **(right)**, and who had his origins with both Chronos and Saturn, the ancient gods of time. The Grim Reaper is their latter day counterpart, who is generally used to warn people of an imminent death.

In Chapter 6 we saw how a myriad of symbols and myths are attached different seasons of the year. Another enduring legacy of our Pagan ancestry is the origins of the ways we gauge time today, be it a month, day of the week, or even hours. They mostly derived from pre-Christian times, and have remained in common usage over the last 2000 years. Let's have a look how our distant ancestors still affect our everyday lives.

Divisions of Time

Hour derives from the Latin *hōra*, although there is good evidence to show that the Sumerians, Egyptians, and the peoples of ancient India, had already divided up the day into smaller divisions of time, centuries before the Roman Empire.

Day comes to us from the Latin *dies*, by way of the Old English *daeg*, which is associated with the god *Dagr,* the Norse personification of the day, as shown in this 1874 painting by Peter Arbo **(right)**. In the Norse *Prose Edda,* the

43

god races across the sky on a white horse, gifting daylight to mankind.

Night comes from the Greek *nux*, the Latin *nox*, the Old Norse *natt,* and finally via the Old English word *niht*.

Week comes from the Old English *wice* and the Germanic *wikon,* meaning *'turn, move, change'.* The captive Hebrews of Babylonia were using the concept of a week as early as the 6th century BC.

Fortnight derives from the Old English *fēowertyne niht,* literally meaning *'14 nights'.* This unit of measurement was based on *nights* rather than days because it was used to denote half (14.77 days) of the average lunar cycle. Its origins can be traced back to the ancient Hebrew word *shvu'ayim,* meaning *'two weeks'.*

Month was first used in Mesopotamia as a natural period based on the motion of the Moon, based on the consecutive appearances of the same phase (29.53 days).

Year comes from the Saxon word *gēar,* the Gothic *jēr,* and the Norse rune *jēran or jera.* *Annual* and *anniversary* come from the Roman *annus,* meaning *'year'.*

Calendar comes from the Roman *Kalendae,* which was Latin for *calends,* the name given to the first days of each month, as well as to signify a new lunar cycle.

Decade comes from the Greek word *dekas,* meaning ten.

Months of the Year

January comes from the Latin *Ianuarius,* and was named after Janus, the god of beginnings and transition, sometimes shown with two faces **(left)**. His name came from the Latin for door, *ianua.* It was named and added to the Roman calendar around 713BC, and became the first month of the Roman year from about 450BC. Saxons knew it as *Wulf-monath,* or the *Wolf Month.*

February was the Roman month *Februarius,* after *februum,* which means purification. The ritual of *Februa* was held annually at this time, and the month is recorded as part of the Roman calendar from 713BC.

March comes from the Latin *Martius,* named after the god Mars **(left)**. As well as being the god of war, Mars was the god of agriculture, and his month signalled the beginning of the activities for both agriculture and warfare. It was the first month of Roman calendar as late as 153BC and many New Year celebrations took place. The *Ides* were the name to which the Romans gave the middle days of every month, and were sacred to the god Jupiter; they were made famous of course by the assassination of Julius Caesar on March 15, 44BC – the *Ides of March.* The Saxons called the month *Lentmonat,* named from the spring equinox, from which derived the term Lent, the forty day period of fasting and preparation prior to Easter.

April also derives from the Romans, from the Latin *Aprilis,* their word for *opening,* which refers to the opening of flowers at this time. The month was sacred to Venus, and her festival of *Veneralia* was held on the first day. April also has origins in the Greek's equivalent of Venus, Aphrodite, which in Greek is *Aphrilis.* The Etruscans knew the month as Apru. April Fool's Day, on April 1, had a precursor with the festival day of

Hilaria, which Rome also took from the Greeks; it was given to any day or season of feasting or rejoicing.

May was named after the Greek and Roman goddess Maia, the daughter of Atlas, who was associated with the Earth Mother (Gaia), motherhood and elder women, and who is identified with the Roman goddess of fertility, Bona Dea. In Roman myth, Mercury was the son of Maia and several festivals were held in his honour in May.

June is thought to be named after the wife of the supreme god Jupiter, the goddess of marriage, Juno **(right)**, and one writer of the time, Plutarch, states that it was a favourable month in which to marry. The image here is a Roman silver statuette.

July is named after Julius Caesar, as it is the month in which he was born (prior to this the month was known as Quintilis).

August was first named in 8BC, in honour of Augustus, the first Roman Emperor.

September derives its name from the Latin for seven, *septem*, as it used to be the seventh month of the Roman calendar.

October gets its name from the Latin for eight, *octō*.

November was the ninth month of the Roman calendar, and comes from *novem*, meaning nine

December is the Latin for ten, *decem*.

Days of the Week

Sunday is quite simply named after the Sun – the Roman *dies Solis*. It was the Egyptians who initially regarded it as the first day of the week, and it is surprising how universal the solar dedication of this day is. The Greeks knew it as *hemera heliou*, in Old Saxon it was known as *sunnundag*, and in Old Norse *sunnudagr*, all of which mean *'Day of the Sun'*. Several traditions now regard it as the *Lord's Day*, and it always has been, the Sun being the original Lord in question. It was in March 321AD that Rome's first Christian Emperor, Constantine I, declared that Sunday should be a day of rest, on what he called the, *'Venerable Day of the Sun'*.

Monday is named from the Old English *Mōnandaeg*, meaning *'Moon's Day'*, and corresponds to the Old Norse *mánaddagr*.

Tuesday is derived from Tiwaz or Tyr, who in Norse mythology was the god of single combat, heroic glory and law. The Romans dedicated Tuesday to Mars, and astrologically that day is still ruled by the planet Mars today.

Wednesday comes from the Old English *Wōdnesdaeg*, meaning *'Woden's Day'*, from the Norse/Germanic god Woden or Odin, shown here in a 1901 drawing **(centre)**. To the Romans it was *dies Mercurii*, *'Day of Mercury'*, reflecting the fact that the Germanic god Wodin or Odin was interpreted as Mercury. European languages today reflect this origin with Mercredi (French) and Mercoledi (Italian). In Scandinavia, Wednesday is still *Onsdag (Odin's Day)*.

Thursday comes from the Old English *Thunor's Day*, meaning *'Thor's Day'*, after the Norse god of thunder **(right)**, who in turn

45

derived from the Germanic god Thunraz, their respective thunder god. The Romans knew this day as *jovis dies* – *'Jupiter's Day',* from their god of the sky and thunder.

Friday derives from *Frigedag,* meaning '*Day of Frigg',* and is the result of an old practice of associating the British goddess Frigg with the Roman goddess Venus (frīg was a common noun meaning *love*). In Scandinavian countries, Friday is Freya's Day (Freya was the chief spouse of Odin), and some authorities say that the two goddesses were in fact one and the same.

Saturday is named from the Roman god Saturn/Saturnus **(left)**, the god of money, wealth, agriculture, liberation and time, and with whom the planet Saturn is associated. He is one of the most ancient Roman gods, said to be the father of Jupiter himself. The origins of Saturn may in turn have evolved from the Etruscan god Satre.

That the first two days of the week honour the Sun and the Moon, and that other events concerned with time have ancient origins, is ample proof that they are survivals from times when the Sun, the Moon and other gods were revered. The persistence of these terms perhaps reflects Constantine's pragmatic approach not to 'rock the boat' when he pronounced the Roman Empire to be Christian. The names of the old Roman months were retained, as well as days named after Pagan gods and goddesses, all of which were the familiar bedrocks for ordering the passage of time.

Originally, shamans of old knew that time can be worked with, and even manipulated, as it is merely one dimension composing apparent realities - time was the evolving Universe. But time later became a means to control people, reminding them that, as sinners, they only had a finite period to repent during their life or else face eternal damnation in Hell. The once mighty gods of Saturn and Chronos, who had represented a wonderment of, and a respect for, the unknown qualities of time, were now represented by generally negative characters, such as the Father Time/Grim Reaper **(centre)** and the Angel of Death, characters who could be knocking on your door any time soon. Time, it seems, really does wait for no man.

12.

The Underworld and Hell

Caves contain some of the earliest expressions of Man's spirituality **(images p. 12)**. These otherworldly places were usually difficult to access, devoid of light, yet were ripe with mystery, home to unknown force, and subterranean creatures such as dragons, trolls, dwarves, and even gods and goddesses. In Greek mythology, Zeus, the primal god, was born in a deep cavern under the forests of Mount Aegeum on Crete **(top)**. Caves are primal earth wombs, where insights may be gained from encountering the dark, which is analogous of exploring the dark spaces within us all. Caves **(images p. 9 and 12)** were naturally regarded as entrances to the Underworld, a place where humans either could not go or rarely ventured, and yet from where the affairs of Man could, none the less, be fashioned. These realms were deep within the body of the Earth Goddess, whose unknown domains were seen as both a birthing womb, or else from where more violent apparitions, such as volcanoes, originated.

Some Mayan and Aztec pyramids, and European temples, were built over sacred caves, to access earth energies as well as to enhance the growing potential of grains (Burke and Harlberg 2005). In later times, Man created artificial caves in the form of chambered tombs, especially in areas where caves could not occur naturally or were scarce, excellent examples being Newgrange, Maes Howe, and West Kennet Long Barrow (Knight 2011). These were built out of the desire to be 'rebirthed', during one's lifetime and after death. These ancestral places were literally doorways to the Underworld of the dead, liminal conduits of the shaman.

Wells and springs were also regarded as entrances and exits of the Underworld, the life-giving waters emanating from the very body of the Earth Mother. Hundreds of such watery places were formerly dedicated to local Pagan deities, but with the arrival of the Church were re-dedicated to saints, more often than not female holy ladies, who replaced local goddesses. A whole temple complex, Aqua Sulis, was built by the Romans around the former Celtic spring site at Bath, and hundreds of tons of votive offerings were made into the warm waters that flowed, as if by magic, from deep within the Great Mother **(centre image)**.

47

Countless myths survive about beings residing beneath the earth, in such places as labyrinths, caves, and even entire subterranean lands and cities. It was a place to where the dead were transported, often to be judged. In Sumerian/Babylonian mythology, the Underworld is a place of no return, to where a person journeyed after death via seven gates, the last of which closed forever. This is surely one of the origins of the *Pearly Gates* of Christian myth. This Underworld is described as, *'Kingdom of Shadows',* and it is not difficult to see from whence Hell or Hades evolved.

Greek myths tell of Tartarus, *a* place deep below the earth which was a prison for giants and gods, imprisoned for misdemeanors on the orders of Zeus. This Underworld was ruled by Hades **(bottom, previous page)**, a god rather than a place name; his cohort was the *Hell Hound* Cerberus. It seems to be the Romans who changed this to a place where humans could be sent. It is from this that the Christian concept of Hell derived, for in the original version of Peter 2:4, we read, *'evil angels were cast down into Tartarus';* modern Bibles have substituted *Tartarus* with *Hell*.

Egyptian mythology devoted more time and effort concerning the concept of the afterlife and the Underworld than any other ancient culture. The god of Duat, the Egyptian Underworld, was Osiris **(left)**, charged with taking the dead to the other side, and whose devotees hoped would grant them eternal life. His co-worker was the jackal-headed god Anubis, who presided over embalmment and funerals, and opened the road for the dead. The *Pyramid Texts* are a set of Egyptian manuscripts designed to navigate the hostile forces of the Underworld. Like the Greeks, the Egyptians believed that spells given to a departed Pharaoh (as in the *Book of Gates*) enabled him to pass through a series of gateways guarded by snakes and deities. (For more gates guarding *Paradise* see Chapter 27.)

To many other ancient cultures, the Underworld was a place of rebirth and renewal, which is ultimately linked to the seasonal cycles of the earth, such as in the myth of Demeter and Persephone/Kore. This myth describes the goddess's captivity in Hades during the winter, and her escape and return in the spring; a statue of Persephone is shown here **(left)** seated on her Underworld throne, dated 460BC. This is echoed by the Phoenician myth concerning the annual Underworld adventures of the gods Mot (symbolising drought) and Baal (the return of fertility).

To the Celts, the Underworld or Otherworld is sometimes described as a *'Golden Realm'* or a *'Land of Eternal Youth'* (Leitch 2007). Annwn is the name generally given to this Otherworld, and Yuri Leitch makes a clear distinction between this and the Underworld; he sees the Otherworld as being present all around us, a world we may interact with, or even stumble upon (Leitch 2007, p. 18). Celtic bard Taliesin spoke of Caer Wydyr, *the Glass Castle,* thought to be the realm of the dead, and which has been associated with Glastonbury in recent times. Irish Celtic tradition speaks of the *Tir fo Thuinn,* or the *Land Under the Waves,* and there are Irish tales of an Underworld called *Ysbaddaden,* a domain of giants, as well as a kingdom called *Scathach,* which was guarded by phantoms and other horrors; Celtic heroes would often have to battle with such supernatural forces. One lord of this realm was Cernunnos, the antlered lord **(bottom image, previous page).**

In Norse myth, the world tree Yggdrasil connects the heavens, the Earth and the Underworld. Valhalla was the Norse *Hall of the Gods,* or *Hall of the Slain,* presided over by Odin/Woden, which had a gateway known as Valgrind, reminding us again of the gates of Heaven. Dead Viking heroes were taken to Valhalla by the winged Valkyries **(image p. 171),** not unlike the role of some Christian angels. In Hindu myth, the legs of the god Vishnu connect Man to the seven realms of the Underworld.

Sometimes it was a hero who went on a quest to the Underworld. Orpheus was a Greek heroic figure who had to enter the Underworld to persuade the gods to heal his wife Eurydice. Hercules was commanded to go down into the Underworld to collect Cerberus, guardian of the *Infernal Gates* (the *Pearly Gates* again!). Orion was the heroic giant of the Greeks, who, after his death, continued to hunt animals in Hades.

In later times, caves were seen as the abode of witches (or, how I like to call them, solitary wise women), who were outlawed because they did not toe the line. The Witch of Wookey, Somerset and Mother Ludham, Surrey, are two English examples. In British mythology, both Merlin and King Arthur are said to lie sleeping deep within the earth until a time comes when Britain is in need of their services again.

Hell and the Devil

The Greek god Hades (also known as Pluto) was the husband of Persephone and master of the Underworld, who appears to have the qualities of both terror and mystery as his attributes. In the original translation of the Old Testament from the Greek, the term Hades (from the Hebrew *shoel*) is used for the abode of the dead, and not a place where the wicked are sent. Only in the New Testament does it become a place of damnation and eternal torment, morphing into a powerful propaganda tool. The word Hell may derive from *hel* of Norse Pagans and Old English, recorded around 725AD, describing the netherworld of the dead. 'Hell' may have reached North European cultures from *Hel* or *Hellenis,* the Norse Queen of the Otherworld. Underworld Pagan gods, such as Cernunnos, shown here on the Gunderstrup Cauldron **(right),** were replaced by the Devil, Satan or Lucifer, the new personification of evil. The horns, tail and cloven hooves of the Devil in Christian art is the demonisation of Cernunnos and Pan, the Pagan *Lords of the Forest.* The ancient *Oracle of the Dead* at Baia, Italy, gets increasingly hotter as one descends underground due to geothermal activity, and this and similar underground sacred places surely fueled the Christian concept of Hell as a place of fire and eternal damnation.

Devil comes from the Greek *diabolos,* meaning *slanderer.* Satan may have derived from the Egyptian god Set, or Set-hen. Whilst Judaism contains no concept of a Devil (although their term *ha-satan* means '*the adversary*'), Islam and Christianity regard the Devil as the fallen angel, seen here at Rosslyn Chapel **(right),** a wayward being who commands an army of evil spirits and who constantly tries to tempt us all from the righteous way. It has

been noted, however, that in Isaiah 14:12, Lucifer simply refers to a Babylonian king, described as a *'falling morning star'*. The name Lucifer only occurs in this one place in the Bible, but has been used to describe the fall of the angel from Heaven, defeated by St Michael as shown in this 1636 painting **(left)**.

In the Bible, Satan is described as a serpent in the Book of Revelations, but is not named as being the serpent in the story of Adam and Eve. Lucifer has also been described as a *bringer of light* by New Agers, who do not recognize the concept of a Devil. Likewise, Hinduism does not recognise any central evil entity that opposes Man or God, even though it does distinguish several entities that can perform negative acts. To Christians, Satan provides a scapegoat for monotheism, which would otherwise place blame for the ills of the world on God.

Countless sites across the world also incorporate the name *Devil* or *Hell*; they are usually ancient sacred sites that were later repainted with a negative brush. Devil's Tower, in Wyoming, is a huge natural monolith, made famous in *Close Encounters of the Third Kind'*. The Devil's Arrows are tall megaliths in Yorkshire, that were thrown by the *Dark Lord*; there is a Devil's Bridge in Wales, and a Devil's Cauldron at Lydford Gorge near Dartmoor; the Devil's Stone is a natural monolith at Abbotsbury in Dorset, and not far away is the Hell Stone, a Neolithic dolmen (Knight 1996, 1998 & 2000); the Devil's Den is a another dolmen near Avebury, whilst in Avebury itself one of the stones, with an inset seat, is known as the Devil's Chair.

Yet, as we saw with festivals, it is amazing how tenacious locals were in preserving pre-Christian practices. For example, a huge mask called the Dorset Ooser **(centre)** survived until Victorian times; prior to this it was regularly paraded around local villages, a reminder of the vanquished horned lord (Knight 2013).

The threat of eternal damnation at the hands of Satan, depicted here at Rennes-le-Château **(left)**, is arguably one of the most successful negative concepts ever used in the dogma of any religion; as a result, fear has been instilled into millions of people for nearly 2000 years. Perhaps we should look back to prehistory, to the writings of the Greek Ptolemy; he regarded Hades as symbolic of the ego, the shadow side of our psyche which can be transcended, for it is mere illusion, a construct of our personal fears and insecurities. Regarding Christianity, the Devil is most certainly the byproduct of Man's generic fears and insecurities.

The Underworld, whether an imagined mythology or physical reality (as in caves), was a place where spirits and gods dwelt, a world into which shamans and heroes ventured for rites of passage. Ancient civilisations knew that myths concerning the Underworld were allegories, metaphorical means through which knowledge could be attained on the road to Gnosis, the *'know thyself'* state of being. Unfortunately, Biblical literalists have fostered a one-way-ticket to a Hell that is a harrowing place of perpetual torment governed by the Devil, where no such place existed before. Indeed, it has been argued that, *'Religion is the Devil's greatest achievement'* (Freke and Gandy 2001, p. 276).

13. Creation – In the Beginning

Myths concerning Creation (known as cosmogonies) seem to go back as far as, well, Creation! They are our primary myths, the first stage of what could be called the psychic evolution of our species. Very few ancient cultures did not seek to express and understand how the world and the Universe came into being. Christianity was to be no exception, as it strove to demonstrate that it was the *'one true God'* that was responsible for all of existence. Whether Creation myths initially involve humans or not, the original man and woman are usually seen as central symbols and themes soon afterwards; I shall deal with the first man and woman in the next chapter, as they are so closely linked to the Tree of Life. Let us, for now, look at some ancient myths that may have a familiar ring to them.

In Hindu mythology, Upanishad texts from 9th century BC speak of the one God creating the Universe by reflecting on nothingness and finding himself; everything was initially a dark and watery chaos, and life developed from a spontaneous heat, called the *tapas*. In the Hebrew text known as The Zohar, we read, *'God began by forming an imperceptible point that was His own thought'*. In Persian cosmogony, the omniscient lord Ahura Mazda pronounced, *'I have created a world where none existed'*. In Maori cosmology, the Universe was originally an eternal night, until the Earth Goddess, Papa, mated with the sky god Rangi. In Norse legends, Odin and his two brothers killed a giant, Ymir, whose flesh became the land - his bones formed the mountains, and the waters flowed from his blood. The Australian Aborigines speak of the Dreamtime, in stories going back 150,000 years. It tells how their creator god, Baiame **(top)**, dreamed up all that exists in the physical world, and how the gods travelled along *song lines*, which Aborigines still walk today. Likewise, Dogon shamans of Mali still perform their creation dances **(centre)**.

Some archaeologists believe that the central figure in the famous Aztec *Calendar Stone* **(right)** is Tlaltecuhtli, a goddess who featured in their Creation myths; she was an *'ocean monster'* that embodied the violent chaos prior to

Creation. To the ancient Greeks, the world was created from an initial dark, formless Universe, referred to as *'Chaos'*. It was Eros who embodied the creative urge, along with Gaia (the Earth Mother) and Uranus.

Egyptian Creation myths tell how Nu or Nun, the original primal water, subsided to expose a mound of land; the image here **(left)** shows the first ever sunrise over that mound, as two goddesses add the waters of the Earth. After the land appeared the Sun god Atum self-generated by masturbation, and from this act all other things were created. The myth was an extension of the annual life-sustaining flooding of the Nile. In Babylonian myths, composed in the 12th century BC, the god Marduk cut the seas in half, creating two ocean goddesses, Apsu and Tiamat, and the two halves became the earth and the sky. This reflected the annual flooding of the Tigris and the Euphrates. It is interesting, therefore, that in Genesis I of the Bible, the Creation story tells us that, *'darkness was upon the face of the deep. And the spirit of God moved upon the face of the waters'*. Subsequently, on the second day, God separated the sky from the waters **(left)**, and on the third day he separated the earth from the sea. He later created *'two great lights'*, the Moon and the Sun, as shown here by Michelangelo **(third image)**. This comes directly from Hebrew tradition, whereby Elohim-Yahweh *(meaning he creates)* is the creator deity (although his name first appears in 13th century BC Egyptian texts). The story told in Genesis has come down to us today via the Babylonian exile of the Israelites; the myths of their captors were absorbed, and later the basic earlier Creation story evolved, for it is now the One God that waved his magic wand **(bottom)**. William Blake's iconic painting, *The Ancient of Days*, now housed in the British Museum **(image next page)**, epitomizes this image of a male God on high, the Creator of all things, whose will still influences humanity.

It is interesting that the Babylonian goddess of Creation, Tiamat, translates into the Hebrew as *Tehom*, meaning *'The Deep'*. So as God banishes the, *'... darkness on the face of the deep'*, Hebrew cosmogony is expelling Tiamat, the goddess of Creation. It is interesting and relevant that there is no word for goddess in the Hebrew language, so anyone reading the Old Testament today may have the impression that the Hebrews had originally worshipped no goddesses at all. Divinity was now a male God, singular, and the Goddess was *on the run*. Unfortunately, with her also went most of the former rights of women. It was, and still is, all desperately chauvinistic.

It is interesting how God is *'The Word'*, which is merely an echo of the Sumerian god Enlil, described here in one text: *'Your word is the floodwater, the life of all lands'*. This is echoed by Ptah, the Egyptian god spoken of as the god of the Universe: *'Ptah spoke on his tongue the utterances of his heart'*. Again, the creative word of divinity alone can manifest the Creation. Hindus believe that the sacred sound *Om* or *Aum* existed at the beginning of time and that vibrations caused by its sounding brought about the Creation of the world.

In Genesis, the Hebrew God Yahweh famously said, *'Let there be light'*. This echoes times when it was once the Mother Goddess who was the creatrix principle; the great ancient Mesopotamian goddess Inanna-Ishtar was known as *Light of the World;* the Greeks regarded the goddess Sophia as the personification of *wisdom and light*. Tiamat, the *Dragon Queen* of Babylonian Creation myth, is described as a *'shining being'*. In Tibetan mythology, the Universe began when two lights were born, one black, the other white (the equivalent of yin and yang – in other words, both the male and female principles were present at the moment of Creation); when these two lights combined they produced five multicoloured streams of light, from which the elements were created. These two lights are of course echoed in Genesis, when God creates the Sun and the Moon.

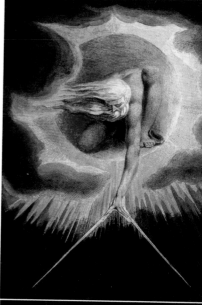

The Big Bang Theory

I hope I have demonstrated that the Christian Creation story is in fact a thinly disguised retelling of the Hebrew/Jewish Creation legend, which in turn was based on many pre-existent myths of how the Universe and the world began. Several of these ancient myths speak of the physical Universe being created from nothing, or from pure spirit. It is interesting that modern cosmologists and mathematicians are embracing the quantum concept that before the Big Bang, that moment when the physical Universe was created **(right)**, there was also a *nothing* that, nevertheless, still possessed creative potential. Ironically, science is confirming the religious concept of Creation from *ex nihilo,* meaning *out of nothing*, which is part of ancient Egyptian myths, and that of others: the Indian Vedas speak of there being initially a, *'... dark and watery chaos, and life developed from a spontaneous heat'*. Is this heat describing the moment of the Big Bang? Likewise, Hebrew texts say, *'God began by forming an imperceptible point'*. The first Greek deity was Chronos – the personification of time; quantum physics tells us that

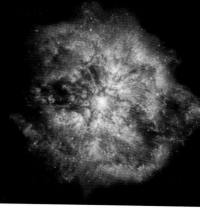

time may only have come into existence *after* the Big Bang. Science has proven that the Universe expanded after the Big Bang, and that all galaxies continue to expand away from each other. In the Qur'an, Muslims read (in verse 47 of Adh-Dhariyat), *'We who have built the universe with our creative power, and verily, it is We who are steadily expanding it'*.

On November 22, 1951, Pope Pius XII decreed that the Big Bang Theory need not conflict with the Catholic concept of Creation. It seems that Creationists and Scientists are finally finding some common ground.

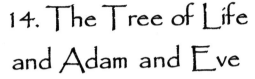

14. The Tree of Life and Adam and Eve

Trees have long been global religious archetypes. In Greek myths, the Golden Fleece was draped across the top of a magical tree, guarded by a serpent or dragon. Buddha achieved his enlightenment after sitting for three days and nights under the Bodhi tree. Oak, in particular, was sacred to the Druids, just as Banyan trees are to Hindus today. The concept of a Tree of Life, also known as the Axis Mundi, World or Cosmic Tree, or World Pillar, is very ancient, and represents the connection between Earth and Heaven, or the realms of the gods. It was the ultimate conduit for the forces that regenerated life on Earth, and is central to many Creation myths. In Norse mythology, Odin hung from the World Ash, Yggdrasil **(top)**, which grew up from the Underworld, and from which he received the vision of the runes; the Wyrd Sisters also dwelt within its roots. Asherah, the oldest Canaanite goddess of Sumerian inscriptions, dated c. 1750BC, is typically represented as the Tree of Life, and an image of her stood in the Temple of Solomon. In the church at Cranborne, Dorset, this concept is Christianised in a wall painting depicting a tree sprouting out of the top of a woman's head (Knight 1998, p. 176).

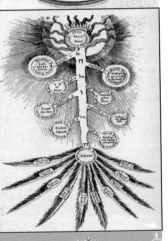

Sometimes the tree is inverted, such as with the Jewish Kabbalah **(second image)**, with the roots in Heaven and the branches extending below, representing God reaching down to Earth. This reminds me of Sea Henge, with its inverted tree stump reaching down into the earth. It also relates to the chakra system, and the connection that exists between the macrocosm and microcosm.

From the earliest times the Tree of Life, or World Axis, has been associated with the first humans of the Creation myth, who were created as part of divine cosmology. Japanese cosmogony has an original couple called Izanagi and Izanami. To the Egyptians, the first couple was Isis and Osiris, who emerged from the Acacia tree of Lusasset. The Tree of Life was central to Egyptian cosmology **(third image)**; the raising of the *Djed Pillar* is depicted in many temples, and represents the phallus of Osiris, the regenerative principle of vegetation, an aspect of the Tree of Life (Baring and Cashford 1991, p. 242). Some depictions have an ankh rising from the pillar, representing eternal life and renewal. The obelisks of Egypt also represent the Tree of Life – the phallus of Osiris. This is echoed by three bronze trees, up to four metres high and dated around 1200BC, found in a sacrificial pit in Sichuan, China. At the base of one was a dragon. Dragons are often associated with the Tree of Life, which may issue from the creature's mouth.

In Crete, trees are worshipped as symbols of the goddess, and the *Tree of Eternal Life* is shown on the Mycenae *Ring of Nestor,* c. 1500BC **(bottom image, previous page)**. Note the couple holding hands walking towards the tree on the lower left! Also shown here is the iconic Lion Gate at Mycenae, which is dated c. 1300BC **(top)**. The two lions stand either side of a pillar, which has been interpreted as the World Axis. On my visits to Malta, I recorded this Tree of Life at the Neolithic temple of Hagar Qim **(right)**. The tree is depicted on all four sides and is thought to be the earliest Tree of Life sculpture. I found a motif carved inside the Neolithic chambers of Des Pierres-Plats in Brittany **(third image)**, which may also depict the tree.

The Yakut of Siberia believe that a tree growing in the primordial Paradise stood in the naval of the Earth, and that the first man was suckled by the tree. In Indian mythology, the first man, Yama, drank with the gods next to a wondrous tree. Magical trees occur in the Bible too, such as the burning bushes of Abraham and Moses.

That Babylonian, Sumerian and Egyptian myths had a powerful influence on the construct of the Old Testament has long been advocated by scholars. The goddess Inanna accompanies a couple and the Tree of Life on rare seals dated 2300-2000BC. A frieze is shown here from c. 900BC from Nimrod Palace, and depicts two Annunaki gods either side of a tree **(right)**. In the Bible, Adam was told to *'till the earth ...dress and keep the garden'.* But the story of the first gardener comes from Sumeria, where kings took the official title of *'Gardener',* embodying the life of vegetation and fruitfulness of the earth, taking on the symbolic role of consort of the goddess Inanna. However, Adam was changed to be, *'son of the great Father',* rather than the symbolic consort of the Great Mother. In Genesis, God placed cherubs with flaming swords between humans and the Tree of Life (Genesis 3:24), which, in effect, erected a barrier between humans and divinity.

In Genesis we read that God created a garden and delighted in its creation. We are told of *two* trees in that garden (Genesis 2:9), one being the *'Tree of Life',* with evil only entering the story with the *'Tree of Knowledge',* the apples of which must not be eaten **(top image, next page)**. The name

Adam is actually from the Hebrew name for soil, *adamah*, a feminine noun that has been interpreted as *Mother* (Baring and Cashford 1991, p. 425). It is interesting that Eve (from the Hebrew *Hawweh, 'to be'*) is described as, *'the mother of all living'*, not the mother of all human beings. She is the divine feminine personified, as the *Mother of All Living* is insidiously changed into a distasteful woman. This was to have far-reaching implications in the rejection of the Goddess, as the divine feminine was demonized into a *fallen* woman. The Genesis version of Creation is almost unique in that it takes all the elements of Creation myths that had gone before (i.e. a garden, Paradise, the Tree of Life, a serpent, and the first two people) and turns them from tales of joy, creative wonder and a celebration of life, into a lesson of fear, guilt and sin. Before there was Aphrodite and Adonis, Ishtar and Tammuz, and Isis and Osiris – and now we have Adam and Eve; from being *Her Creation*, the natural regenerative and sexually-charged

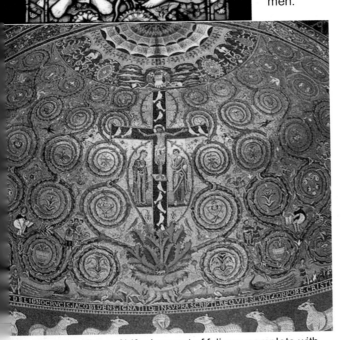

powers of Nature have become Eve's 'sin', and therefore womanhood's eternal burden.

Gone now is the ever-renewing God/Goddess as *the source of all life, for whom no atonement was necessary*, replaced by the curse of a wrathful God. What a depressing and ultimately malevolent dogma, and one that sets the tone for the rest of the Old Testament.

As a final insult to the Goddess and Nature, Eve is created from Adam's body, which is contrary to Nature, where it is the female who births life. This shift of power marked the replacement of the Goddess with God/Yahweh as the Creator and renewal deity. The consequence of this is that if women came from a man, then they belonged to men.

I am not specifically knocking Christianity, for as I have already shown, the die was cast in the Hebrew sacred texts where (Sir. 25:24) we read, *'Of the woman came the beginning of sin, and through her we all die'*. The goddess Lilith **(image p. 37)** was an ancient sexual trickster, spoken of in Sumerian myths as *'Queen of the Night'*. She was the darker aspect of the goddesses Inanna and Ishtar, who are both described as, *'Divine Lady Owl'*. One version from Hebrew mythology tells how Yahweh (God) made Lilith (Eve) from the earth, but that he then, *'took filth and impure sediments from the earth, and out of these he formed a female'*. I think it speaks volumes that the words *filth* and *impure* are used in the conception of the first woman.

The Christian Tree of Life rises out of foliage, complete with serpent, and spiraling branches. St Clement, Rome.

56

In the Bible, the serpent that guards the Tree of Life had the ability to speak, a gift from God. In ancient Aramaic, the word Eve is very similar for the word for snake, and in Arabic, Eve is *hawwa,* meaning '*snake*'; Eve could indeed be the derivation of the ancient snake goddess (see Collins 2014). The story of Eve's creation from one of Adam's ribs is probably a corruption of a Mesopotamian myth in which the Mother Goddess Ninkhursag healed the injured rib of the god Enki. From this healing was created the goddess Nin-Ti, whose name means '*Lady of the Rib*'. Male and female figures sitting either side of a tree, like Adam and Eve, can be seen on a Sumerian cylinder seal dated 2500BC.

Other vestiges of the regenerative powers of the Tree of Life can be found in the Bible. In the Book of Revelations, the Tree of Life will bear fruit, '*... for the healing of the nations*'. Then there is Adam's death; he pleads for some of the *Oil of Mercy* that oozes from the Tree of Life, that it may save his life; this is the same oil that was prophesied would again be used when Jesus incarnated.

In his book, *Gőbekli Tepe – Genesis of the Gods,* Andrew Collins surmises that a holy relic, an actual fragment of the Edenic Tree of Life, is held by the monks of Yeghrdut, a monastery in the foothills of the Taurus Mountains, a place said to be located in, '*... one corner of Eden'* (Collins 2014). Collins goes on to add that Adam was apparently created out of, '*red clay',* and that this may collate with the extreme redness of the earth in this area. In one Mesopotamian myth, we learn how Enki, one of the Annunaki gods, created the first man, called Adapa (which sounds similar to Adam), by modelling him from clay the colour of blood.

One of the megaliths (Pillar no. 31) at Gőbekli Tepe is adorned with carvings of snakes, and may possibly symbolise the Tree of Life. Andrew Collins proposes that the Garden of Eden, stories of which we know originated in the Middle East, was situated in the Armenian Highlands, and that Gőbekli Tepe was one of its temples (Collins 2014). Myths about this temple complex, and the area's association with Eden, may have been absorbed by the captive Hebrews in Babylon, and the rest, as they say, is history.

Perhaps the woeful story of Adam and Eve can be taken as a metaphor for the loss of innocence of our species, caused by our discovery and adoption of agriculture. Man is not only being constantly judged by God, but has also chained himself to the land, by divine decree it would seem.

One of the finest Christian examples of the Tree of Life as the Axis Mundi is the Apprentice Pillar at Rosslyn Chapel, near Edinburgh **(right)**. This beautifully crafted masonic wonder has leaves ascending in a spiral, mimicking both DNA strands and the serpents of old. Dragons encircle its base, representing the regenerative forces of the earth; a dragon called Nidhogg resided at the base of Yggdrasil, the Norse World Tree. Hardly any space is spared in Rosslyn, as trees and foliage adorn every inch of the walls and ceiling, all vying for our attention. Dragons and serpents are not in short supply at Rosslyn either, and we shall return to both of these mythical icons in more detail later. Yuri Leitch has recently highlighted two fine examples of the Tree of Life in the Glastonbury landscape, namely at the church at Hornblotton (on a floor mosaic), and at Stoke-sub-Hamdon (Leitch 2013).

Christmas trees are in fact the Tree of life or World Tree. Its decorations remind us of the regenerative fires of the Underworld, which will eventually proclaim victory over the dark of winter. The concept of decorating trees goes back to at least Roman times when celebrants at the festival of Saturnalia observed the rebirth of the year. The cross of the Crucifixion marks the death of nature in its dying phase before the rebirth of the Sun in spring (mirroring the rebirth of the new solar god, Jesus); in ancient Crete, trees were cut down to represent the dying solar god. A Byzantine image, c. 1500, in the Basilica of San Clemente in Rome, shows the body of the tree **(lower image, p. 56)** with Jesus issuing from its trunk – the Osiris resurrection myth reincarnated. From this tree spiralling branches unfurl, encompassing all of life. Pope Benedict XVI once described the cross of the Crucifixion as, *'... the true Tree of Life'*. The other image here **(top image, previous page)** is another Crucifixion scene, at Corsham, Wiltshire, which shows Jesus hanging on a cross with a knobbled bark and which sprouts *living leaves*; it bears the inscription *Arbor Vitae,* meaning *Tree of Life.* Some speak of Jesus being the *New Adam,* as things come full circle it would seem, as Jesus makes amends for Adam's failures.

The maypole, of village green and fete, represents the World Axis, around which all revolves; it is a phallus which rises from, as well as penetrates, the Earth Mother; maypoles were erected in ancient Rome to the fertility/sun god Attis. Trees are still dressed with offerings around the world today, reminding us of a primal urge to honour the creative principles of Nature. Tree rings **(below)** are symbols of nature's *'long term policy',* of the perpetual cycles that come and go.

Left: *Elohim Creating Adam,* by William Blake. Note the winged God, the serpent and the Sun, all ancient mythological icons. Right: *circles of life* - tree rings in Savernake Forest, Wiltshire.

15. The Green Man

The Green Man **(right)**, is the mysterious character who issues foliage from his eyes, ears, mouth or nose. He gazes down at us from lofty roof bosses and many a dark recess, and is an image widely found in churches all over Europe, and beyond. The earliest Christian example of the Green Man may be that at St Abre, in St Hilaire-le-Grand, thought to date from c. 400AD.

The Green Man reaches to us from a time long gone, when magic was everywhere, an age when the land was abundant and green. Sometimes it is a lion or cat that is the focus of the foliage, at other times a dragon, implying that the meanings of the Green Man are multifaceted, and somewhat hidden. Heads that do not have foliage growing out of them, and are merely bordered by greenery, are known as Jack- in-the-Green.

Apparently, there are more images of the Green Man in churches than there are of Jesus (Broadhurst 2006, p. 35), an amazing statistic, and one that reminds us that although empires and civilisations come and go, the power of Nature, which is what the Green Man symbolises, is eternal. In pre-Christian eras it was the gods of old that had been responsible for the fecundity of the land. Many depictions of the Green Man (or Green Lady) have vines or fruit sprouting from them, so they are clearly not demons or the Devil. Bringing this ancient and potent image into churches was ample proof that it was now God, singular, that blessed the fields.

The concept of the disembodied head is a relic of older myths concerning magical decapitated heads, and the *Cult of the Head* was one of the cornerstones of Celtic spirituality. Legend tells of the magical and protective properties of the head of Bran the Blessed, which was buried beneath the site of the Tower of London in order to keep Britain safe. The head of John the Baptist, known as the *Baphomet*, became a mystical sigil of the Knights Templar **(image p. 202)**.

Osiris (the son of Geb, the earth god) is shown with a green face in *The Judgment Scene* of the Egyptian *Book of the Dead*, c. 1375BC; Osiris is also green in the tomb of Nefertari (1295-1253BC) – to the Egyptians, green was the colour of life and regeneration. On some temple paintings Osiris is shown with ears of wheat issuing from him. The example shown here **(second image)** is from a tomb in the Valley of the Kings, where he is accompanied by Anubis and Horus. The earth god Geb is also often depicted green **(image p. 63)**. However, green was not always viewed positively; in Egypt, cats with green eyes were feared, and in Medieval Europe it was considered unlucky to wear green, as the colour had become associated with the Devil.

In Tibet, Amogha-siddhi is a god often depicted in green. Green Tara of Buddhist/Hindu tradition has a green body and is thought of as the, *'Mother of All Buddhas'* **(bottom image, previous page)**. In the Temple of Swayambunath Gompa, Nepal, a Green Man with marigolds pouring from his mouth is directly above an image of the Buddha. In Buddhist temples in the Indian Himalayas, there are many wall paintings of a semi-human figure with Green Man affinities, with foliage issuing from his mouth.

In the Jain temple at New Delhi, India, there are stone carvings of foliage and fruit, and a Green Man appears on one of the columns. Interestingly, when the temple was turned into a Muslim mosque in Mogul times, many decorations around the site were smashed, but the Green Man was left intact (Harding 1998). Elsewhere in India, foliated heads from the 8th Century decorate other Jain temples. On buildings in Borneo, elaborate green-faced heads act as a protective spirits.

The Greek god Attis **(third image, previous page)** was associated with the cycles of Nature; his birthday was on December 25th and large pine maypoles were erected in his honour. The Greek Sun god Apollo is sometimes depicted as a youth, wearing a headdress or garland of leaves and flowers, as do May Queens today. Adonis was born from a tree, and, likewise, Osiris was *reborn* from one. Dionysus of the Greeks, and his Roman counterpart Bacchus, are both often shown with leafy beards, surrounded by foliage. The Greek fertility god Pan represents the wildness of nature; he reappears as Peter Pan, who is both immortal and dressed in green.

There are parallels between these classical fertility gods and the British deities Lugh/Lud and Nodens. Cernunnos was the Northern European *Lord of the Forest,* who has a fertility aspect. The word Druid means *'Men of the Oaks'*, demonstrating their close connection with trees and the wild wood. Previously, I have commented that although the Long Man of Wilmington and the Cerne Giant are defined by white lines, their bodies are green (Knight 2013).

The Green Knight, the gatecrasher at King Arthur's court, requested that someone hack off his head, signifying the death of the old year; the one here is in Winchester Cathedral **(top)**. May Day festivities involving *Jack-in-the-Green* **(centre)** were once commonplace, as this 18th century drawing testifies.

The Woodwose, Wodehouse or Wildman, a human-like figure covered in leaves living deep in the forest, features in many medieval illustrations and texts; he is most excellently carved in the choir area of Christchurch Priory in Dorset (Knight 1998, p. 242), where he holds a club like the Cerne Giant. Robin Hood is another legacy of the *wild man* of the forest, as are Irish Leprechauns, which are usually clothed in green attire. Unfortunately, trees are no longer regarded as beings of wisdom and intelligence, such as the Ents of Tolkien, and Nature worship in general has been outlawed; fierce religious propaganda transformed forests into the domain of the Devil, where evil creatures lurked behind every tree.

The Knights Templar

Foliated heads in Lebanon and Iraq date back to the second century AD, whilst some 11th century examples have survived in Jerusalem; to Muslims, the prophet Mohammed's green cloak represents Paradise. The Knights Templar crusading in the Holy Land would probably have known of the Osiris myth, and of the Muslim *Green One,* al-Khidr **(bottom image, previous page)**. Al-Khidr was an inspirational, legendary Islamic figure, always clothed in green and who left green footprints in his wake - wherever he went the earth was made green. In one tale, al-Khidr comes across the severed head of a king, which he restores to life, reminding us of Gawain and the Green Knight. From Iraq comes an 11th century image of al-Khidr spearing a dragon, which closely resembles St George slaying the beast. We know that the Knights Templar absorbed and embraced the mysticism of Islam, known as Sufism, during their visits to the Holy Land, and they would have recognized the similarity between the tales of al-Khidr and the Green Man; he mirrored their own concepts of nature, and they later incorporated foliated heads into Christian architecture.

The ultimate shrine to the Green Man is arguably Rosslyn Chapel, near Edinburgh, where it is said there are over 100 carvings of the foliated fellow. One is impressed with the sheer opulence of the carvings at the chapel, as faces both peer and leer from between leaves and branches at every turn. The main focus of the whole building, for me, is the amazing Green Man **(top)** that projects out from the walls of the Lady Chapel; it was suspended over me as I stood beneath, and I felt subservient, as if it was looking into my very soul.

Four of my favourite and outstanding images, in terms of both artistic merit and hypnotic effect, can be seen in Britain, at Rochester Cathedral **(second image)**, at Kilpeck, in Herefordshire **(third image),** whilst at Cattistock, Dorset (another shrine to the Green Man, and dragons for that matter) the Green Man is beautifully and realistically carved on an external Victorian door. Again,

his eyes seem to penetrate into one's very soul **(image, below right)**. The fourth is at Sutton Benger, Wiltshire, where the Green Man inside the church is of such high quality, and possesses such realism, that it has featured in many books **(image, below left & p. 232)**.

Today, the Green Man offers us a reconnection to Nature, back to the spirit of the green wood, and to a more conscious way of connecting with the cycles of the Earth, one in which we acknowledge our reliance on them. The Green Man now has a festival named in his honour, and many carnivals and folk festivals feature Morris dancers who don the green of the wild wood once more **(bottom image, previous page)**. The Green Man/Lady is the personification of the fertility and ever-changing phases of the turning year, and his or her face reminds us of natural forces that cannot be tamed. We are offered glimpses, reminiscences, of times when trees had personalities, when they were seen to possess magical attributes. Trees were once revered as sacred entities, and not viewed as a mere commodity or resource. The eternal gaze of the Green Man can ignite our conscience, that we may once again respect all that we once did, for when we look up at a Green Man, it is the very soul of Nature that returns our gaze.

The Green Man at Sutton Benger, Wiltshire (left), and at Cattistock, Dorset (right).

16. The Phallus – the Staff of Life

In his authoritative book *'Phallic Worship'*, George R Scott emphatically stated that, *'The study of phallicism is the study of religion'* (Scott, 1966). Worship of the male member is very ancient and universal, and this reverence and the belief that the phallus possessed magical potency began way back in the Palaeolithic; our distant ancestors frequented caves that were filled with stalagmites and stalactites, emergent rigid phalli within the dark interior of the Earth Mother **(image p. 9)**. Numerous Ithyphallic cave art from these distant times has been found in many such environments **(image p. 12)**.

Later, the Greeks, Romans, Hebrews, Babylonians, Egyptians, Chinese, and many other cultures (including the ancient British), all held the phallus to be representative of the fertility of Nature. The name of the Sumerian god Iskur means *'erect'*. The Biblical phrase, *'Yahweh Sabaoth'* comes from *SIPA-UD*, meaning *'penis of the storm'* (Allegro 1970, p. 24); *'Yahweh was everywhere represented by images which were man-like in outline... All these images possessed, in comparison with their size, enormous phalli'* (Scott 1996, p. 110).

The gods and goddesses of ancient cultures were all-powerful beings that ruled over Mankind, and were often sexually active, even promiscuous. Their myths echoed the forces at play in Nature, so to honour their sexual merging was to honour deity and the natural world.

In the Egyptian Creation myth, the god Atum sat on the primeval mound grasping his phallus. He ejaculated into his mouth, from which issued the first man and woman. Osiris was the Egyptian god most associated with the phallus, as numerous obelisks built in his honour testify. He was the god of the dead, the afterlife and the Underworld agency that granted the sprouting of vegetation and the fertilising floods of the Nile. But Osiris was by no means the only Egyptian ithyphallic god; Geb was a phallic earth god, usually shown as a man reclining, sometimes with his phallus pointing upwards to Nut, the sky goddess **(top)**. Yet another was Min **(centre image)**,

63

whose cult originated in the 4th millennium BC. He was worshipped in many temples as the god of regeneration and as the deity who influenced procreation of the human species. Min was represented in many different guises, but was often in male human form with an erect penis in one hand and an upheld flail in the other.

The association between phallic worship and serpents is well proven; Bacchus, Thoth and Hermes are all associated with serpents, and the staff of Hermes, the caduceus, has two entwined serpents around the rod (itself a phallus) and was said to be the axis around which the whole universe revolved; Hermes was an ithyphallic god **(left)**. The Roman fertility god Priapus deserves special mention, as he is considered to be the equivalent of both Hermes and Mercury. He is usually shown exhibiting his phallus, and orgiastic festivals were held in his honour. In Pompeii, his image is painted on the walls of brothels, and in this example he also carries a caduceus **(bottom, previous page)**.

In terms of ancient sites, many of the Neolithic megaliths of Brittany are decidedly phallic-shaped, some of them over 5m (16ft) tall, such as the Dol Menhir **(centre)**; many were later Christianised with inscribed crosses **(image p. 20)**. Even in modern times, French women seeking to have children would visit such stones, such as is recorded at the Stone Mare of Locronon. I have also found phalli at some of the Neolithic temples on Malta (Knight 2011 and 2013), where at some sites, notably at Hagar Qim and Mnajdra, a tall ithyphallic stone was set into the temple walls **(bottom centre, p. 13)**. The British Isles was not excluded from the ritualistic celebration of fertility in which phallicism was often a central component. This is hardly surprising really: *'It was natural that the ancient Britons should worship stones and pillars, as emblems of the male principle, just as did the ancient Hebrews, Greeks, Romans, Egyptians, Japanese, et al'* (Scott 1966, p. 184).

In Ireland, a hand-held phallic artifact was found at Knowth, a Neolithic tomb complex in the Boyne Valley. At the same site a 2.1m (7ft) pillar stone stands outside one of the entrances, marking an equinox alignment (Brennan 1994, p. 104-5). Another ithyphallic stone, called the *Stone of Destiny*, stands at Tara, the sacred centre of Ireland **(image p. 31)**.

Around Britain, phallic stones once stood in the centre of our towns and villages, right up until times when such objects began to cause offence. Derek Bryce comments: *'The fact that stones of this kind survived through many centuries of the Christian era may indicate that they were not seen as offensive or embarrassing until the nineteenth century... most of them were quietly made to disappear'* (Bryce 1994, p. 15-16). This kind of thinking can also be applied to the Cerne Giant **(left)** – couples had made love on the Giant's phallus for generations and the figure did not cause offence until relatively recently (Knight 2013). Bryce also advocates that the high crosses of

Christianity are the new phalli, replacing the ancient ones that were once an important element of every community.

The tallest stone known in Britain, the 8.5m (28ft) Rudstone monolith, is ithyphallic, as are some of the bluestones at Stonehenge, which might have been selected, or shaped, to achieve this effect. Expanding this further, several chambered tombs (such as West Kennet Long Barrow, Newgrange and Stoney Littleton) were designed to enable thin beams of light to pierce the dark interior, like a shaft or phallus *penetrating* the womb of the Earth Mother (Knight 2011). Today we speak of a *'shaft of light'*, and this term may once have had a quite literal meaning.

Phallicism was a recurring theme to the Celts, symbolic of regenerative life-force. On the continent, images of ithyphallic warriors have been found at Val Camonica and Le Donon. Some nude war-gods of the Brigantia tribe of Northern England were both horned and phallic, as at High Rochester, Northumberland, where a naked horned god displays large genitals, demonstrating the link between manhood and sexuality. Roman phalli have turned up in several British excavations, symbolising manhood and pride; the phallus was a good luck charm for soldiers stationed on Hadrian's Wall, where they were carved into stone at the forts of Maryport and Chesters. At the fort at Birrens is an inscription, *'the phallus of Priapus'*, demonstrating how legionnaires wished to associate themselves with this virile god.

Kokopelli was a phallic, seed-carrying god of the Amerindians. There was an ithyphallic shrine near the Moqui village of Mushangnewy, Arizona, and at Colhuacan, California, phalli images were once said to be *'extremely prevalent'* (Allen 1966, p. 96). Further south, the Aztec fertility god Xopancale was represented by a pillar.

Across India, ithyphallic pillars or posts called *lingam* are still worshipped today as a symbol of Shiva. The shaft of the lingam is the Axis Mundi, the Tree of Life, connecting Man to the divine. Some temples in India are covered in sexual imagery **(image p. 221)**, playing out myths of creation and regeneration. This is typical of ancient cultures, which saw no conflict between sexual imagery and religious faith: *'The failure to associate sex with obscenity sufficed to cause the ancients, and especially the Pagans, to enliven their temples with phallic images'* (Scott 1996, p. 43).

At Tyrnavos, Greece, there is a yearly *Phallus Festival*, and at Kawasaki, in Japan, an annual Shinto festival called Kanamara Matsuri is held, central to which is the parading of a 2.5m high pink phallus **(top)**. These and others are enduring memories of ancient Pagan rites that have survived to this day. In temples across the ancient world, male exhibitionist carvings were displayed to honour and commemorate the divine act of procreation, and fertility objects were even regarded as possessing magical powers. The maypole is a relic of phallic worship, from the veneration of Osiris and Roman fertility festivals. The one shown here is erected annually for the Padstow May Day festival, Cornwall **(right, and p. 25)**.

Christian Phallicism

The Hebrew Old Testament has abundant references to phallic worship among the Israelites, Canaanites and the Assyrians. Abraham erected pillars to Yahweh (God), whereas previously they had been for Pagan gods, such as Baal. Yahweh himself was originally a phallic deity, indicated by the rite of circumcision; in Exodus we read how Zipporah stood at the feet of an enraged Yahweh, offering the foreskin of her son as an appeasement. Yahweh is referred to as *The Bull of Israel,* indicating his association with fertility. Joshua worshipped a pillar at Shechem, and Solomon paid homage to another

stone at Gibeon. Two pillars, named Boaz and Jachin, were erected at the doorway to the Temple in Jerusalem; these pillars are central to Freemason ceremonies today. Following Jacob's dream, he set up a stone pillar and poured oils upon it. Moses himself forbade the erection of pillars, indicating how phallic worship, probably honouring the god Baal, was rife in his day. At times the distinction between Baal and Yahweh was vague, for in the Book of Psalms we read, *'To show that the Lord is upright, he is my rock'.* The cross, the prime symbol of Christianity, was once regarded as a phallic symbol and its use was forbidden by early Christians. In 4th century, Lamblichus wrote, *'crosses are signs of productive energy and provocation to a continuation of the world'* (Scott, 1996, p. 206).

The concept of obscenity and sin was born of religious piety. With the growth of Christianity, phallic worship was looked upon as something to be hidden, a taboo subject, and one that was subject to many ecclesiastical condemnations. Sex became sinful, and with it countless rites and ceremonies that had been carried out for thousands of years by King and rustic alike. Phallicism became isolated, suddenly seen as the cult of a minority of sexually-obsessed deviants spurred on by the Devil. Although some phallic symbolism *is* connected with coitus and orgiastic gatherings, most is not. Phallicism was more than titillation and penis adoration, but unfortunately Rome's version of Christianity did not see it as such. Yet despite St Peter's rumblings against every form of sexual practice, and his fanatical glorification of celibacy, people continued to indulge in sex rites at every opportunity afforded to them, such as at religious festivals, most of which were Church hijackings of Pagan events. It is interesting that nowhere in the Old Testament are there any references to nudity being associated with obscenity; King David, for instance, danced naked before the Ark of the Covenant!

The tenacious nature of phallic worship is proven by the numerous and widespread carvings of the phallus on Christian architecture; literally hundreds of ithyphallic images have been recorded across Europe **(left, and next page).** Male exhibitionist carvings lurk in countless churches, to surprise and even shock the unsuspecting onlooker. *Images of Lust* by Weir and Jerman (1999) is an excellent reference work on the subject. Such images are complemented by *female* exhibitionism, comprising nudes with exposed yoni, as at Kilpeck, Herefordshire (see Chapter 37).

Upper: Maillezais, France.
Lower: Santillana del Mar, Spain.

Sexual carvings were later regarded as images to remind parishioners of the dangers of the *'sins of the flesh'*. Sometimes, however, things were done in a more clandestine manner, proven by a number of phalli that have been found inside pre-14th century church altars; these were clearly not intended for-public display.

Old habits, it seems, die hard (no pun intended). In 1282, a priest in Fife had to appear before the Bishop to explain why he had led a fertility dance around a ithyphallic figure at an Easter dance! From 1786 we have a record of an unusual figure called *Jack of Hilton* **(centre)**. In his left hand he holds his penis, which is composed of a stump covered in oak leaves. Perhaps this is the origin of the term *wood,* the slang term for a phallus! This hollow brass statuette is 30cm (12ins) high and is believed to be Etruscan in origin, and was used in a curious New Year's Day Staffordshire custom. Two wooden phalli found during the demolition of a Welsh farmhouse were dated as late-17th century, whilst on the Isle of Eriska, ithyphallic pillars were revered as late as the early 18th century (Scott 1966, p. 186).

The early French church even had several so-called *'Phallic Saints'*, in whose shrines and chapels people sought fertility blessings. One such saint was St Foutin, whose name comes from the verb *foutre* – *'to fuck'*.

The Cerne Giant **(image p. 64)** is Britain's most obvious display of an ancient phallus, and I have dealt with this hill figure, and phallicism in general, in my book on the Giant (Knight 2013). There are numerous records telling of couples who would make love on the Giant's phallus to procure fertility. Complementing this, there are many tales from around Britain of fertility practices associated with sacred monuments, places where it was advantageous for women to visit if trying to conceive. Amongst these are Bride's Chair, a depression in a crag in Lancashire, the Kelpie Stane in the River Dee, and the Cradle Stone in Grampian. Some places were also said to aid the fertilizing powers of men, such as the cross at Boho near Enniskillen, and the ancient cross shaft at Clonmacnoise, Ireland.

Perhaps the inclusion of these sexual and exhibitionist images in medieval churches, like this one at Sopley, Hampshire **(right),** was originally intended to somehow tap into these primal forces, and only later seen as a tool to repel the forces of evil, to avert the maleficent gaze of the *Evil Eye*. In Church architecture, this former celebration of life was metamorphosed into warnings of the sins of sexual practice, visual propaganda to keep illiterate masses on the moral high ground. However, in the process, the act of sexual union, central to the survival of life on this planet, was castigated and virtually demonised – spiritual castration no less.

17. The Cosmic Egg

Every year, children around the world look forward to receiving Easter eggs. We have already seen how Easter replaced former Pagan spring festivals concerned with regeneration of the land (p. 24). The egg is testicle-shaped, the yoke representing the womb, the white the sperm. Yet the concept of the egg as a symbol of birth, rebirth and resurrection is much older than Christianity, for its use as a universal symbol for creation can be traced back thousands of years. Eggs were painted on Palaeolithic artifacts, and engraved ostrich eggs dating back 60,000 years were found in Africa. Vessels with egg decoration were made during the early civilisations of Sumeria, Crete and Egypt. A decorated ostrich egg from Ur, Iraq, is preserved in the British Museum, and is dated 2600 – 2200 years old **(top)**. The ancient Zoroastrians painted eggs for their New Year celebrations, around the Spring Equinox, and this is recorded back at least 2500 years, and sculptures on the walls of the Persian city of Persepolis show people presenting eggs to the king.

In Greeks myths, the *World Egg* was laid at night, imagined by a black-winged bird, and from it hatched the god Phanes/Dionysus. The Orphic Egg **(left)** is entwined by a serpent, representing the life force of the Universe (see also Chapter 24 regarding serpents).

According to Egyptian mythology, the solar god Ra was contained within an egg laid by a celestial Goose, said to be a gift from Thoth. Later myths change this bird to an Ibis, another bird associated with Thoth. Gold and silver eggs were placed in Egyptian graves as a sign of rebirth, a tradition that goes back 5,000 years.

In India Vedic myths, the cosmos is egg-shaped, known by the Sanskrit word Brahmanda (from *Brahm* meaning '*cosmos*', and *anda*, meaning '*egg*'). In ancient China, the god Pangu was birthed within an egg.

The concept of the World Navel/World Egg, or omphalos, is an ancient one. The omphalos (from the Greek for *navel*) is also associated with Creation and birth; in the human body, the navel is the point from which the embryo starts to grow. Several omphalos stones have been found around the ancient world, most notably at Delphi and Delos, both in Greece, and at Pergamum, Turkey. The famous Delphi omphalos **(left)** has a knotted decoration and is hollow. It was said to have been found by Apollo, and that it enabled direct communication with the gods via the oracle priestess. Ancient omphaloi were often positioned on holy hills, or in the centre of cities at temple sites, and some developed into oracle centres, as at Delphi. A village or market cross, a town fountain, or a statue are today's equivalents – the latter day focal points of a community. Temple Mount in Jerusalem is the omphalos of Christianity. Jewish tradition says that it was here that God revealed himself to his people through the Ark of the Covenant, on a stone that is very similar to that at Delphi. Today, this *Foundation Stone* (right) is a true omphalos, standing on the holy site in the Church of the Holy Sepulchre. To Muslims, Mecca is the omphalos of the Islamic world.

The cosmic egg also has links to the legends of the Grail, as the Philosopher's Stone. An ancient omphalos stone was unearthed during the excavations of Glastonbury Abbey (bottom). It lies, almost forgotten, at the rear of the Abbot's Kitchen. It is egg-shaped and has a depression in the centre, similar to those spoken of at ancient sites; the oracle, often a menstruating woman, would sit on a stone with a depression, which would catch her blood, to be used in further rituals. I often wonder if Mary Magdalene, who many believe could have been a priestess and may have come to Glastonbury, ever sat on the very same stone.

There is an old tradition in the Eastern Orthodox Church to give red eggs at Pascha, Easter. The legend goes that Mary Magdalene was taking some eggs to the other ladies who were keeping watch over the tomb of Jesus, but when she saw him resurrected, the eggs turned red. Is this an echo of the ancient Middle East practice of presenting eggs to a king at New Year, the time of new beginnings? Later, there was a conversation between Mary Magdalene and Tiberius Caesar in Rome. Because of her family's high standing she was given an audience with the Emperor, presenting him an egg. He scoffed, saying that no one could rise from the dead as Mary said Jesus had, no more than the egg she carried could turn red. With these words the egg in Mary Magdalene's hands turned red (centre). She then used this apparition to explain how Jesus rose from a sealed tomb, the red egg representing both the stone that covered it, and Jesus' blood. This developed into the tradition of giving red *Paschal Eggs* by Orthodox Christians in Russia, which later spread to the West when the Tsars presented Fabergé Eggs to the British monarchy.

Ancient myths, such as those from Egypt, speak of the Phoenix being born out of a red egg made of myrrh. This links us further to Mary Magdalene, in that she and the other ladies present at the tomb are known as the '*myrrh carriers*', as they were to have anointed the body of Jesus after his death. It is amazing how the much-loved tradition of Easter eggs actually developed from tales of a mythological bird, Mary Magdalene, and an anointing fluid.

69

18. Round in Circles

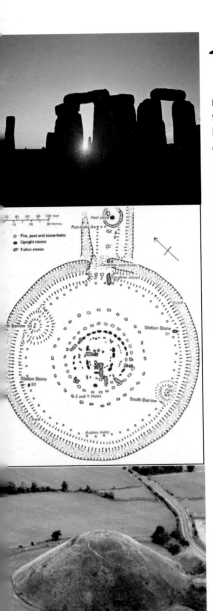

The circle is part of the basic building template of the Universe, a symbol of harmony and balance around a dimensionless point. It is present everywhere in the natural world, either as a flat concept or its 3-D extension, the sphere. Ripples on water, bubbles, the pupils of eyes, berries, spiders webs, tree rings **(image p. 58)**, the layers of a dissected onion, fungi fairy rings, and the disc of the Sun and the Moon were all circles observed and recorded by our distant ancestors. Of all the shapes studied by the Greeks, which included squares, triangles and spirals, they considered the circle to be a perfect shape, possessing no beginning nor ending – it represented eternity. Every religion has used circles to express their take on the nature of reality, and how the cosmos works. A circle emphasizes that which it encircles, such as on road signs, or the way a teacher might encircle writing on a blackboard. Although the circle is the shape of 'zero' and would appear to be empty, it is also a vessel, a container of limitless potential. In many sacred ceremonies, to step into a circle that has been cast on the ground is to enter a sacred or magical place, a space which possesses a deeper significance to that outside of it; those casting a circle partake in a profound and ancient rite.

Our early ancestors saw the zodiac as a great circle around the sky, and later on Man laid out the orbits of the planets as circles, also discovering that the Sun, Moon and the planets are spheres. The ancient Greek astrologer and alchemist Hermes Trismegistus said, 'God is like an intelligible sphere, whose centre is everywhere and whose circumference is nowhere'. The German theologian and mystic Jakob Böhme (1575-1624) thought that, 'The being of God is like a wheel, wherein many wheels are made one in another'. Ancient temples and stone circles were often laid out to a circular design, most famously at Stonehenge **(top & centre)**. Although complex sacred geometry can be found inside this and other circles, perhaps the basic form was meant to reflect wholeness, the nature of the Sun, the Moon, and the bowl of the heavens above; Native American medicine wheels are likewise circular. The plan of Silbury Hill, **(left)**, the Neolithic mound in Wiltshire (Knight 2013), is

70

very nearly circular in plan. On a grander scale, many huge landscape circles have been advocated, defined by sacred sites, churches and hills, most famously around Rennes-le-Château in the south of France (Lincoln 1991). Chris Street has mapped several landscape circles, usually enclosing hexagrams or pentagrams, around the London landscape (Street 1990 and 2000), whilst David Furlong has similarly championed two interlocking circles, vesica piscis, in the Avebury landscape (Furlong 1997). Three vast roughly-circular configurations called the Perpetual Choirs, are laid out on the landscape of England and Wales, first recorded in the *Welsh Triads;* at each of the holy sites, continuous chanting was carried out, said to maintain the enchantment and peace of Britain (Gibson-Forty 2012). The concept of Perpetual Choirs was known to the Egyptians, and may well have come to Britain by way of the Druids.

Burial mounds across the world are often circular, a simple design to build for sure, but also representing the circle of life and the swollen belly and womb of the Earth Mother. Newgrange **(top)** and Knowth, both in Ireland, are superb examples. Concentric circles decorate prehistoric burial tombs across the world, and many of the ancient cup and ring marks found on rocks across Britain are of a circular design. The Egyptians often depicted gods and characters with discs on or around their heads, and we shall look at this metamorphosis into haloes later in Chapter 20. The Dendera Zodiac, found on the ceiling of the Temple of Hathor, is a circular Egyptian zodiac map (Knight 2013, p. 113). The Biblical Tower of Babel, told of in the Book of Genesis, was of a spiralling, circular design. Its name comes from the Akkadian word *bab-ilu,* meaning '*Gate of God'.*

Romulus founded the City of Rome with a ceremony involving a circle. The huge semi-circular arches and domes of classical temples were divinely inspired, and many temple plans were circular, such as is well seen at Delphi, and Epidaurus, which reflected the dome of the sky and the movements of the gods. The example here **(centre)** is the Tholos at Delphi, which was dedicated to Athena. In Britain, the circle is magnificently represented on the Battersea Shield, found in the River Thames, which is dated Iron Age, 350-50BC **(right)**. This was a ritual object, too flimsy for combat, which is on display in the British Museum.

The eastern yin-yang symbol **(top, next page)** is enclosed within a circle, and represents the union of the dualities of the cosmos, a symbol of perfect balance. A yantra is a series of sacred mandalas involving triangles and hexagrams, and yet it too is encompassed by a circle.

In prehistoric times, the cross symbolised the Sun; the Celtic wheel cross **(second image, next page)** often has an orb at the centre, which once represented the Sun, yet now symbolises the non-moving divine light of God, around which all else revolves. The early Celtic crosses are excellent

examples of circular design **(image p. 217)**.

Domes are circular, comprising half a sphere, and many Greek, Roman and Christian buildings incorporate them, sometimes to spectacular results; St Peter's Basilica in Rome, and St Paul's Cathedral in London, are two superlative examples. Hindu and Buddhist temples also contain circles and wheels, and to Zen Buddhists, the circle as a wheel represents enlightenment and human perfection. The Buddhist Dharma Wheel symbolises the endless cycles of reincarnation. The wheel was the symbol of Fortuna, the Roman goddess of fortune; even today there are countless game shows that involve a *wheel of fortune*.

The Catherine Wheel is associated with the martyrdom of St Catherine of Alexandria in the 4th century; Catherine **(third image)** was to be executed by means of a spiked wheel, but the instrument of torture was miraculously destroyed at her touch. Is this act symbolic of the destruction of the old Sun-worship cults, whose symbol was a Sun disc or wheel? Many chapels dedicated to Catherine are on high places, ancient Sun hills, which are complemented by the fact that angels carried her corpse to Mount Sinai after her death. Some depictions of Catherine wheels have eight spokes, which denote the eight divisions of the Celtic year. Note how this 10th – 11th century Celtic cross from Margam, in South Wales, **(left)** contains eight spokes. Again, motifs very similar to this can be found at European Neolithic and Bronze Age sites. We shall return to crosses later.

The Knights Templar brought back the techniques and styles of Islamic architecture from the Holy Land; building churches that were circular in design, or else had a circle somewhere in their construction, was foremost in their thinking. Their English headquarters at Temple Church in London, built in the late 12th century, demonstrates the classic Templar *round* **(bottom)**. The Templars observed that the circular patterns and arabesques in Muslim buildings were not just for decoration, but demonstrated the mathematical order of the Universe, of God.

Many writers agree that they were copying the Holy Sepulchre in Jerusalem, whilst others think the octagonal Dome on the Rock (image p. 20) was the template. They recreated the symbolism of the Temple in their *New Jerusalem,* which was a mathematical plan involving sacred geometry within circles enclosed within a twelve sided figure, symbolic of the twelve gates of Jerusalem. The circular design meant that the knights sat around the perimeter democratically. This of course mirrors the Round Table of Arthurian myths, such as the copy shown here, from Winchester **(top, next page)**. The Templars would have been familiar with this, as they would also have been acquainted with the circular Roman and Greek amphitheatres. Jackie Queally has perceived a circle incorporated in the key elements of the architecture of Rosslyn Chapel, Edinburgh, with its centre at the Mar Pillar (Queally 2007). The chapel comprises many elements that appear to have been inspired by the legacy left by the Knights Templars.

The superb rose windows that are incorporated in churches and cathedrals across Europe **(centre)**, are magnificent examples of circular design, geometrical expressions of Man's view of the cosmos. The rose was the ultimate symbol of love and eternity, the symbol of enlightenment and redemption. This flower is the chief symbol of Aphrodite, Venus, the Virgin Mary, and Mary Magdalene, and is the sigil of the Rosicrucians **(image p. 145)**. To Carl Jung, rose windows represented the, '... *Self of Man, transposed onto the cosmic plane"* (Jung, 1964). The commonest expression in a rose window is of a round centre with radiating spokes. Arguably the finest rose windows are three magnificent examples in Chartres Cathedral; the fine window here is at Corsham, Wiltshire **(right)**.

The Freemasons continued the traditions of the Templars, employing the circle in buildings and symbolism. Many seals, medals and badges of Freemasonry incorporate the circle, and globes are an important element, which are usually in pairs at Masonic lodges – one celestial, the other terrestrial; this derives from a tradition that the two pillars at the entrance to Solomon's Temple were capped by globes. The discs of the Sun and the Moon are also key Masonic symbols, representing power, goodness and wisdom. Remnants of ancient solar and lunar worship survive today in the circular 'Obby 'Oss at Padstow **(image p. 25)**.

As late as the Renaissance, philosophers illustrated cosmic order using spheres, representing the various perceived levels of the Universe, and Man's place in it. Leonardo da Vinci placed the figure of a man inside a squared circle **(right)** in his *Vitruvian Man,* demonstrating the principle of *as above, so below;* the circle represents order in the Universe, with Man seen as the crowning glory of God in the heart of this 'circle of life'.

Today, we can all be co-creators of the divine circle, as shown here in this circle made from the quartz intrusions in these beach pebbles **(below)**.

19. Vesica Piscis
and the Aureole

The vesica piscis (meaning *'vessel, or bladder, of the fish'*) is created by the intersection of two equal circles, whose centres are dissected by the perimeter of the other, producing a central lozenge or almond-shaped area. In mathematics, the ratio of the height of the vesica piscis to its width from the centre is the square root of three. Where the circles overlap, two equilateral triangles can occupy the space, creating not just abstract geometry, but a form that is present in the patterns of Nature and studied by many mystery schools. The vesica piscis represents perfect equilibrium, regarded by many as the interpenetration of the worlds of Earth and Heaven, matter and spirit. From the vesica, one can overlay triangles, pentagons, hexagons and hexagrams as the act of creation unfolds (French 2012). Certain reptiles and amphibians have vesica-shaped pupils, and the shape can be observed in total eclipses of the Sun, displayed at the moment when Moon is halfway across the solar disc.

Earth Mysteries pioneer John Michell found the dimensions of Great Pyramid, at Giza, to be related to the vesica (Michell 1983). He also found its shape reflected in the dimensions of the Lady Chapel of Glastonbury Abbey, and that a large vesica determined the placement of some of the sacred buildings of Glastonbury. Gary Biltcliffe found that the positioning of churches and a castle on the Island of Portland, Dorset, inscribed a vesica piscis, and one which is aligned with the solstices; he concludes that, *'The Vesica Piscis is the seed from which all geometry is born'* (Biltcliffe 2009). Chris Street has found vesicas in London (Street 1990), and Roma Harding has suggested a vesica associated with the Wessex Astrum **(top)**, the huge landscape hexagram involving Stonehenge, Glastonbury and Avebury (Knight and Perrott 2008). And all of these landscape alignments are not the result of 'New Age' imagination, for one antiquarian overlaid a vesica piscis onto the plan of Stonehenge as early as 1723!

The vesica was known to early civilisations in Mesopotamia, Africa and Asia, sometimes revealed in the form of magical doors and portals. The Greek mathematicians Pythagoras and Plato both studied the vesica piscis, and even back then related the image to a fish; their name for the figure was *'meaning of a fish'*. It represented the

74

intersection of the divine and mundane worlds, the merging of different polarities and dimensions.

The Flower of Life, or Seed of Life, is composed of interlocking vesica piscis, and is seen at the temple of Osiris at Abydos, Egypt. Called the *Genesis Pattern*, some say it demonstrates how Creation unfolded. The example shown here **(bottom image, previous page)** is a Greek mosaic from the temple complex at Ephesus, c. 400BC. Examples of the Flower of Life were found at Mount Sinai and Masad, Israel, showing they were familiar to the Jewish/Hebrew mystery schools and may have reached Christianity through these traditions.

The Egyptians used the vesica in their *crux ansata* cross, better known as the ankh. Vesica is also the Sanskrit word for yoni, and the association of the space where the two circles overlap has long been associated with the vulva. To Muslim mystics, the vesica piscis is the womb of the Universe, which holds the secrets of the black stone, the Ovum, at Mecca. In the Hebrew Kabbalah, the vesica represents the feminine principle, the goddess of ancient cultures. The shape of the human eye forms a vesica, as in the *Eye of Horus* (front cover). Keith Critchlow has done an excellent study of ancient sites relating to the vesica piscis (Critchlow 2007).

The vesica piscis was taken on board in medieval Christian architecture, championed by the Knights Templar. Gothic arches and doorways express the upper halves of the vesica, as do huge vaulted ceilings. To Christians, the vesica is reflected in the shape of the fish, the symbol of the Piscian Christian age, as well as representing the womb of the Virgin Mary. We know the vesica was adopted by early Christians in the catacombs of Rome, symbolising to them the interaction between material and spiritual worlds. Two vesicas in the Chalice Well Garden, in Glastonbury, are both perfectly positioned to energetically interact with its healing waters **(top and centre)**.

An image often encountered in churches and cathedrals is that of God, Jesus or the Virgin enclosed within a vesica, often illuminated with rays radiating outwards. This is called an aureole, also known as a mandorla, and is a type of nimbus that encloses a whole figure, like a person's aura in esoteric schools. It is, however, a much older concept; in Hinduism, the goddess Kali and Bhairava are often shown in sexual union inside an aureole. An example here **(right)** is from Tibet, and shows this divine marriage taking place within the aureole, the space of rebirth, where the divine and mundane meet within the yoni. The god Shiva may also be depicted dancing inside a flaming aureole. A Greek vase is illustrated here, showing Medea on a chariot

enclosed within an aureole, and dates from 400BC **(bottom left)**. Buddhists depict the aureole as a lotus blossom petal **(bottom centre)**.

The space within the overlapping circles was always a space where spirit and matter overlapped and interacted, and in Christianity this space is now occupied by God or Jesus (or sometimes Mary the Mother), all now centre stage, as shown here at Brighstone, Isle of Wight **(bottom right)**; only through these Christian superstars, apparently, can one's salvation be assured.

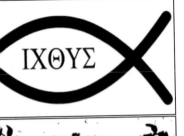

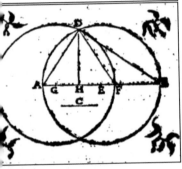

When turned sideways, the vesica becomes the *'Jesus Fish'* logo of Christianity, sometimes containing the words *Jesus* or *Christ* in Greek or Latin **(left)**. Fish are connected with Jesus several times in the New Testament, most famously when he says, *'I will make you fishers of men'*. It became popular after St Augustine extracted the word *ichthus*, meaning *fish*, from the prophecy of an Erythraean sibyl.

Even today the sacred geometry of the vesica is represented by the bishop's mitre, which in itself resembles Egyptian and Mesopotamian headdresses, and the Phrygian cap of Mithras **(image p. 41)**. For centuries, Freemasons have been fascinated by the vesica piscis, as this drawing from 1663 demonstrates **(left)**. The vesica is embodied in the shapes of the collars worn by Freemasonry officiates, as well as the shape of many Masonic seals.

The similarities between (left to right) the Greek, Buddhist and Christian vesica/aureole.

20. The Halo

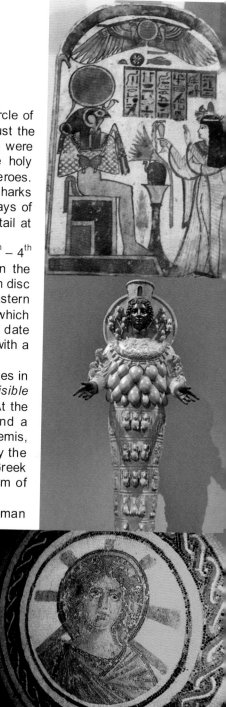

The halo, also known as a nimbus, is a ring or circle of light that surrounds a person, most commonly just the head, in religious art. Before Christianity, haloes were used in the iconography of other religions to indicate holy figures, such as gods, goddesses, and even rulers or heroes. Jesus is universally depicted sporting a halo, which harks back to the solar gods he replaced, who had glowing rays of the Sun emanating from their heads. (I shall look in detail at solar gods and Jesus in Chapter 38.)

Here is an Egyptian scene showing solar god Horus (8th – 4th century BC) from Thebes, which I found on display in the National Museum of Scotland, Edinburgh **(top)**. The sun disc on his head is a precursor of the halo. The Middle Eastern goddess Ishtar is often shown with a headdress on which rests a circle with a star insert, some examples of which date from the 8th century BC. The god Baal may be shown with a halo, as can the Hittite goddess Arinna **(image p. 194)**.

Homer describes seeing glows around the heads of heroes in battle, and Sumerian literature speaks of, *'a brilliant, visible glamour which is exuded by gods, heroes and kings'*. At the Greek temple complex at Ephesus, there used to stand a multi-breasted statue of the fertility Earth Goddess Artemis, who was decidedly black, and later renamed as Diana by the Romans. Here is a Roman alabaster copy of the Greek original, dated 2nd century AD, now housed in the Museum of Naples. Behind her head is a halo **(right)**.

The goddess Juno was the consort of Jupiter in Roman mythology, and is sometimes shown with a halo-type headband, known as a diadem. On a 2nd century AD Roman mosaic floor preserved at Bardo in Tunisia, a haloed Poseidon appears in his chariot. A late 2nd century AD floor mosaic from Thysdrus, also in Tunisia, shows Apollo/Helios sporting a halo, which represents the Sun. The example shown here is from a Roman mosaic floor unearthed at El-Jem in Tunisia. It shows a youthful Apollo, with a halo and sun-rays **(right, and p. 206)**. Sometimes Emperors were shown with haloes, such was the extent to which they regarded themselves as divine.

In Indian mythology, the goddess Durga has a halo in

an 8th century painting of her slaying a demon. She is also sometimes depicted with tongues of fire issuing from her head. It is not uncommon to see various Hindu deities with haloes. Images of Buddha with a halo pre-date Christianity, and he is sometimes depicted with a halo whilst he sits obtaining enlightenment under the Bodhi tree **(image p. 137)**. The golden Bimaram Casket in the British Museum is dated 60AD and was found in Afghanistan, and depicts Buddha with a halo. The Kanishka Casket is a gilded copper reliquary dated 127AD from India, a faithful copy of which is in the British Museum **(top)**; on the lid sits Buddha adorned with a halo, whilst either side of him stand Brahma and Indra, also with haloes. Another image of Buddha with a halo (or mandorla), symbolising his *'light and blessedness'*, is shown here from Japan, now in Edinburgh Museum **(bottom left)**.

The Japanese solar goddess Amaterasu has a halo with the sun's rays behind her head. In the Museum of Scotland, Edinburgh, I found a Mayan statue of a *'Mother Goddess'* from Mexico, dated 900AD; she is wearing is a halo-like headdress **(centre)**. Haloes are found in Islamic art from many periods, especially in Persian and Ottoman art, and Mohammed has also been shown with a simple halo.

The Gnostic Gospels speak of people possessing crowning haloes of light; *'The light has become a crown on my head'* (Pistis Sophia, 1.59), and Christianity has a variety of characters all deemed worthy of a halo, from angels to saints **(bottom right)**. A cruciform halo, one that contains a cross, is reserved for God or Jesus **(images p. 211 & 220)**. Later, during the Renaissance, the urge for realism meant that haloes were a problem for artists, who largely stopped depicting them, even for important Biblical characters. Leonardo da Vinci's *The Last Supper*, for instance, has no haloes, although an arch above Jesus' head is symbolic of one. In 1563, the Church ordered that haloes must be included in all works of sacred art, and some artists got around this edict by putting natural light sources or glowing luminosities behind heads. So the halo was reborn as a sigil of divinity and holy virtues, just as it had been thousands of years before.

78

21. The Spiral

A spiral is a curve that emanates from a central point and gets progressively further away from that point as it revolves around it. It represents energy, movement, and growth, *'the creative principle at work in the Universe'* (Ward 2006). The curve may be three-dimensional, a helix, which turns around on a central axis. When two spirals rotate around an axis it is known as a double-helix, such as in DNA strands, and shown in classical art as the double-serpents of the caduceus, which I shall look at in Chapter 24. Examples of natural unfolding spirals include the sunflower floret, the pineapple, artichoke, pine cone, an unfurling fern, and a spider's web. Most snail shells have a spiral form **(top)**, plus the extinct fossils known as ammonites. On a larger scale, whirlpools, tornados and most galaxies **(right)** are spiralling. Snakes occur in many ancient myths, and this may have had much to do with the spiralling they exhibit when coiled; the spiral is the originator of the labyrinth, which symbolises the path of a snake.

The mathematical ratio of spirals, known as the Fibonacci sequence, or Spira Mirabilis, unfolds to the proportions of phi and was noted by the Greeks as early as 450BC. It gets its name from Leonardo of Pisa, also known as Fibonacci, who wrote of it in 1202. A Nautilus shell shows this sequence well **(image p. 7)**.

Spirals have been depicted by Man from the earliest times. Perhaps the oldest known examples are those carved on a Mammoth ivory medallion from Siberia, which dates from 18,000-23,000 years ago, on which several spirals are depicted, the largest of which has seven turns. In the Grotto des Hôteaux caves of France, a woman's skull, dated c. 15,000 years old, was surrounded by carefully laid snail shells. There is evidence that snail shells were ritually deposited at Neolithic burial and ceremonial sites, such as Stonehenge and at sites in the Avebury area (Meaden 1991); at West Kennet Long Barrow, an *inland* site, *marine* shells were deposited (Knight 2011). The ritual offering of snail shells is a phenomena recorded at Pompeii, and on a Mayan pyramid in the Yucatan,

Mexico. Spiralling fossils were found in Neolithic sites on Malta, and other examples associated with burial occur across Europe, such as the large ammonite set into the entrance of the Stoney Littleton tomb, near Bath. Ammon Ra is the ram-headed god of Egypt who sports spiralling horns, and gives us the word ammonite; spirals adorn this fine Neolithic Egyptian pot **(bottom image, previous page)**, on show in Birmingham Museum.

At the Neolithic passage grave of Newgrange, Ireland, several spirals were carved on megaliths as long ago as 5,700 years **(images p. 79 & 170)**. More can be seen on the kerbstones at Knowth nearby, and others are known from across the British Isles. Spiral decoration was found on pottery at Stonehenge, and other examples have been unearthed across Europe.

Double and triple spirals have further meaning: they are connected, 'flowing' from one to the other, representing energies moving in different directions simultaneously – birth and death, the eternal cycles of the cosmos. The triple spiral **(image p. 170)** may have represented the Triple Goddess, later to be morphed into the Holy Trinity. I have personally marvelled at the intricate spirals carved on stones at some of the temples on Malta, the examples shown here being from Tarxien **(top)**. Terence Meaden has produced an excellent study looking at the prehistoric significance of the spiral (Meaden 1991).

Small stones bearing geometrical symbols have been found at Neolithic sites in Scotland, and have been interpreted as representing the *Platonic Solids;* incredibly, they were made 1000 years before the life of the Greek mathematician. I had the privilege to see some of these in the National Museum of Scotland, Edinburgh; the Towie Ball **(centre)** was found in Aberdeenshire and is dated to 3000BC; another sphere bearing spirals was found at Skara Brae.

The ancient ziggurat towers of Mesopotamia and Iran were often ascended by means of spiralling staircases or ramps, as it was thought that the towers linked Earth and the heavenly realms; the Biblical Tower of Babel is one such example. It has been suggested that Silbury Hill may once have had a similar spiral path to its summit. In a similar manner, the ancient path that spirals up Glastonbury Tor may be 5,000 years old (Ward 2006, p. 5).

On the other side of the world, spiral geoglyphs can be seen among the Nazca Lines of Peru, dated 200BC-500AD, as seen with this monkey **(bottom)**. The famous Serpent Mound in Ohio features a spiralling design in the tail of the geoglyph **(image p. 122)**. A spiralling Anasazi carving from the American southwest, dated 1000 years old, was worked into a rock face so as to interact with shafts of sunlight at midwinter. Spirals also occur in Pre-Columbian Central America, and are depicted on some of the petroglyphs dated 750-1200AD.

Mycenae vessels and Greek pottery were often decorated with spirals. The Greek mathematician Archimedes penned a work entitled '*On Spirals*', and one of his iconic inventions was of course the *Archimedes Screw*, a rotating spiral which raised water to a higher level. In Egypt, another name for the Great Sphinx is *Neb,* which means, *'the spiralling power of the Cosmos'.* Egyptians regarded spiral seashells as good luck amulets, worn to protect them from evil.

A Bronze Age statuette from Romania has spiral motifs, and many Bronze Age and Iron Age pins have been found with double-headed spirals, such as at Cadbury Castle, Somerset, dated 750BC. At Maiden Castle, the huge Iron Age hillfort in Dorset, spirals were found on a piece of chalk (Knight 1998, p. 53). At another Iron Age site, at Rainsborough, Oxfordshire, large quantities of ritually-deposited snail shells were unearthed. Later, Romano-British mosaics display spirals, as do pots from this period. The Norse also used spiral decoration, and several *Picture Stones* bearing spirals were found on Gotland, Sweden.

Spirals are depicted in tattoos and carved figures of the Maori, who see them as representing creation, and spirals are believed to be a key to immortality in Polynesia. Australian Aborigine symbolism is rich in spirals, and the Pueblo Indians chant *Spiral Songs* at their New Year; they also partake in spiral dances, as do the Sufi *Whirling Dervishes* of Turkey, which to them symbolises the patterns of life's flow and constant change.

Dowsers often map earth energies as flowing and emanating in a spiraling nature, especially at vortices or nodes. I have described previously the spiralling patterns of energies at West Kennet Long Barrow (Knight 2011) and at the Cerne Giant (Knight 2013). Crop circle researchers have long commented on spiral patterning in the flattened crop.

Classical Greek and Roman columns were often capped with capitals displaying spiralling scrolls, called volutes **(top)**. As Rome was Christianised, it was only to be expected that the Church carried on the reverence that the classical world regarded for the spiral, especially in Church architecture **(right)**. But there also seems to have been some remembrance of the early sacred significance of the spiral, bearing in mind the large number found on grave stones and early crosses, such as the Pictish stones **(image, p. 17)**. As late as the 9-11th century AD, two grave stones on Anglesey were decorated with large double spirals (Meaden 1991, p. 202). Many Celtic crosses incorporate spiral designs, side-by-side with Celtic knot work. Later still, mazes often had spirals at their centre. Spiralling branches associated with the Tree of Life can be seen on p. 56, and in both Classical and Christian art, unicorns are frequently depicted with a spiralled horn. The spiralling nature of the foliage of the Apprentice Pillar at Rosslyn Chapel has already been commented on **(image p. 57)**, and the doorway at Kilpeck church, Herefordshire, is beautifully framed with spiralling serpents. On the font at Lostwithiel, Cornwall, is a carved grotesque head **(right)**, that shows a spiral on the forehead, in the position of the *third eye* chakra of Eastern spiritualities;

across the top of its head there are two serpents (Miller and Broadhurst 1989). I have stood in front of this head and the effect on the psyche is profound. It is interesting that in Tantric yoga, the Sanskrit word for spiral is *kundalini*, describing the serpent power that rises through the chakras of the body. At Stoke Trister, Somerset, I found spiralling snakes on an old floor monument **(left)**, hidden under a carpet; it seemed to explain the spiralling vortex of energy that I had earlier dowsed at that point.

I have had the pleasure to stand before the cross at Whalley church, Lancs **(centre)**, which is adorned with beautifully carved spirals and triangles, so reminiscent of the imagery at Newgrange **(image p. 79)**; the church stands on the Belinus Line (Biltcliffe and Hoare 2012). Another Christian example so reminiscent of the Neolithic spirals and triangles at Newgrange is shown here, this time on a cross at Kelly, Devon **(bottom right)**.

Spirals have even been involved in Christian 'miracles'. At Whitby, Yorkshire, spiralling ammonite fossils were said to have been snakes that were turned to stone by St Hilda when she founded a convent there; at Keynsham, near Bristol, the prayers of St Keyna similarly turned snakes into ammonites.

In the Cornish village of Rescorla, the tradition of the *Snail Creep* has persisted into modern times; in springtime, people partake in a spiral dance which eventually leads into a packed centre, which is followed by an unwinding. It represents conquest of the Sun over winter, the defeat of death by means of a ceremonial *Resurrection*.

William Blake's *Jacob's Ladder,* painted in 1805 **(below left)** is now in the British Museum, and shows how he regarded the ascent to Heaven to be more like a spiral staircase than a ladder. He is acknowledging the ancient mystical importance of the spiral, and its place in the grand design of the cosmos. The spiral has never been just an abstract, meaningless symbol or mere decoration, but rather a potent image of death and rebirth, of productiveness and creation, of movement and evolution — it represents the very rhythm of life.

22. Labyrinths and Mazes

The terms labyrinth and maze are often used interchangeably, yet this is a misnomer, as there is a clear distinction between the two. A labyrinth has but one (unicursal) path to the centre, although it may be complex, whereas a maze is a puzzle, and can have multiple (multicursal) paths, along which it is possible to get lost. The word maze comes from the Old English *amasian,* which means, *'to confuse'.*

To ancient cultures, the labyrinth was a liminal, ritual space that must be walked, offering a gateway between this world and the realms of spirit, as well as a bridge between our everyday lives and our subconscious. Early labyrinths appear to have been routes for the soul to journey to the Underworld, providing the gateway between life and death. The earliest known reference to a labyrinth was made by the Greek historian Herodotus, who wrote of an underground labyrinth built as a memorial to twelve Egyptian kings, and accompanied by a pyramid. Labyrinths appear on several Egyptian seals and were used to plan pharaoh's tombs, in the hope of fooling tomb robbers. The Roman writer Pliny also mentions Egyptian labyrinths, and he recollected labyrinth patterns marked out as children's games.

Petroglyphs featuring labyrinths have been found at Goa, India, dating back to 2500BC, and labyrinths also appear in ancient Indian manuscripts. On the Solovetsky Islands of the White Sea, 30 stone labyrinths have been discovered, dated 2000-3000 years old. At Rocky Valley in Cornwall, two small but beautifully crafted labyrinths can be seen inscribed into the vertical rock face **(top)**, and which are officially dated to the Bronze Age.

The simplest form of labyrinth is the *Cretan* or seven-fold design, and the name labyrinth itself is from the *labrys,* the double-headed axe of ancient Crete. These axes were often held by the figure of a goddess who would guard the entrance to a labyrinth, which was the route to the Underworld; the main deity of the palace at Knossos was Labyrinthoio Potnia, known as *'Mistress of the Goddess'.* The most famous labyrinth was that of the Minoans of Knossos, who reached the peak of their civilization around 1600BC. In the celebrated myth, Theseus descends into a labyrinth to slay the bull-headed Minotaur in a rite of passage for both his body and his mind. A labyrinth was drawn on the floor of the palace at Knossos, and a coin from the site is shown here, displaying a labyrinthine design, dated 1400BC **(bottom)**. Archaeologists have recently conducted a search of the nearby Skotino Cave system, and some think this may be a contender for the origins of the labyrinth myth.

Labyrinths are associated with the womb and rebirth, a symbolic journey into the body of the Earth Mother, followed by a subsequent rebirth on one's return. The Tapu'at labyrinths of the Hopi Indians represent a curled up baby inside the womb, the entrance being the birth canal. This feminine link can be traced right back to Crete, where the hero Theseus **(left)** was aided by the goddess Ariadne, who assists the hero by providing him with a long thread to aid his return – it is an umbilical cord no less. The hero's journey and the goddess connection all mirror ancient Palaeolithic journeys down into the labyrinthine passages of caves, in order to reach the inner sanctum of the Goddess.

It has recently been suggested that some of the Neolithic enclosures of Wiltshire, comprising of masses of wooden posts, may have been symbolic labyrinths (Williams 2010). At the Tholos temple at Epidaurus, the Greeks constructed a labyrinth beneath the floor of the temple, linked with passages, and the Romans carried on the tradition from the Greeks through labyrinth floor mosaics and wall illustrations. A Roman mosaic unearthed at Rhaetia, Switzerland **(top)** comprises a labyrinth with Theseus and the Minotaur at the centre, and at other Roman sites labyrinthine mosaics were clearly large enough to have been walked.

Dowsing has detected powerful earth energies associated with the Chartres labyrinth, which has a potent effect on the psyche of pilgrims walking it. Similarly, on the summit of St Catherine's Hill, near Winchester, a square labyrinth, called the Mizmaze **(second image)**, has been set into the turf midst an Iron Age hillfort, next to the site of a Norman hilltop chapel. Powerful energies associated with the Belinus Line can be experienced in the labyrinth, as the male and female flows converge at the centre (Biltcliffe and Hoare 2012, p. 70-1). On Glastonbury Tor, a three-dimensional prehistoric labyrinth was fashioned through the enhancement of the natural ridges of the hill's geology; the hill is sacred to the god of the Underworld, Gwyn ap Nudd. Labyrinths inscribed into rock dating back to the Iron Age have been found at Val Camonica in Italy, and Native Americans have long created labyrinths as part of their ancestral ceremonies.

The Church adopted the labyrinth as early as the 4th century AD, and they became ever more common from the 9th century onwards. Large designs were incorporated into Gothic Cathedrals, most famously around 1230 at Chartres, France **(third image and left)**. A six-petalled central flower at its heart is said to signify, *'the healing union of Christ and Mary the Mother'*. Medieval pilgrims and penitents alike would trudge to the centre in the hope of salvation, and people too weak to partake in a geographical pilgrimage could walk the labyrinth. It represented the tortuous path of human existence, and some traversed the labyrinth on their knees. What is wonderful about the Chartres labyrinth is that if the adjacent north rose window was hinged and was somehow dropped on to the labyrinth, it would cover it exactly; the thirteen-fold design of this labyrinth also mirrors the annual number of lunar months.

Chartres is not unique in housing labyrinths that can be walked; other examples can be seen in the Basilica of St Quentin and Amiens Cathedral, both in France, in St Lambertus, in Minglosheim, Germany, at Grace Cathedral in San Francisco, and yet another is laid beneath the tower of Ely Cathedral. Another fine English example is laid into the floor of St Mary's church at Itchen Stoke, Hampshire, which is a copy of the Chartres design, and has the altar at its centre; the church is only a few miles from the labyrinth on St Catherine's Hill. Another one close by is the geometrical labyrinth in Winchester Cathedral **(top)**.

Sometimes medieval *'finger labyrinths'* are inscribed onto walls, such as at Lucca in Italy. A small labyrinth is carved onto the font **(right)** in the church at Lewannick, Cornwall, accompanied by a spiral and a pentagram. The Watt's Mortuary Chapel at Compton, Surrey, is a late 19th century wonderland of esoteric architecture fusing art nouveau and Celtic influences. Included are the Tree of Life and five labyrinths, all of which are held by angels, one of which is shown here **(right)**.

Mazes developed from ecclesiastical labyrinths, and these further symbolised the difficulty that poor sinners have in getting to Heaven. From the Middle Ages, mazes came into fashion with the wealthy as novelties and status symbols on their huge estates. It is thought, however, that they were inspired by the great medieval cathedrals that feature them. Mazes continue to be constructed today, to confuse those curious enough to be lured in.

Walking a labyrinth today can be a profound experience, as I have found several times at St John's church in Glastonbury **(bottom)**, St Catherine's Hill, and Winchester Cathedral. We are required to bring ourselves into the here and now, to focus on reaching a sacred centre, and one that is not merely on the ground on which we walk, but within the depths of ourselves.

23. All Creatures Great and Small

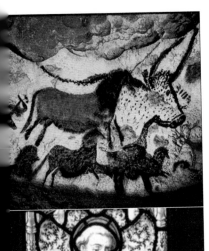

Man's relationship with animals had its genesis at the very birth of our species, when we hunted them for food and clothing, as we still do. But evidence suggests that from very early times we were regarding them as more than merely a resource, and that a spiritual relationship between us and other creatures was forged as far back as the Ice Ages. Ancient cave paintings **(left, and p. 12)**, often depict animals which are thought to represent sympathetic magic, as shamans sought to connect with the spirits of the animals they hoped would sacrifice themselves during hunting **(image p. 92)**.

Let us compare the animal symbolism most often seen in churches, as well as some of the Biblical stories that involve animals, and see where the origins of these lie. We shall deal with two creatures, the dragon and the serpent, in much more detail in subsequent chapters.

The Evangelists

Matthew, Mark, Luke and John are the four apostles who are credited with writing the Synoptic Gospels of the New Testament, and are thought to have been amongst the twelve Biblical followers of Jesus. Although we now know that other, both profound and esoteric, gospels were written, these four are the ones that were projected to the forefront of the Christian agenda.

Three of these four apostles are commonly represented as animals in Church imagery, whilst Matthew is shown as a man or angel. Mark's sigil is a lion, shown here with him in St Edmund's, Glastonbury **(left)**; the lion is regarded by Christians as a symbol of both courage and monarchy. Luke's symbol is a bull or winged oxen, symbolising sacrifice, service and strength. The icon of St John (the Divine) is that of an eagle, a creature that sees the bigger picture or overview from his lofty position in the sky; it is symbolic of the tenet that Christian's should look upward and onward, never flinching in their ultimate goal of union with God. But, as we shall now see, all of these symbols were already in use thousands of years before they adorned Christian manuscripts.

Lion

Lions, in particular the male of the species, have been an important symbol for cultures throughout the world for thousands of years. They are often associated with sovereignty, stateliness, and bravery, for lions are the *kings of the beasts,* the *kings of the jungle.*

Lion statues and reliefs provide a sense of awe and majesty, especially when used on public buildings or statues. Lions appear in cave paintings dating back 32,000 years, and several are depicted in Palaeolithic cave art of Lascaux, France, which are dated to 15,000 years ago. Lions have been found on pillars and stones at *Gőbekli Tepe* (Collins 2014).

In Egypt, the Great Sphinx of Giza **(right)** once had a lion's head; it also faces to where the constellation of Leo rose at the time it was constructed. The Egyptian war goddess Sekhmet is typically shown as a lioness **(centre)**, and the gods Debun and Maahes were likewise depicted as lions. Hathor had lion heads that looked both backward and forward, symbolising time.

The Mycenae Lion Gate is a famed use of lion symbolism **(image p. 55)**, and similar lion images were incorporated into the gates of the Hittite city of Bogazkoy, Turkey, as well as the entrances of the Persian cities of Persopolis, Hyrcania and Susa. In ancient Babylon, the lion was the supreme symbol of royal power, and sculptures of winged lions were popular on important civic buildings. At the Hittite city of Yasilakaya there is a spectacular image of a 6ft high goddess mounted on a lion. At Catal Hüyük, Turkey, one sculpture features a goddess sitting on a throne flanked by lions, and has been dated c. 6,000BC **(image p. 193)**.

In Greek mythology, Heracles (Hercules) defeated the Nemean lion, and he is often shown with the beast's skin over one arm (Knight 2013), whilst several other Greek fables also feature lions. In Islamic tradition, the lion is a figure of courage, chivalry and royalty, and was used in Muslim architecture in Spain. The lion commonly features in Chinese myths and architecture, and people partake in a Chinese New Year *Lion Dance* to ward off evil spirits. Tibetan culture features lions, and a pair of Snow Lions are portrayed on the Tibetan flag. In India, the name Singh comes from the Vedic name for *lion,* and one of the avatars of the god Vishnu is Narasimha, *'Man Lion'.* The entrance to Sigiriya (*Lion Rock*), Sri Lanka, was through *Lion Gate*.

The famous Biblical story relating to lions is of course that of Daniel, who was thrown into a den of lions and yet miraculously survived, as shown here at Corsham, Wiltshire **(right)**. As already mentioned, St Mark's icon is a lion, often winged, and which is said to originate from a legend that the Roman's also threw him to the lions; but the beasts went to sleep at his feet, at which point his captors released him. Other authorities contend that the lion is

Mark's symbol because it represents the Resurrection, as lions are said to sleep with their eyes open, and that Jesus is the 'King'. The example here **(left)** from Chippenham, Wiltshire, is a window that shows Leo in the circle of the zodiac (with the scales of Libra), both being held by an angel. The next image is also of St Mark's lion, from Gussage St Michael, Dorset **(second image)**.

In the Bible (Judges 14), strongman Samson kills a lion with his bare hands, which echoes the Hercules myth. God himself is compared to a lion in Amos 3:8: *'The lion hath roared, who will not fear? The Lord God has spoken'.* In Proverbs 28:1, we read, *'the righteous are bold as lions'.* And again, in Hosea 11:10, *'They shall go after the Lord; he will roar like a lion'.* The Israelites' time in captivity in Babylon (where the goddess was associated with lions), influenced them greatly, for we read in Ezekiel 18:32 – 19:1, *'O house of Israel… What is thy mother? A lioness',* and in Psalms 34:10, *'The young lions suffer and want and hunger, but those who seek the Lord lack no good thing'.* In Solomon's Temple itself we are told that, *'… set in the frames were lions and oxen',* and, *'… twelve lions stood there one on each end of a step'* (1 Kings). The lion was indeed the symbol of the tribe and kingdom of Judah, and today the beast is the symbol of Jerusalem; in Genesis 49:9, we read that, *'Judah is a lion's cub'.* The supplication of the old ways is brought to the fore, however, for in Jeremiah 12:8 we read, *'My heritage has come to me like a lion in the forest; she has lifted up her voice against me; therefore I hate her'.* However, centuries later, some Christian depictions of Mary the Virgin show her accompanied by lions; the long association of the divine feminine with the beast continues.

Lions are common icons in heraldry, symbolising courage, and triple lions represented King Richard the Lionheart. Today, three lions feature on the shirts of the English national football and cricket teams, and lions can be seen on the emblems of many sporting and corporate bodies. The four iconic bronze lions on the base of Nelson's Column in London must be amongst the most photographed felines in the world.

Bull/Cattle

Bulls, or aurochs, appear on the Palaeolithic Lascaux cave paintings, c. 15,000 years old **(image p. 86)**, and they were carved on pillars and stones **(third image)** at the ancient site of *Göbekli Tepe* in Turkey (Collins 2014). In Sumerian mythology, the *Bull of the Heavens* plays a role in the *Epic of Gilgamesh,* which dates back to around 2150 BC; here the goddess Ishtar sends a heavenly bull to gore Gilgamesh, who had scorned her. The zodiac sign of the bull, Taurus, appears on the Egyptian Dendera Zodiac, and

Isis is often depicted as a horned *Sacred Cow*. In Greek and Roman religions, bulls were associated with the anger of Zeus/Jupiter, perhaps because thunder reflected the roar and stamping hooves of a bull. In one myth, Taurus the bull was tamed by Jason the Argonaut. The god Mithras slaying a bull is a common motif of ancient Rome **(image p. 41)**, as was Apis the Bull. Hercules is frequently shown killing a bull, as in this mosaic from Madrid **(bottom, previous page)**. Bulls were carved at the Neolithic temple at Tarxien in Malta, and Michael Dames has suggested that the blocking stones at West Kennet Long Barrow form the shape of an ox (Knight 2011, p. 132); it has also been suggested that the plan of the barrow is laid out as a bull's head (Knight 2011, p. 92).

From the Minoans of Crete comes the celebrated myth in which Theseus descends into a labyrinth to slay the bull-headed Minotaur in a rite of passage; the same culture held bull-vaulting and bull-running festivals. At Catal Hüyük, Turkey, several bull images and relics were uncovered, and the animal seems to have been central to worship of the Goddess; the nearby Taurus Mountains were named after the bull. The creature has also been a continuous feature of zodiacs for thousands of years ago.

In Indian mythology, the god Shiva rides a sacred bull called Nandi, and giant statues were erected to the beast, as shown in this 1901 photograph **(top)**.

The Hittites and Phoenicians had a weather god that was carried along on a chariot pulled by bulls. One Egyptian obelisk at Thebes declares, '*Horus the mighty bull*'; the god Buchis was another Egyptian bull deity venerated at Hermonthis, and the goddess Hapi was worshipped as a bull at Memphis. In Romano/British Iron Age Britain, bull-worship was prolific; to the Celts, the bull represented fertility and prosperity, and was sometimes depicted with Cernunnos; indeed, the magical powers of the bull, and its horns, pervaded the consciousness of the Celts; the Romans recorded that Druids used to sacrifice bulls for divination purposes. Remnants of bull worship survive with the Dorset Ooser **(image p. 50)**.

The sacrifice of bulls was a central theme in the Egyptian worship of Ra, a rite repeated by cultures across the ancient world, including Jews and Christians. Yahweh is referred to as *The Bull of Israel,* indicating a fertility association. Evidence of bull worship is found in the Bible, as well as bull/cattle sacrifice: '*...sacrifice a bull each day as a sin offering to make atonement*'. God told Moses to partake in several sacrifices, including that of a bull, whose blood was poured over an altar (a very ancient, Pagan and shamanic practice). In the well known Moses myth, the Israelites worshipped a golden calf in his absence **(second image)**. We read in Numbers 23:22, that, '*God brings*

89

them out of Egypt and is for them like the horns of the wild ox.' And in Psalm 22:21: 'You have rescued me from the horns of the wild ox!' St Luke's icon is a bull, often winged, and two examples shown here are from Cattistock, Dorset, and Sutton Benger, Wiltshire **(bottom two images, previous page)**. St Mark's bull is shown on the 8th century *Book of Cerne* (Knight 2013), and not far from the Cerne Giant is Bulbarrow, relating to more ancient bull worship (Knight 2013).

Eagle

To the Persians, Babylonians and Assyrians, the Griffin was a mythical beast that had the body of a lion, and yet possessed the head, wings and talons of an eagle, combining strength with clear vision and far-sightedness. The Griffin can be found in Church iconography, sometimes representing Satan, although in medieval heraldry it symbolised strength and protection. The eagle-headed human-like god Nisroch can often be seen carved on Assyrian walls and stele in Mesopotamia **(top)**. Horus is the Falcon-headed god of the Egyptians, and the eagle is a close relative. In Hindu mythology, the god Vishnu rides on the back of Garuda, who was half man/half eagle. The eagle was known as the *King of Birds,* and was the symbol of Jupiter **(image p. 220)**, who was ruler of the gods, and it became a symbol of Rome, and of the Roman legions **(left)**; the doubled-headed eagle was in fact a popular symbol of emperors. In many cultures it has a long association with the Divine, and its many attributes include faith, courage, power and vision.

The Eagle was the symbol of the Israelite tribe of Dan. The bird is also highly revered by the Native Americans and was adopted as the emblem on the seal of the USA; *Eagle* was the name of the lunar lander on the Apollo XI moon landing.

The Eagle is the frequently encountered symbol of the apostle St John the Divine **(left)**. In Revelations, which he wrote, the Eagle is one of the creatures grouped around the *'Throne of the Lamb'.* The connection with St John may have come from St Jerome, who said John's gospel begins, *'... like an eagle hastening to lofty things',* as John relates the Creation. John's gospel is the most mystical, as John, *'... contemplates God in the same way that the eagle was meant to be able to look unflinchingly into the eye of the sun'* (Taylor 2003). This stunning example **(bottom)** is at Sutton Benger, Wiltshire.

It was thought that Eagles could look directly at the Sun, and as such became a symbol of Jesus' Ascension, their gaze fixed on the *'glory of the light'*. It was also thought that Eagles re-birthed by flying into the Sun, and therefore are often depicted on fonts, signifying new life. Lecterns often take the form of an eagle with outstretched wings, on which the Bible rests, symbolising spiritual power and divine inspiration. Many of these are gold and glitteringly spectacular, reminding us of Imperial Rome.

Sheep/Ram/Lamb of God

Aries, the ram, has an ancient tradition as one of the zodiac signs. Sacred rams were very popular in ancient Egypt, chief amongst these being Ba Neb Djedet, for in him was incarnated the soul of Osiris. The god Khnum, who was originally the god of the Nile, had the head of a ram. Ram's heads were found in Neolithic shrines at the ancient city of Catal Hùyùk, Turkey, indicating their spiritual significance. The Sumerians had a sheep goddess named Duttur, who was an oracle deity, hence our modern association between dreams and getting to sleep by counting sheep. The ram enjoyed considerable prominence among the Celts and they would frequently be associated with the horned god Cernunnos; sometimes the god is associated with ram-headed serpent. Ram horns sometimes adorn images of gods, usually in the context of fertility or aggression. The

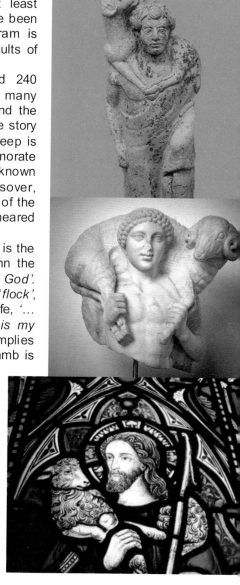

Greeks and Romans used sheep for sacrifice, and in Greek mythology the fabled Golden Fleece is central to the tale of Jason and the Argonauts, and dates back to at least 800BC. In Chinese Buddhism, a ram is said to have been present at the birth of Buddha, and in Tibet a ram is annually released into the wild to release human faults of the previous year.

Sheep and shepherds are mentioned on around 240 occasions in the Bible. The Old Testament has many stories involving sheep, such as on Abel's altar, and the ram caught in a bush that served as a sacrifice in the story of Abraham's test of faith. In Islamic tradition, a sheep is sacrificed during Eid al-Adham, a festival to commemorate Abraham's obedience to Allah. In Judaism, a lamb, known as the Pascal Lamb, was sacrificed on the eve of Passover, to celebrate how God took the lives of the first born of the Egyptians, yet spared the Israelites, who had smeared lamb's blood on their doors.

Jesus is often represented by a lamb or a ram, for he is the Agnus Dei, *'Lamb of God'* in Latin, from when John the Baptist sees Jesus he says, *'Behold the Lamb of God'.* Jesus is the *'Good Shepherd',* sent down to tend his *'flock',* and who even describes himself as laying down his life, *'... for the sheep'.* Psalm 23 tells us that, *'The Lord is my shepherd, I shall not want'.* His portrayal as a ram implies that he is leader of the herd, yet his link with the lamb is ultimately about the altruism of his self-sacrifice.

Hermes Kriophoros was the *Ram Bearer* of the Greeks, who was protector of flocks and herds and is shown here on a statute c. 5-6th century BC **(top)**. His cult was very widespread in Arcadia, and myths tell of how he would lead his animals to fresh water, sometimes carrying beasts on his shoulders. By the fourth-century AD, the Romans were transforming their version of Hermes Kriophoros **(centre)**, into Christ, the new *Good Shepherd,* which is the icon that has come down to us today. These two ancient images can be compared to the similar and typically Christian imagery of Jesus **(right)**, from Sutton Benger, in Wiltshire.

Deer/Stag

For early Man, the deer was a valuable resource, providing nourishment and clothing. But, more than this, the animal played an important role in many shamanic practices. Even today, Lapland Shaman feed their reindeer the psychoactive Fly Agaric mushroom, and then drink the animal's urine, which by then has increased in potency. The famous cave painting called the *'Sorcerer of Trois Freres'* **(left)** was found in a French cave in 1914, and is dated c.12,000BC. It is thought to be a shaman shape-shifting into a deer, or at least depicts a man imitating a stag as part of a sympathetic magic rite. Stag antlers have been found in countless Bronze Age and Neolithic burials, such as at West Kennet Long Barrow (Knight 2011, p. 107-8). The stag has a long association with fertility (in particular the male principle), and with fecundity, rebirth and longevity.

The Scythians, Iron Age horsemen of the Eurasian steppes, had great reverence for the stag, which is one of the most common motifs in their artwork, especially at burial sites. This swift animal was believed to speed the spirits of the dead on their way, which may explain the curious antlered headdresses found on horses in Iron Age burials at Pazyryk, Siberia, as well as Scythian figurines featuring stags **(left)**.

Deer have significant roles in the mythology of various peoples. The Huichol people of Mexico hunt and sacrifice deer in their ceremonies; they make offerings to both the *Deer of the Maize*, that it might care for their crops, and to the *Deer of the Peyote* for spiritual guidance and artistic inspiration. According to the Hindi *Aitareya Upanishad*, the goddess Saraswati takes the form of a red deer called Rohit, and a golden deer plays an important role in the epic *Ramayana*. Deer were considered messengers to the gods in Japanese Shinto culture, and it is the emblem of the city of Nara. In various parts of northeast Japan, an annual deer dance called *'Shishi-odori'* is traditionally performed as a surviving Shinto ceremony.

The Hittites revered the stag alongside the bull at Alaca Höyük, and in their mythology there was Kal, a protective stag deity. Other Hittite gods were often depicted standing on the backs of stags. In Hungarian mythology, Hunor and Magor, the founders of the Magyar peoples, chased a white stag in a hunt, which lead them into unknown land that they named Scythia. To this day, an important emblem in Hungary is an antlered stag with its head turned back over its shoulder.

In Greek mythology, the deer is particularly associated with Artemis in her role as virginal huntress, as deer drew her chariot. After witnessing the nude figure of Artemis bathing in a pool, Actaeon was transformed by Artemis into a stag, and his own hounds tore him to pieces. A Greek silver gilt libation vessel in the form of a stag is shown here, dated 4th century BC **(bottom)**. One of the Labours of Heracles (Hercules) was to capture the antlered *Cerynian Hind,* sacred to Artemis; as hinds bearing antlers were unknown in Greece, the story suggests it was a reindeer, which, unlike other deer, can be harnessed and has antlered females; so the myth may relate to Hyperborea, a land to the north that was a natural habitat for reindeer. The infant son of Heracles, Telephus, was nurtured by a doe on the slopes of Tegea, and shown here is a Roman copy of a Greek statue showing all three characters, found at Tivoli in Italy **(right)**.

The insular Celts held deer to be supernatural animals, *'fairy cattle'* that were herded and milked by a benevolent fairy giantess (*bean sidhe*) in each Celtic land, and who could shape shift into a red deer. Several Celtic mythological figures, such as Oisin, Flidais and Sadb, were given connections to deer, and the Celts believed that a white stag would appear when one was transgressing a taboo. The Celtic imagination produced gods who could transform into animals; Cernunnos was the god that possessed deer antlers, and early evidence for the god goes back to the 4th century BC on an Italian rock carving. He was known as *The Horned One* or *The Horned God* - antlers are technically horns. Cernunnos is also known as *The Stag Lord, Lord of the Forest*, and *Lord of the Animals,* although it is impossible to know exactly why this is so, as there is not one ancient myth concerning him. He famously appears sitting cross-legged on the Gunderstrup Cauldron, an Iron Age relic from Denmark **(image p. 49)**, and is named alongside his image on a stone found under Notre Dame Cathedral, Paris, in 1711, which is dated 17AD **(right)**. The torcs hanging from his antlers signify his authority.

An Anglo-Saxon royal sceptre found at the burial site at Sutton Hoo, features a depiction of an antlered stag. In the Old English saga *Beowulf*, much of the first portion of the story focuses on events surrounding a great mead hall called Heorot, which means *'Hall of the Hart'*. In the *Prose Edda* poem *Grímnismál,* four stags of Yggdrasil graze on the world tree. In another tale, the god Freyr killed Beli with an antler, and in yet another saga, Sigurd was nursed by a doe. The font at Melbury Bubb, Dorset, is thought to be a re-used Saxon cross **(right)**, and shows an inverted stag (see Knight 1998 and 2000).

Turkic peoples from the Eurasian Steppe that converted to Islam brought with them their beliefs and cults involving horns, deer, antlers, hides, etc. So that in the Ottoman Empire, more specifically in western Asia Minor and Thrace, the deer cult seems to have been widespread and much alive, no doubt as a result of the meeting and mixing of Turkic with local traditions. A famous tale from the 13th century tells how holy man Geyiklü Baba, *'Father Deer'*, lived with his deer in the forests of Bursa and gave hind's milk to a colleague (compare with Saint Giles below).

In Judaism, the Naftali Tribe bore a stag on its tribal banner, and a hind is poetically described in the *Blessing of Jacob*. In Songs 2:9 and 8:14, for instance, we have *'young hart'* literally, *'fawn of the roe deer'.* In Jewish mythology, a giant

stag named *Keresh* dwelt in a mythical forest called '*Bei Ilai*'. Furthermore, the term *Ya`el* or *ya`alah* occurs four times in the Old Testament, and was thought to mean '*wild goat*', but several scholars now take this to mean either roe deer, doe or even ibex. The Hebrew term *Tsebhi* is translated as roe or roebuck in the King James Bible, whilst in the Revised Version it is usually *gazelle*. The Bible generally associates deer with grace, swiftness and beauty; Ayyalon, meaning *deer*, is the name of several towns in Palestine.

In Arthurian legend, the white stag or hart has the perennial ability to evade capture, and that the pursuit of the animal represents Mankind's spiritual pursuits; its appearance signalled the time for knights to embark on a Quest.

Unfortunately, the horned and antlered gods of pre-Christianity, such as satyrs, Pan and Cernunnos, were metamorphosed into the Devil and other ungodly creatures. However, there are several later myths in which deer are seen in a more favourable light.

Saint Giles, a Catholic saint from Athens, who is especially revered in the south of France, is reported to have lived for many years as a hermit in a forest near Nîmes, where his sole companion was a hind, who in some stories sustained him with her milk. Legend says that when hunters shot an arrow at the deer it hit the saint instead, injuring him. In art and church windows, he is often shown with that hind **(top)**.

A stag was partly responsible for the conversion of the martyr St Eustachius or Eustace, who saw a vision of Christ between a stag's antlers, as told in a 13th century manuscript, where he was informed that he would suffer for Christ; the stag is often depicted with a cross on its head, seen here at Tavistock, Devon **(centre)**. That said, St Hubertus (or Hubert) is a French saint who is the patron saint of hunters, mathematicians, opticians and metalworkers, and could also be invoked to cure rabies. His legend concerns an apparition of a stag with a crucifix between its antlers, effecting the aristocrat's conversion to a more saintly life. The obvious similarities between the stories of Eustachius and Hubertus have led some scholars to suggest that the attributes of one of them may simply have been transferred to the other, which is not unknown in Christian mythology, just as it had commonly occurred in ancient cultures.

St Faber, the Irish saint mentioned in 9th century manuscripts, had a deer for a pet, and the beast was entrusted with carrying her sacred books. The saint and her deer companion are shown here in a window at the Sacred Heart church at Boho, Ireland **(left)**.

Yet another legend concerns Le Puy-en-Velay, France, where a church replaced a megalithic dolmen. When its founder, Bishop Vosy, climbed the hill, he found that it was snow-covered even though it was July; in the snowfall he saw the tracks of a deer around the dolmen, which he took to be a sign as to where to lay the foundations of the church. This is echoed by the founding of the church at Llangar, in Wales, which was built where a white stag was seen (Whitlock, 1979).

In the 6th century, the Bishop St Gregory of Tours wrote his Chronicles about the Merovingian rulers, in which appears the Legend of the King Clovis I, who, in one of his campaigns, prayed to Christ that he might find a place to cross the River Vienne. A huge deer appeared which was considered a divine sign, showing where his army should ford the river.

In the 14th century, a deer appears once more, probably in keeping with Saint Eustace's legend. The manuscript known as the 'Chronicon Pictum' tells a tale of King/Saint Ladislaus I of Hungary and his brother, King Géza I, who were out hunting in a forest when a deer appeared to them adorned with candles on his antlers. King Ladislaus said to his brother that it wasn't a deer but an angel of God, and that his antlers were wings and the candles shining feathers; the place where the deer stood was where a cathedral was built.

Christians take the stag **(top)** and the hart to symbolise hidden strength and the soul's yearning to be united with God: *'As a deer longs for flowing streams, so longs my soul for thee, O God'* (Psalm 42:1). Because of the more positive virtues, deer have been common motifs on medieval floor tiles, in heraldry, and on the armorial emblems of many towns and cities. The most commonly perpetuated myth concerning deer is the annual fascination with Santa and his flying reindeer; although few people realize it, this connects us back to the goddess Artemis and her chariot, which was pulled by flying deer.

Monkey/Ape

In Egyptian religious symbolism, as well as having the head of an Ibis, the god Thoth can also be shown as a baboon, or as a dog-headed ape in his aspect of the god of equilibrium. There is a fine statue of Thoth as a baboon in the British Museum **(right)**. Hanuman, the Hindu monkey general of India, is said to have been an incarnation of the god Shiva, and at the temple of Shimla stands a 33m (108ft) tall statute of the monkey-headed god; in India, monkey lore goes back to at least 500BC.

One of the animals of the Chinese zodiac is the monkey, which gives rise to the *Year of the Monkey* every twelve years. In Buddhism, it is said that a monkey offered Buddha a bowl of honey. Delighted that it was accepted the monkey was overjoyed and fell dead from the tree, and yet was instantly reborn as the son of a Brahman. The well-known adage *'See no evil, hear no evil, speak no evil'* originated in the Far East, from the writing of Confucius, and occurs in texts dating to 2-4th century BC. A monkey with a spiraling tail is featured in the iconic Nasca Lines in Peru **(image p. 80)**.

To Christians, monkeys and apes signify self-indulgence, sloth, malice, cunning, greed and even lust. This originated

95

from observations that they are similar in appearance to us, with humanlike desires, yet they lack the human capacity for restraint. In the Middle Ages the Devil was sometimes depicted as an ape, such as in a scene of the Temptation of Christ at Santiago Cathedral. An ape depicted in chains symbolises the defeat of sin and evil, a fine example of which is shown here **(bottom image, previous page)**, from San Quirce, Burgos, in Spain. It is interesting that Thoth, who was depicted as a baboon, was the Egyptian god of moral law; in Christianity, apes represents opposite attributes.

Horse/Mythical Horses/Donkey

The horse often symbolises speed and grace, but also virility and lust, particularly the stallion. They are depicted on some of the oldest cave paintings from around Europe **(images p. 12 & 86)**. A white horse was the emblem of the ancient Saxons, and has been linked with the White Horse of Uffington **(image p. 13)**. In Viking mythology, Oisin and Lanval are transported to the Otherworld on white horses, and the god Odin rode his eight-footed steed, Sleipner, as he carried the souls of dead warriors to Valhalla **(left)**. To the Celts, horses were highly revered and prestigious animals, valued for their speed, bravery, loyalty and sexual vigor. Various heroes are featured riding horses, particularly in tales concerning hunting. The goddess Rhiannon is associated with a white horse, and the rhyme, *Ride a Cock Horse to Banbury Cross* may be a reference to the goddess. Several other Celtic and European Iron Age gods rode horses, and horse/rider motifs were common across the Roman world. Several white horses appear in Hindu mythology, and in Buddhism the prince who was to become the enlightened Buddha rode a white horse. Perhaps the most famous horse myth is that of the Trojan Horse, which enabled the Greeks to capture Troy.

In classical mythology, Pegasus **(left)** was the winged stallion of the Muses, which could magically manifest a spring to rise from the earth at the striking of his hooves; it was transformed into the constellation of that name by Zeus. Sometimes Bellerophon rides on the back of Pegasus, as he kills the Chimera. Horses are often the preferred mode of transport for the gods; Jupiter is shown riding a horse on top of the famous Jupiter Column from Mertz, now reconstructed in Stuttgart; this horse was born from the neck of Medusa after she was decapitated by Perseus. To Greeks and Romans, the horse generally stood for contemplation, poetic inspiration and eloquence.

In Greek mythology, Centaurs were beasts that had the torso and legs of a horse and a man's upper body. It can portray how Man is torn between evil and good. Heracles/Hercules slays the centaur named Nessos in one myth, and centaur images go back to at least the 8th century BC. We shall look at this creature in more detail soon, such is its importance.

The Unicorn is a well known fabled creature, a horse that is usually white and adorned with a single, spiralling horn on its forehead. It often signified longevity and fertility, and in Roman mythology the Unicorn was powerful, wild and beyond capture. It is represented in the night sky by the constellation Monoceras. Its association with Christianity is that the untamable beast could only be captured by a virgin, hence the unicorn became associated with chastity and purity, and thus Mary the Virgin **(bottom image, previous page)**. It also represents Jesus, who *'raised up a horn of salvation for us'* (Luke 1:69), a symbol of his power over sin. The Unicorn was very popular in heraldry and in Renaissance art, although Leonardo de Vinci clearly had a different opinion of the beast, perhaps with an agenda to push, for in his paintings the beast represents lust. The horn of the Unicorn was said to bestow healing and purity on anything it touched, and ancient prescriptions often used the horn, such as an antidote to poison; Jesus was thus the antidote to the sins of Man. The Unicorn can be seen today as a supporter of the Royal Arms of the United Kingdom, and past royals have similarly had the mythical beast as their emblem.

In Islamic culture, a white horse named Al-Buraq carried both Mohammed and Abraham. In Jewish tradition, coloured horses are mentioned in the Book of Zechariah, including four horses pulling a chariot, which is a theme found in ancient myths. In Christian symbolism and art, the horse can be an emblem of generosity and courage, but also of lust, such as in Jeremiah 5:8, during God's condemnation of the Israelites: *'They are well-fed, lusty stallions, each neighing for another man's wife'.* In Revelations, *The Four Horses of the Apocalypse* make their appearance; they are white (for pestilence), red (war), pale (death) and black (famine). These four horses are merely the re-branding of very similar ancient stories. St George is often depicted on a white horse, as he subdues the dragon, as is shown here in St John's, Glastonbury **(top)**. The saint miraculously appears to Crusaders at Antioch, astride his steed, inspiring them to victory. St James, patron saint of Spain, also rode a white horse.

Donkeys are depicted on Egyptian paintings, sometimes as a sigil of the solar god Ra, and some kings were buried with several of the beasts for use in the Afterlife. Donkeys or ass are mentioned several times in the Bible, often as a symbol of humility and hard work, and they frequently appear in churches in images of the Nativity, the Flight to Egypt, and Jesus' triumphant entrance into Jerusalem on Palm Sunday. It is interesting that the Hindu goddess Kalaratri rides a donkey in triumph **(centre image)**, and the Greek god Silenus likewise rides the beast. Jesus' choice of this non-kosher animal was a clear insult to the Jewish establishment, and also showed that he came in peace **(right)**, rather than if he had ridden on the warrior's choice of transport, the horse.

The *'prancing horse'* is the symbol of both Porche and

Ferrari cars. A white horse called Shadowfax was Gandalf's steed in Tolkien's *'Lord of the Rings'*, where he is described as *'King of the Horses'* of Middle Earth. This, and the various 'obby 'osses that are paraded at festivals today, are cultural relics of times when horses were revered and worshipped.

Bear

Bears appear on ancient prehistoric cave paintings, and clearly had both a hunting and spiritual association; several bear cults are known, and some Siberian tribes considered the bear to be the spirit of their ancestors. The Greeks and Romans believed in the ability of men to shape-shift, or be turned into, bears. One of Zeus/Jupiter's children, Callisto, was turned into a bear by Zeus' jealous wife, Juno. Years later, her son Arcas was out hunting and came upon a bear, but failed to recognise that it was, in fact, his sister. Just as he was about to strike, Zeus intervened **(left)**, transforming them both into the constellations of the Little Bear, Ursa Minor, and the Great Bear, Ursa Major. The Arcadians of Greece worshipped Callisto as *Bear Mother*.

The Ainu, who once inhabited many of the offshore islands of Japan were another bear cult, as were several Native American tribal nations. Folklore from around the world tells of people turning into bears, which may have derived from shamanic rituals concerning the animals. The legend of Jean de l'Ours, from the French Pyrennees, tells how he was born in a cave from the union of a woman and a bear.

The Welsh name for bear is *arth,* which perhaps led to the animal's association with King Arthur. The name of St Ursula means *'little she-bear'*, whilst the Swedish name Björn literally means *'bear'*.

In Christian myths, St Corbinian tamed a dangerous bear that had killed his horse; the saint then made the bear carry his baggage over the mountains **(centre)**. St Romedius, the 4th century Austrian saint, also subdued a bear, which then carried him from his hermitage to the city of Trento. Another bear encounter is connected with St Gall, an Irish saint who, when travelling through Switzerland, was charged by a bear whilst sitting at his campfire. He quelled the bear, which then collected firewood and became a lifelong companion of the saint. However, the bear motif is also used as a symbol of evil powers, and Christianity's (perceived) victory over Paganism.

In the churchyard at St Andrew at Dacre, near Penrith in Cumbria, stand four mysterious stone bears, known locally as *The Dacre Bears*. Each bear clings to a pillar **(left)**, and they may have celestial connotations, representing Ursa Major, the Great Bear, who guards the polar north (Biltcliffe and Hoare 2012). The symbol of a bear and a pole is a common icon of Middle East civilisations, representing a celestial gateway to the Otherworld, protected by the Great Bear. Perhaps there may also be some local connection to King Arthur, who was,

'... *sovereign protector of the sacred North'* (Op. cit. p. 329). *Goldilocks and the Three Bears* and *Winnie the Pooh* help perpetuate Man's connection with these magnificent animals. The bear is also the symbol of Russia and Finland, and a Giant Panda is the well-loved icon of the World Wildlife Fund.

Dog/Wolf

As the result of Man's taming of wolves and wild dogs, canines are probably the oldest domesticated animals. In fact Man may have learnt his hunting skills by watching wolf packs pursuing game back in the Ice Age. Much later, gods are sometimes portrayed as being accompanied by a dog, such as Orion, Silvanus, and Nodens/Cunomaglos (Knight 2013, p. 97). These myths were sometimes transferred to the heavens; in the sky, Orion the Hunter is accompanied by his two dogs, Canis Major (the Great Dog) and Canis Minor (the Little Dog). Sirius is the brightest star in the sky and is known as the Dog Star, and was of vital importance to the Egyptians, as its appearance would signal the arrival of the Nile floods. Anubis **(right)** was the Egyptian jackal-headed god of the dead, and the god of embalming, who led souls to their judgment.

The dog was one of the days of the Aztecs farmers' calendar, and the Maya buried dogs with their masters so they could guide them to the Afterlife across the *River of Death*. The ancient Chinese god Erh-lang drove away evil spirits aided by the *Celestial Dog,* and the dog is one of the years of the Chinese horoscope. In Homer's *Odyssey,* Argos is Odysseus' faithful dog, and Cerberus was the watchdog of the Greek Underworld, and of Charon, the ferryman. Coyotes are North American and African wild dogs that can appear as divination allies, and even as cultural heroes.

The Greeks and Romans associated wolves with the solar god Apollo. The Roman god Mars is sometimes shown in the company of wolves, and it was a she-wolf that nursed Romulus and Remus, the founders of Rome **(centre)**. Norse mythology also speaks of the wolf Skoll, who would pursue the setting Sun in an effort to eat it. The Norse god Odin is often accompanied by wolves, shown here next to the enthroned god **(right)**, and wolves were also considered harbingers of victory in battle (Knight 2013, p. 89).

Wolf bones have been found in Neolithic tombs, and grain farmers in Japan worshipped the wolf and would leave offerings at shrines dedicated to them. To the Mongols and the Ainu, wolves were the ancestors of their culture, and wolves appear in Babylonian myths. Wolves were often painted with a negative brush, such as with the Zoroastrians, who saw them as a creation of evil. Wolves can be portents of an imminent death, and in shamanic lore a wolf may take the role of guardian of, and even a guide through, the Underworld, such as in Native American culture; the Black Foot nation have a myth that describes the Milky Way as the *Wolf Trail.*

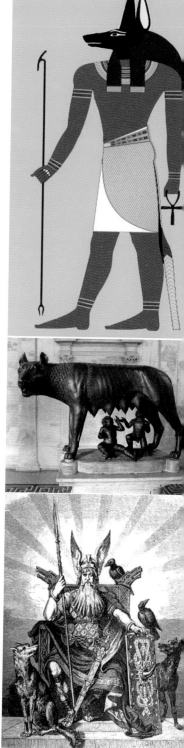

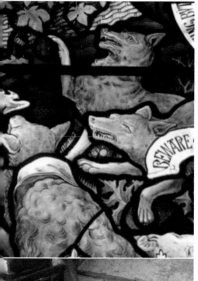

In the Bible, dogs and wolves often represent violence, cruelty or are seen as lowly creatures; Jezebel is killed and eaten by dogs (2 Kings 9: 33-37). Aesop features wolves in several of his fables, playing on the fears of sheep-herders, the most famous fable being *'The Boy Who Cried Wolf'*. Aesop uses wolves to criticise and moralise human behavior, and they feature in thirteen stories in the Bible, usually as symbols of destructiveness and greed.

Shown here is a window at the church at Box, Wiltshire, in which wolves cower in subservience **(left)** below Jesus. Some scholars believe that Jesus' comparison of wolves to treacherous people (such as, *'Beware wolves in sheep's clothing'*) legitimized the persecution of wolves.

In Dante's *'Inferno'*, a she-wolf representing greed and fraud. *'Little Red Riding Hood'*, written in 1697, furthered the bad press for wolves, symbolising the predatory male, as do horror movies concerning werewolves. It is ironic, therefore, that wolves became popular in heraldry, drawing on their reputation for courage, victory, and as a communal beast.

Dominican friars are sometimes symbolised by a black and white dog, which is a pun on their name, which means *'Dogs of the Lord'*, and the fact that they wear black and white attire. To Christians, dogs can also be a symbol of faithfulness, and they are commonly incorporated on tomb symbolism as a confirmation of fidelity. Here, a dog guards a lectern in Exeter Cathedral, Devon **(left)**.

Foxes are canids that have an ancient association with Man. In Mesopotamia, the fox was one of the sacred animals of the Goddess Ninhursag, acting as her messenger. In Chinese, Japanese and Korean folklore, foxes are powerful spirits known for their mischief and cunning, which take the form of human females in order to seduce men. The Dogons of Africa see foxes as tricksters, possessed with magical powers, whereas in Christian iconography regards foxes as symbols of gluttony or cunning. Foxes are mentioned in the Bible, such as in the *Song of Solomon* and in Aesop's fable *'The Fox and the Grapes'*.

Hare/Rabbit

Hares and rabbits have an ancient association with Man's myths, folklore and symbols; a record of a rabbit's foot carried for good fortune comes from 600BC. The Greeks would present rabbits and hares as gifts **(third image)**, to represent love and high libido; they also had many myths associating fertility and sexual desire with hares, which can be shown with Dionysus, Artemis, Eros, Aphrodite, as well as Venus. The well known *'Hare and the Tortoise'* story comes from the Greek storyteller Aesop (620-560 BC). The satyr Marsyas was able to enchant woodland creatures, including hares, with magic pan pipes **(left)**. The constellation Lepus (Latin for hare) was recorded by the Greeks, and lies just below Orion the Hunter in the sky. The Egyptian hieroglyph *Un,* depicts a hare, and means *'opening, becoming, to spring up',* representing creation and the cycles of Nature. One aspect of the god Osiris was Osiris Unnifer, who was sometimes shown with the ears of a hare, representing the Underworld; he is the young god, associated with dawn and sunrise, when hares emerge from underground. One of the megaliths at Avebury (stone 50) has been compared to a rabbit or hare, and one wonders if its selection was due to its simulacral features.

Rabbits and hares often appear in folklore as the trickster archetype. Native Americans speak of the Great Hare, Manibozho, who created the Sun and the Moon, and from whose house the sun rises each morning. Buddhists have a story in which the young Buddha went into a forest to meditate and was brought food by a hare. The hare is traditionally associated with Eostra, the spring goddess, and the Easter Bunny is a popular symbol at this time. The moon-gazing hare is a Pagan icon today, although the animal's association with the Moon is very ancient; some cultures, such as those in China, Tibet, India and Mexico, believed they could perceive a hare on the Moon's disc, rather than a human face. The Egyptians had a lunar hare goddess called Unnu-it, *'Mistress of Moon City'.* The Japanese moon goddess, Gwatten, often holds a crescent moon on which sits a hare (Cater 2010), and the Aztecs likewise had several rabbit gods.

In Judaism, rabbits and hares are *'unclean'* animals, and this may have led to derogatory statements about them. Some images of Mary the Mother with the infant Jesus also have white hares or rabbits in the scene **(top)**, which may be a relic of Moon goddesses, whom Mary replaced. Such images represent Mary's purity (many thought that rabbits and hares were hermaphrodite), compared to the association of hares and rabbits with sex. This is echoed by the Christian folklore of St Melangell, the patron saint of hares **(second)**, who was a virgin hermit who lived in North Wales in the 7th century. She saved a hare from a prince's hunting party, and her piety so impressed him that he built her a sanctuary; she founded a community for women, becoming their first Abbess.

The Christian concept of the Holy Trinity is often expressed as three hares running in a circle **(right, and image p. 24)**, their three ears forming a triangle. But this image has a long history, the earliest so far found being from China dated the 6th century AD. Other examples occur across Europe, Asia, and Africa, and transcend religious boundaries; ironically, they can be even found in synagogues, and the hare is considered a semi-divine creature to some Shi'ite Muslims. It has been suggested that the triple hares signify the feminine aspect of divinity and fertility (Cater 2010), connecting us back to the hares' association with the Moon, so long associated with goddesses; the triple hare motif has been adopted by modern Pagans, women in particular. Devon is a good place to study triple hares, as 17 churches house them on the *Three Hares Trail.* A leaflet has been produced to enable one to follow the trail of these icons, most of which are in churches around Dartmoor; rabbits and hares were the

favoured food of miners on the moor. In the 17th century, during the persecution of women, hares became associated with witches and evil magic; *'mad as a March hare'* is still used today. It was long thought to be a bad omen if a hare crossed your path, as witches were thought to take the form of the animal. However, even today it is still considered good luck to carry a rabbit's foot. More recently hares and rabbits seem to be faring rather better, their folklore being perpetuated in such stories as *'The Hare and the Tortoise'* and *'The Tale of Peter Rabbit';* Lewis Caroll's *'Alice's Adventures in Wonderland'* famously features the March Hare, and Kit Berry's *'Stonewylde'* series includes a girl who dances with hares. *'Watership Down'* dares to suggest that it is not just humans that have spiritual awareness, but that rabbits do too.

Whale

In Africa and in the Pacific Ocean, the whale is linked with rebirth, and numerous tales from Southeast Asia speak of spiritual heroes being saved by whales. The Maoris of New Zealand tell the story of Paikea, the *Whale-Rider*, who escaped drowning on the back of a whale, seen here atop of a Maori sacred building **(top)**. Whales also appear in Aborigine Creation myths of Australia. The Inuit of Alaska believe that the whale was formed from one of the fingers Sedna, the goddess of the sea. In China, a whale called Yu-Kiang is said to have human hands and feet, and rules the Oceans. In Icelandic myth, a magician shape-shifted into a whale in order to spy on the opponents of his king. The constellation of Cetus (the *Whale*) is a straddling group of faint stars below Pisces and Aries, named after a sea monster of Greek mythology.

The image of a whale shown here **(left)** is in the choir area of Exeter Cathedral. The whale is used by the Church as both a positive and negative icon. Its open mouth represents the Devil and the gates of Hell. Herman Melville's *Moby Dick* epitomized how the whale symbolised evil and death to sailors. Ironically, the Church also holds up the whale as an icon of rebirth and resurrection, demonstrated by the Biblical whale that swallowed Jonah (who had disobeyed God) only to be disgorged by it **(centre)** after three days and nights, a story that is also told in the Qur'an. This can be compared to Jesus' three days in the tomb. In St Matthew's gospel, Jesus himself draws a parallel between Jonah and his own impending resurrection. Some theologians also see the story of Jonah as an allegory of the deliverance of the Jews from Babylon.

Centaur/Sagittarius

In Sumerian, Greek and Roman mythology, centaurs are beasts with the head and torso of a human, and the lower body of a horse. Centaur images go back to at least the 8th century BC and in many stories they symbolise how Man is torn between evil and good. Heracles (Hercules) slays the centaur Nessos in one myth, and in other tales they represent chaos, adultery and the degradation of morals - a man trapped by his sexual urges; the Roman statue shown here **(right)** depicts a centaur with Eros on his back; like Eros, centaurs often wield a bow and arrow. One centaur, Chiron, represented more positive attributes, and the Greeks told of him being exceptionally wise and gentle, as he was taught by both Artemis and Apollo. He was wounded by Heracles and gave up his immortality rather than living in pain, making him a fine example of the *'wounded healer'.* Zeus later placed him amongst the stars, represented by the constellation Sagittarius (whose glyph is an arrow, signifying projection). This constellation marks the centre of our galaxy as viewed from Earth; is this mythical archer directing his arrow towards the galactic centre?

Pictish stones from Scotland show centaurs, notably on carved stones at Maiden Stone and Glamis.

In Church iconography, the centaur is generally taken to represent lust, one of the *Seven Deadly Sins.* The creature is often found representing Sagittarius in zodiacs, and the Sun is now in that constellation at the winter solstice. Some depictions, such as at Kencot in Oxfordshire, have been found associated with the centaur-slaying dragons, which may be symbolic of the slaying of the Earth dragon at this time of year (Biltcliffe and Hoare 2012, p. 140). Biltcliffe and Hoare have suggested that centaurs releasing arrows in churches on the Belinus Line may be firing them along the alignment itself (op. cit. p. 143).

Centaurs can be found in churches if one gets one's eye in, such as on floor of the Chapel of Mary Magdalene in Chichester Cathedral, on the floor zodiac at Canterbury Cathedral, and at Kencot, Salford and Burford, all in Oxfordshire (Biltcliffe and Hoare, 2012, p. 140-3). They can also be seen on tympanums at Stoke sub Hamdon **(second image)**, Somerset, and Ault Hucknall (Derbyshire). The fonts at both Hook Norton **(right)**, (Oxfordshire) and Luppitt (Devon) also display centaurs aiming their arrows.

Two fine European examples can be seen in the Cathedral of Compostela, and, representing Sagittarius, in the magnificent *Zodiac Window* at Chartres Cathedral **(bottom)**.

In esoteric circles, the landscape zodiacs at Kingston (Surrey) and Glastonbury (Somerset) both feature a centaur, thought to represent the constellation Sagittarius. Some researchers, such as Katherine Maltwood, equate the Chiron/Sagittarius image in the Glastonbury vicinity with King Arthur; the *Temple of Stars* can thus be perceived as the Knights of the Round Table, relating each Grail knight to an appropriate sign of the zodiac. The archer figure at Stoke sub Hamdon **(second image)** certainly appears to be sporting a medieval

knight's helmet, and is accompanied by the Tree of Life, inviting arcane links with the Knights Templar, as well as to the Arthurian mythos. This links with the esoteric concept that Sagittarius/Centaur represents the perfect being, a combination of human and animal, symbolising spiritual power, higher wisdom, the spiritual seeker, and divinely-led potential.

Rodents

To the Greeks, mice were associated with female sexuality and lechery, although to the Romans white mice were regarded as bringing good fortune; one of the aspects of Apollo was *'Prince of Mice'*. Ancient cultures sometimes compared timid humans to mice as an insult, which is perpetuates today with the adage, *'quiet as a church mouse'*. To the Celts, mice were associated with dark, destructive forces and cunning; in Africa, mice were used for divination because it was believed that they understood the mysteries of the Underworld, and Native Americans have several myths involving mice. In medieval Europe, mice became linked with witches; infestations were regarded as a punishment from God, and British folklore tells us that death would come if a mouse was seen leaving a house.

A rat named Krauncha was, paradoxically, the chosen steed of Ganesh, the elephant-headed god of Indian mythology; the god made himself smaller and lighter so the rat could carry him **(top)**. Rats were nocturnal raiders of Middle Eastern granaries, and therefore linked with the Underworld, and ultimately with the Christian concept of the Devil. Rats were symbols of fecundity and avarice in many cultures, and generally have a bad press, such as their association with pestilence and plague. However, they can also represent knowledge; in Asia, for instance, they are associated with gods of wisdom and success. In China, it was a rat that first presented rice to mankind, and anyone born in the *Year of the Rat* is considered to be adventurous and possess a zest for life. In Japan, a rat is a companion of Daikoku, the god of prosperity. In Christian art, rats signify avarice, one of the *Seven Deadly Sins*. Mice and rats may be seen carved in the choir area of churches, mostly on wooden seating **(second image)**, and many congregations add a token mouse to their Harvest Festival displays.

Small Creatures

It certainly isn't all down to size when it comes to the veneration of animals. The scarab, or dung beetle **(left)**, was highly revered by the Egyptians. The insect's activity of pushing balls of dung reminded them of the sun-god Khepri, who pushed the sun across the sky. Another beetle, the Ladybird, was named after the Virgin Mary, the spots representing her *Seven Sorrows*. Cancer, the crab, is one of the most ancient of zodiac signs. In Greek mythology, in Crete the god Zeus fed on bee's honey, which was known as the nectar of the gods.

Egyptians held the bee as solar symbols, born from the tears of the Sun god Ra, and there is a hieroglyph in the form of a bee. The Minoans associated bees with the goddess, and several images of *'bee goddesses'*, dating from around 1500BC, were unearthed at Knossos; the close association between this insect and the goddess is proven by the fact that priestesses dressed as bees; shown here **(bottom, previous page)** is a bee goddess on a gold plaque from Rhodes, dated 7th century BC. Apollo was given his gift of prophecy from three bees called the Thriae.

The sacred geometry of the bee's hexagonal honeycombs was noticed by the Ancients, and used by them as an example of perfection.

The beehive is the symbol of St Ambrose **(right)**, in whose mouth a swarm of bees settled without harming him, even leaving him a drop of honey of his tongue. Christians also use the beehive to symbolise hard work, prudence and purity. In Freemasonry, the bee and beehive represent industriousness as a virtue, as well as wisdom and obedience; beehives are sometimes depicted outside banks and other businesses.

Butterflies are one of the oldest archetypal icons of transformation; images of them have been found on Neolithic pottery from the 5th millennium BC. Psyche, of Greek mythology, is sometimes shown as a butterfly, and Australian Aborigines believe that they are the spirits of the dead who are returning. Butterflies signify resurrection and change, having the ability to cast off a previous existence, and they are sometimes shown with images of the infant Jesus.

Flies have been used a symbols of the Devil; another name for Satan is Beelzebub, which is a Hebrew word that translates as, *'Lord of the Flies';* flies were the third plague to beset the Egyptians as foretold by Moses. However, in the Egyptian New Kingdom, flies were noted for their bravery and persistence and were used as a symbol by warriors, and fly symbols have also been found on wands from this period.

One of the huge geoglyphs at Nazca, Peru is that of a spider **(right)**. Hopi Creation myths speak of *Grandmother Spider*, who created all living beings, for she was able to secrete the world from her body, as the spider produces its web. Australian Aborigines say that *Great Spider* is a solar hero, whilst many cultures, including the Celts, believed that spiders' webs represented the unseen forces that held life together, the pattern of the grand design, the *Web of Wyrd.* This is mirrored today by the *World Wide Web,* whereby everyone is connected. In Egyptian myths, the goddess Neith is the weaver of destiny, Some cultures believe that it was spiders that gifted Man the skills of weaving, whilst in some Native American myths, it was the spider who taught humans the alphabet. In Cretan myths, Ariadne leaves a trail of red thread by which the hero can escape from the labyrinth; the latter has been related to a spiders' thread. Arachne is the *Spider Woman* of European mythology, represented in Britain as Ana, who weaves the web of life; in Greek myth, Arachne and Athena compete in a weaving competition. In Islam, the prophet Mohammed was

being pursued by soldiers and hid in a cave. Allah commanded a spider to weave a web across the cave entrance, and the soldiers passed him by; this is mirrored by David in the Bible, who, when chased by King Saul, also hides in a cave, the entrance of which is similarly covered by a spider's web. A spider in a chalice is the symbol of St Conrad of Constance, the 10th century saint, **(bottom, previous page)**. He fearlessly drank from a chalice into which a poisonous spider had fallen, which was taken as a sign of his faith. Buddhists and Hindus see webs as symbolic of the illusions of the world, and this was taken on by Christianity, whereby spiders are signs of evil and the Devil, spinning webs to ensnare sinners.

The scorpion appears as an icon of the goddess Inanna on Sumerian seals dating back to c. 2800BC. They are often linked with the Underworld, and astrologically the constellation of Scorpio is ruled by Pluto, the Underworld god. This constellation seems to be represented by the scorpion on the Vulture Stone at Gőbekli Tepe, dated around 9,000BC (Collins 2014, p. 102-3). The Egyptian scorpion goddess Selket protected the dead Osiris, and in one myth Isis was accompanied by seven scorpions. One Egyptian king, Selk or Weha, was known as *The Scorpion King* and is often shown with the creature **(top)**.

In Greek mythology, Artemis and Gaia sent a scorpion to kill Orion. This Roman vessel **(second image)** was found at a site associated with the cult of Mithras, and depicts a scorpion. Scorpions symbolise evil and death in medieval Christian art, and because of their *'sting in the tail'* came to symbolise Judas, betrayer of Jesus. This is countered by the scorpion being a symbol for St John, as well as Dan, one of the Twelve Tribes of Israel. The image shown here is from a 15th century astrological manuscript and shows the scorpion as being far from fearsome **(left)**.

Bats are often a symbol of death and fear, and have been linked with witchcraft and the occult. In Africa and ancient Greece it was a symbol of someone who acts and understands concepts quickly and has keen vision. Bats occur as a divine creature of the Underworld in Central and South American mythology. An old English belief is that if you see a bat flying three times around a house it signifies the death of an inhabitant. In Christian and Jewish tradition, bats symbolise the Devil and idolatry, as well as madness. They can often be found on misericords **(left)**.

Even the humble worm has been used in symbolism; Chinese myth tells us how humans had their origins in worms that fed on a primordial being, which mirrors a legend from Iceland which tells us how worms feeding on Ymir, a frost giant, developed into humans. Irish myths speak of the Celtic hero Cuchulainn, who was born from a worm. Folklore around Britain and Europe often features an

Otherworldy, mythical *'worm'*, although the Anglo-Saxon term *'wyrm'* and the Norse *'Orm'* are poetic terms for large legless serpents or dragons. Worms are mentioned 95 times in the Bible, usually in a negative sense, as analogies of moral corruption and decay, often comparing people derogatively to a worm, or else reminding us how worms will devour our flesh when we die.

Fish

I have already looked at how fish, in the form of the vesica piscis came to represent Christianity and the Piscean Age (see Chapter 19), and yet how this was merely the continuation of many ancient mythologies involving fish. Images of a *Fish Goddess* have been found at European Neolithic sites, and shamans shape-shifting into fish appear in ancient rock art. The phallus of Osiris was swallowed by a fish, thus returning rejuvenating powers to the Nile. The initial incarnation of the Hindu god Vishnu, known as Matsyavatara, was as a fish **(top)**, who saved humanity from the Flood; fish are one of the eight auspicious symbols of India. Fish feature on many Greek works, as well as on Roman mosaics, and dolphins and fish were painted on wall frescos at Knossos, Crete. In China they represent fidelity in marriage, whilst in Japan they are a symbol of freedom, love, and well-being; in both these countries, Carp are good luck icons and imagery of them is placed on ship masts and houses. Fishes shown on the soles of Buddha's feet symbolise freedom from worldly constraints.

Pisces is the 12th sign of the zodiac and is described by the Greek Ptolemy, who regarded it as representing Aphrodite and Venus, who turned into two fishes to escape Typhon the sea monster; Triton was another Greek mythical being who was half-man, half-fish. The legends of mermaids **(second image)** and mermen may have had their origins with these types of ancient myth, perpetuated by later Celtic/Norse tales of gods, men and women who could shape-shift into fish. The Piscean symbol of two fishes, however, goes back much further, for an Egyptian coffin lid c. 2300BC shows the classic twin fish motif. Christian versions illustrated here are at Kilpeck, Herefordshire **(bottom)** and the Zodiac Window at Chartres **(top image, next page)**.

Fishes have also been symbols of fertility and virility, and, in the case of salmon, of wisdom and courage. In Irish myth, Tuan mac Cairill takes on the form of a salmon and impregnates a queen; Irish hero Finn cooked the Salmon of Knowledge and, after scalding his thumb, acquired the salmon's gift of wisdom and prophecy.

Hebrew tradition prepared the way for Christianity, as fish symbolised the faithful and were the food of the Sabbath. In the Old Testament, we read of how Dagon **(third image)**, god of the Philistines, was half-man and half-fish (the merman again), and the Babylonian god Oannes was also part-fish, part-human. The Hebrew holiday of Purim was also set by when the Moon was in the constellation of Pisces. The loaves and fishes miracle is one of the most well known of Jesus, who made analogies between fishing and conversion, such as, *'I will make you fishers of men'*. This, however, was predated by Buddha, and Orpheus of the Greeks, who were both known as *'Fishers of Men'*. The other story involving Jesus and fish is on the Sea of Galilee, when he tells his disciples to cast their nets on the other side of their boat, which results in their nets being laden with fish. This was symbolic of the number of souls that the disciples were to save, as fish were symbols of the soul. I find it

fascinating that at Roman processions in honour of the god Bacchus, whom scholars say has many similarities to Jesus, women would carry the symbol of the fish alongside the phallus; Bacchus was also proclaimed a *'Saviour'*.

The Resurrection of Jesus has parallels with the regeneration of the wounded Fisher King of later Grail legends, which itself probably derived from older Irish and Welsh myths. Legend also tells that Joseph of Arimathea entrusted the Grail to a Britain named Bron, who was called *'Rich Fisher,'* after he caught the fish that was eaten at the Grail table. The fish is also a symbol of eternal life in the Qur'an of Islam.

The Christian baptismal font is known as a piscina, meaning *'fish pond',* and Christian converts have been known as *'little fishes'*. As we saw earlier with hares, three entwined fishes can represent the Holy Trinity, and are illustrated here in John the Baptist Church, Frome **(left)**. Fish are sometimes used as symbols of the disciples St Peter and St Simon, as they were fishermen, and are also shown with the Franciscan monk St Anthony of Padua, who was such an outstanding preacher that fish would poke their heads out of the water when he preached near the River Brenta.

The *'great fish'* that swallowed Jonah in the Bible is now generally regarded to have been a whale (see p. 102), and although not technically fish, dolphins and porpoises are often shown in ancient works of art, symbolising wisdom and prophecy, possessing the attributes of divine messengers. Sometimes dolphins carry gods on their backs, and are symbols or companions of Aphrodite, Venus, Poseidon and Neptune.

Shells

Gastropod, ammonite and nautilus shells demonstrate an element of sacred geometry known as the Fibonacci Series **(image p. 7)**, the self-replicating growth in Nature. The use of perforated shells for beads (especially as necklaces) is both widespread and ancient, and includes finds at Palaeolithic and Neanderthal sites. Oyster and scallop shells were used as lamps at Kent's Cave, Devon, and prehistoric peoples also used scallop shells as receptacles when painting with ochre, the natural dye. Seashell beads have been unearthed at various Neolithic chambered sites, such as at West Kennet Long Barrow (**bottom**, and Knight 2011, p. 103-4). A burial site in Brittany, dated

108

5000-7000BC, contained the skeletons of two women, both adorned with necklaces made of shells.

The enclosed, hidden nature of shells has led them to be associated with birth, creation and the womb, and in art as symbols of the vulva/yoni. Pagan cultures originally held the shell to be a symbol of fertility. In Greek and Roman myths, Venus/Aphrodite stands on huge sea shell, as in Botticelli's famous painting *The Birth of Venus* **(right)**; although Venus shields her genitals from view with her hand and hair, her womb is nevertheless symbolically depicted as the *open* shell carrying her triumphantly to the shore. Botticelli's Venus is also so similar to later Christian depictions of Mary Magdalene. I will mention, in passing, that the emblem of the family of Diana, Princess of Wales includes a scallop shell, and one is also included on the personal coat of arms of Prince Harry; both seem fitting motifs for those championing compassion, and Diana, *'Queen of Hearts'*.

The god Triton's special attribute was a twisted conch shell, which he blew like a trumpet to raise or calm the seas. Nerites was a sea god who was transformed into a shellfish by the gods. Nigerian mythology speaks of Yemaya, the *Goddess of the Ocean*, whose first gift to mankind was a seashell. Conch shells were used as ceremonial horns by the Aztecs and the Maya, and shells symbolise the origin of the world to Hindus.

Native American Creation myths speak of *White Shell Woman.* The scallop shell is the emblem of the 1st century saint, James the Greater of Compostela, patron saint of Spain and pilgrims, shown here **(centre)** at Cherhill, Wiltshire (Knight and Wallace 2014). He was one of the first missionaries, and the first apostle to suffer martyrdom. The Church of Santiago de Compostela claims to house his relics, and is the third most visited Christian pilgrimage destination after Rome and Jerusalem. Pilgrims still wear a scallop shell on their hat or clothes to signify they are walking the pilgrimage route, which is marked by the shell **(right)**. The origin of this association is said to come from when the St James' remains were being

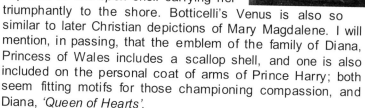

transported from Jerusalem to Spain, when the horse of one of the knights fell into the water and emerged covered in shells. Another version says that the association started when the sides and bottom of the boat transporting his body became covered with scallop shells. When the scallop is used to represent St James it is the outer surface that is depicted, whilst when it refers to Venus it is the interior, concave form.

The scallop shell is also a symbol of the Virgin Mary. This is due to the story that the Virgin appeared to St James on the banks of the Ebro in Spain, after which he returned to Judea. Some shrines show Mary surrounded or covered by a shell-like structure. These occur mainly in North and Central America, and are sometimes known as bathtub

·it igitur exemplum nob quia auctor et c

shrines, due to their shape; sometimes grottos are constructed around old baths, which protrude vertically out of the ground. The Virgin Mary has also been compared to an oyster shell, the pure white pearl of which symbolises Jesus. Raphael the Archangel is the guardian angel of pilgrims and may sometimes be shown with a shell. The stoup containing holy water near the entrance of a church is sometimes scallop-shaped.

Other Birds

We have already looked at Eagles, due to their importance in Christian symbolism (p. 90). Let us now look at other birds. Prehistoric paintings and relics of birds and bird-headed beings show the long association between birds and Mankind's spiritual nature, and birds generally represent goodness and joy, freedom and shamanic flight. A bird mounted on a shaman's staff is one of the paintings inside the Lascaux Caves in France, dated 15,000-12,000BC. Many cultures use feathers when attempting to converse with the ancestors and other spirits, as they seek higher realms of knowledge. The expression, *'A little bird told me'* may be an ancient relic of such spiritual connections. The Romans used bird flight for divination purposes, and Native Americans consider feathers to be powerful ceremonial tools. The Egyptians often depicted the goddesses Isis and Maat with bird wings **(top and p. 36)**.

Dove

Doves have an ancient mythological history, such as in the Middle East, where they symbolised the Goddess; Iron Age shrines dedicated to Astarte and Asherah had dove imagery on them, and some Roman votive offerings found at a shrine in Gaul, brought as gifts for Apollo, depict pilgrims holding doves. The dove was a companion of Semitic and Greek/Roman love goddesses, and images of Persephone show her with doves. The dove is an attribute of Daibosatsu, the Buddhist bodhisattva, who symbolises peace and is a protector of communities.

Because of all this ancient iconography, the dove plays a central part of Christian symbolism; I have already spoken how it represents the Holy Spirit/God **(second image, and p. 34 & 35)**, and how the bird appears above Jesus at key moments in his story. It was a dove that returned to Noah with an Olive branch, and is sometimes shown flying out of the mouths of saints, representing their purified soul or chastity. It is a dove that is often depicted above the head of Mary the Virgin at the Annunciation, representing the Holy Spirit.

The dove is a symbol of the people of Israel (from the *Song of Songs)* and the white dove is almost universally used today as an icon of peace, love and pacifism.

110

Phoenix

The Phoenix is a mythical bird, long used as an archetypal icon for symbolic death and rebirth (often of the Sun). The bird achieves transformation and immortality as it burns, only to be reborn out of the ashes **(right)**. This has its origins in ancient Egypt, where it was called the Bennu Bird. It is said to return every 1400 years (some sources say every 500), and is willingly set alight on a pyre that is ignited by the sun's rays; it is cremated, only to rise again as a young bird. Although originally a myth marking the cyclical nature of the Sun and the seasons, it became an emblem of *Ka,* the concept of a person's immortal soul. In Jewish tradition, the phoenix dies every 1000 years, turning into an egg from which it is reborn. The bird also features in Persian, Chinese, Greek and Japanese myths, usually connected with positive attributes and as a solar symbol. It was featured on Roman coinage as a symbol of the never-ending Empire, and it is easy to see why this ancient solar icon of perpetual renewal would be taken on by Christianity; it is often seen in churches and other Christian art as a symbol of hope, of the triumph over death, and of the Resurrection **(third image, previous page)**. A fine example, in stone, graces the exterior of St Paul's Cathedral, London **(bottom, previous page)**. The bird can also represent charity, and is a popular symbol in heraldry. In alchemy, it is an important symbol of transformative and purifying fire, and of the element sulphur. In occult circles, it is a sign of symbolic death and reincarnation **(top)**.

Pelican

Pelicans were an element of Egyptian mythology, as shown in this relief from the temple of Abu Gorab **(centre)**. The goddess Henet was shown in pelican form, associated with death and the Afterlife, for it was thought that the bird had the ability to aid safe passage to the Underworld. Pelicans also feature in myths from Peru and India, and in the folklore of the Aborigines of Australia.

In Medieval bestiaries, the pelican was said to peck at its own breast to feed its young with its blood; with such a large beak this would seem a difficult thing to achieve, and as such reinforces it as an act of self-sacrifice and parental love. Images of a pelican feeding her young with her blood are known as *'Pelican in her Piety'* **(bottom)**. In one variation of the tale, the father kills the offspring, and the mother returns three days later to bring them back to life with her blood. This is seen as an analogy with Jesus' sacrificial blood and the Resurrection. An Old Testament prophecy (Psalm 102) speaks of Jesus, *'... like a pelican of the wilderness'.* The pelican was an emblem of Elizabeth I, signifying the sacrifices she made for England. Shakespeare (Hamlet Act IV) wrote, *'To his good friends thus I wide open my arms, and like the kind life-rendering pelican, refresh them with my blood'.* The pelican is the emblem of Corpus Christi Colleges at both Cambridge and Oxford and is the symbol of the Dutch and Irish blood transfusion services. It is a frequent heraldic emblem, based on its reputation for altruism and service. The bird's meaning in

alchemical circles is that the growth of Man's spiritual nature must be through acts of service and compassion.

Wading Birds

Large waders, including storks, herons, ibis and cranes, have all been associated with folklore and myths. To the Egyptians, the ibis was a sacred icon of wisdom. The god Djehuty, usually known as Thoth, is sometimes depicted with the head of either a baboon **(image p. 95)** or that of an ibis. He was the god of occult knowledge, of writing

and mathematics, and is often shown in Egyptian art as an ibis-headed man; this example **(left)** is from the tomb of Ramses II at Khaemwaset, from the 12th century BC **(see also image p. 54)**. He was worshipped at Hermopolis as the divine ibis that created the earth by hatching the world egg, and after the young Moses had built Hermopolis, he taught people the sacred values of the bird; in the Bible we are told how he used ibis to eat potentially dangerous snakes that lay in the path of his army on the way to defeat the Nubians. The ibis was sometimes mummified in royal tombs to aid the deceased in the Otherworld. In Turkey, local tradition says that ibis were amongst the first birds released by Noah after the Flood, and because of this people have helped ibis colonies in Turkey to survive, long after the demise of others across Europe.

The stork is the Egyptian hieroglyph for 'soul'. The Greek word for stork means to have strong affection, and the bird was sacred to the goddess Hera, protector of childbirth; in many cultures the bird heralds good news. Its Hebrew name, *hasidah,* means pious, and the bird's attributes of devotion and service come from ancient beliefs that they feed their parents when they are too weak or old to fend for themselves. In Rome there was a law called *Lex Ciconaria, 'Stork's Law',* which ensured that the elderly were cared for by their children.

The European tradition that storks deliver babies may have derived from a belief that the souls of the unborn resided in marshes and ponds prior to birth, and that storks retrieved the infants as they dipped into the waters. Birthmarks on the back of the head of newborns are known as *'stork bites',* and a stork bearing a baby is a popular image today.

To Christians, the stork is a symbol of prudence, purity and chastity, and due to its habit of migrating early in the year, is a symbol of the Annunciation. The bird's association with an impending birth seems to be confirmed by this passage in the Bible (Jeremiah 8:7), *'Yea, the stork in the heavens knoweth her appointed times'.*

Cranes are symbols of loyalty and watchfulness; legend says they gather nightly in a circle surrounding their king, one leg raised and the other holding a stone which, should they fall asleep and drop, would wake them up. Cranes appear in Celtic art, and to the Chinese they are a symbol of longevity and immortality. One of Aesop's tales is *'The Fox and the Crane'* and the bird is mentioned twice in the Old Testament; Christian iconography links it to the Resurrection, and the image shown here **(centre)** is from a bestiary c. 1240.

The heron is another wading bird, which has sometimes symbolises the morning Sun, featuring in the mythology of many cultures around the world; some believe that the Bennu Bird (p. 110) may have been a heron. In Christianity, the bird is mentioned in the Old Testament. A wading bird **(bottom, previous page)** was recently found on a mosaic at a Byzantine church site at Aluma, Tel Aviv, Israel. It is around 1500 years old, and marks the time of transition between Pagan belief systems and Christian Rome.

Corvus

The Corvus family of black birds includes jackdaws, ravens, crows and rooks, which have ancient spiritual associations with Mankind. Their black colouration has led to them generally having a bad press, associated with the *'dark side'*; but, as usual, deeper mysteries are hidden beneath the veneer, for they were formally birds associated with the gods, high magic, and the Underworld. Gods such as Cronus, Apollo, Bran, Lugh and Odin, as well as King Arthur and Merlin, have all been associated with the raven or crow, and there is even a constellation called Corvus, just below Virgo.

Raven

In ancient Greece, the raven was the messenger of Apollo and Athena, and also had associations with the cult of Mithras. The Amerindians have hero ravens in their myths, such as depicted on this ceremonial hat **(top)** and some think ravens brought fire to mankind. The Inuit believe that killing a raven will lead to bad weather, as *Raven Father* is their creator god. The Vikings also regarded the bird to be a powerful icon, often embellishing their sails with raven imagery. The Norse god Odin, known as the *Raven God,* had two companion ravens named Munin and Hugin, who served as his eyes and ears **(right)**. A raven banner is carried by a Norman knight on the Bayeux Tapestry, and the bird has also been associated with King Arthur (Broadhurst 1992).

The famous ravens at the Tower of London are said to be the *'Birds of Bran'*, associated with the prophetic head of *Bran the Blessed* (Bran means *'raven' or 'crow'*); a *Raven Master* looks after these iconic birds **(right)**, to ensure they never leave, as legend says Britain will fall if they ever do. The name of the god Lugh derives from the Celtic for *'raven'*, and the bird is associated with the visions and soothsaying of Celtic deities, such as Morrigan and the battle-raven Badb Catha; some Celtic coins bearing ravens riding on the backs of horses may signify the latter deity. Near the Celtic/Gaulish mithraeum at Sarrabourg, France, was found an altar bearing a raven, and the bird is also depicted alongside a healing god at Mavilly, also in France (Green 1992, p. 26 & 65).

In the Islamic version of Cain and Abel, told in the Qur'an, a raven is the creature that showed Cain how to bury his murdered brother. In Hindu mythology, the god Shani may be depicted mounted on a giant raven or crow.

In Judeo-Christian tradition, the raven can be seen as the dark counterpoint to the white dove of love, and as such has often

been depicted as birds of ill-omen and death in literature and art. The Bible sometimes mentions ravens disparagingly, such as, *'The eye that mocks a father and scorns mother, the ravens of the valley will pick it out'* (Proverbs 30:17). In the tale of the Flood (Genesis 8), it was a raven that Noah first sent out from the ark in an effort to find land, but the bird did not return **(bottom image, previous page)**. The dove, however, did return, and this is a thinly disguised attempt to give the raven (a symbol of Paganism) a bad reputation compared to the dove (a symbol of the Holy Spirit). A better story concerning ravens as good characters are those sent by God to deliver bread and meat for Elijah, the Old Testament prophet, who (1 Kings 17) was hiding from a king in a remote ravine **(left)**. There are other stories of saints being fed by ravens during their time as a hermit, such as St Paul, as shown in this Renaissance painting **(centre)**, although this probably derived from the tale of Elijah. St Vincent of Saragossa, patron saint of Lisbon, is associated with the bird, for after his death, a raven protected his body from being eaten by wild animals, as shown in this 15th century painting **(bottom)**; anyone who later tried to destroy his holy relics would again be driven away by a raven. The bird now features on the coat of arms of Lisbon, recalling this legend. A raven is also said to have protected St Benedict of Nursia, as the bird snatched away a deliberately-poisoned loaf the saint was about to eat. In both instances, the raven was sent by God, echoing ancient myths of the bird's connection with deity.

Jesus used ravens in one of his parables: *'Consider the ravens; they do not sow or reap... yet God feeds them. How much more valuable you are than birds!'* (Luke 12:24).

Crow

Roman statues of Saturn and Cronus show them armed with a dagger or knife in the shape of a crow's beak (Biltcliffe 2009, p. 132), and the birds were sacred to the goddess Athena/Minerva. Crows were consulted by augurs and seers in Rome and Greece, and became associated with longevity. In Native American and Aborigine myths, the crow is seen in a more favourable light, as too in Japan and China; a three-legged crow on a Sun disk was the Chinese imperial symbol, representing the rising, zenith and setting of the Sun. The bird was associated with the goddess Morrigan, goddess of death and war, as was the raven, and in Australian Aborigine mythology the crow is a trickster.

Crows are often mentioned in Buddhism, and three-legged crows are featured in both Korean and Japanese mythology. To Hindus, the birds are considered to be the ancestors and carriers of information, giving people omens of future events.

The crow has since acquired many negative attributes in Europe, becoming an emblem of war, evil, death and ill-fortune. It is believed by scholars that some of the Biblical passages referring to *'ravens'* may have been about crows, as in many cultures little distinction is made between the two species.

114

Jackdaw

Jackdaws feature in several ancient myths. The Roman poet Ovid saw them as harbingers of rain, whilst Princess Arne, who was bribed with gold by King Minos, was turned into a jackdaw as punishment for her avarice. A Greek and Roman adage says that, *'Swans will sing when jackdaws are silent'*, meaning that the wise will speak after the foolish quiet down.

Swan

Cygnus, the Swan **(right)**, is a prominent constellation, also known as the Northern Cross, which has featured in legends for thousands of years. Many researchers have found Creation and other myths associated with this group of stars; the Great Rift which it houses was taken as an entrance to the Otherworld, a place of the ancestors. The star formation is aligned with many sacred sites (Collins 2006, Mann 2011, Biltcliffe and Hoare 2012), and in two of my previous works I have shown alignments of Cygnus with West Kennet Long Barrow (Knight 2011) and the Cerne Giant (Knight 2013). Christianity turned the constellation into an icon of the Crucifixion; a 17th century astronomical map made by William Schickhard shows Cygnus overlain with the crucified Christ; this may have had its origins in the Classic legend of Orpheus, who was also associated with Cygnus, and was crucified. The stars were now the Christian *'Christi Crux'*, a tradition that goes back to at least 592AD. In some depictions, St Helena, mother of Constantine the Great, is shown with this re-mythologised *Northern Cross* **(second image)**.

In the *'Hymn to Apollo'*, Callimachus tells of how Apollo rode on the back of a swan **(right)** to the land of the Hyperboreans during the winter; this alludes to the Sun being low in the daytime sky, and with Cygnus being low in the night sky at this time of year. Mark Bolan's song, *'Ride a White Swan'* hints at such mystical associations; Apollo is shown riding his swan on this classical vase, dated 3rd century BC.

Palaeolithic swan pendants made from mammoth ivory have been discovered in Siberia, dated around 13,000BC; linking this with the Orphic myths of the Underworld, the swan symbolises the Siberian shaman's journey into the realms of the ancestors. Swan images were made during the Neolithic, Bronze and Iron Age, showing its iconic spiritual status. As well as symbols or attributes of Apollo, as mentioned above, they are also associated with both Aphrodite and Venus, and are thus linked to romantic love; in Greek and Roman art the two goddesses can be seen riding on the backs of swans. The Greek god Zeus disguised himself as a swan in order to seduce Leda, wife of the King of Sparta **(right)**, depicted here by a student of

115

da Vinci. This has lead to an the association between the swan and the ebb and flow of love; perhaps the image of the heart formed when swans face each other has helped perpetuate this connection with love. Some researchers believe that the bird sitting atop the rod of Mercury and the staff of Hermes is a swan, linking it to a cosmic axis that receives consciousness from the stars (Biltcliffe and Hoare, 2012).

In Celtic myth, a pair of swans drew the Sun across the sky, and at Samhain the *Swan Maidens* and *Swan Princes*, who had been living for a time as humans, reverted back to bird-like beings. In the Irish legend of the *Children of Lir,* a stepmother transforms her children into Swans for 900 years. This is echoed in the ballet of *Swan Lake,* fashioned from Russian folklore, wherein a princess is turned into a Swan by a sorcerer's curse. The Valkyries, or *'swan maidens',* of Scandinavian sagas were also shape-shifters associated with swans (see Trubshaw 2011 for an excellent discussion on swan mythology). Also in Norse mythology, two swans drink from the sacred Well of Urd, in the realm of the gods; this is because it was said that the waters of the well were so pure that anything that touched it turned white.

The swan usually represents perfection, grace, feminine beauty, innocence and purity, and legend has it that the mute swan only sings just before it dies, as it partakes in its *'swan song';* Chaucer suggested that the singing of a swan foretold a death. Due to the virtuous attributes of the bird, it naturally became associated with the Virgin Mary, which is complemented by her other symbol, the white lily. As swans mate for life, they have also been icons for fidelity in Western folklore. St Hugh of Lincoln, the 12th century holy man, is often shown with a swan **(left)**, and is the birds' patron saint. This comes from the story that the saint had a deep and lasting friendship with a swan, which would follow him around and even guard him as he slept. Swans have a long association with sovereignty across Europe, and today the Queen claims ownership of all unmarked mute swans. Swans are also highly revered in the Hindu religion, and several swan deities are featured in Indian folklore.

Owls

The Owl is traditionally associated with wisdom and knowledge, as was the companion and familiar of Athene, the Greek goddess of wisdom and the arts, and her Roman equivalent Minerva. The bird is the symbol of Athens, the city named after the goddess, and the owl shown here **(centre)** is Greek and dates to 630BC. Silver coins bearing owls were issued in Athens to celebrate Greek victories over the Persians in 479BC. The *Burney Relief* from Babylonia, dated 1800-1750BC, shows Inanna-Ishtar in her guise as Lilith **(left)**, and the goddess is flanked by two owls **(full image, p. 37)**; this close up of that image shows Lilith's clawed, owl-like feet and two attendant owls. The

116

Sumerian word for owl was *ninna*, and Nin-ninna was a goddess whose name meant *'Divine Lady Owl'*. Like Lilith, the Hindu goddess Lakshmi is often shown with owls.

Owls are depicted on a host of Neolithic pots and vases, and models of an owl goddess were laid inside Mycenae tombs, Greece, in the 15th century BC, and may have represented the worlds beyond death. The owl was the bird of death in ancient Egypt, Japan, China and India, and yet in other cultures its excellent night-vision linked it to prophecy. Native Americans wear owl feathers as magical talismans and nocturnal protectors and believe owls represent the ancestors. There is, however, a great variation amongst Amerindian nations as to whether owls are positive or negative; some tribes saw it as a harbinger of death. The Maya and Aztecs also considered the owl a symbol of death. A legacy of owl reverence is evident in the fact that three of Canada's provinces have owls as their emblem.

The *Owl of Cwm Cowlwyd* is one of the *Three Elders of the World* in the Welsh Triads. In another British tale, the goddess Blodeuwedd was turned into an owl by her husband Gwydion after betraying him.

Hebrew mythology speaks of the day of Yahweh's vengeance, when, *'... the screech owl also shall rest'*, which refers to Lilith; Hebrews believed that the evil Lilith could fly out of the night at any time and snatch their young children. This encouraged Christians to adopt the owl as a symbol for the night and, with its haunting call and its ability to see in the darkness, to represent evil and the supernatural; on some scenes of the Crucifixion, owls are symbolic of the darkness to which Jesus gives light. Owls are often depicted in churches **(top)**, and in Exeter Cathedral, Devon, there are over 50 of the birds carved in the Chapel of Bishop Oldham.

There is, however, a positive spin on the owl in terms of its association with wisdom; the owl is connected with St Jerome, who was regarded as a wise scholar, as shown in the detail of this 15th century painting **(second image)** by Cosimo Tura (the owl is perched, top right).

Peacock

The wonderfully extravagant and beautiful plumage of peacocks **(right)** has led to them being associated with many mythical characters and legends, and an almost universal association with good fortune, serenity and protection. Its plumage has been compared to the radiance of the Sun and was a frequent emblem of royalty, high-status and prosperity. In Greek and Roman mythology, the peacock is sacred to Hera, the wife of Zeus, and to Juno, the Roman *'Queen of the Gods'*.

117

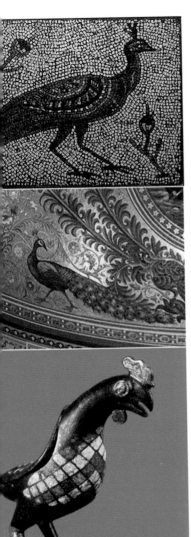

There is a constellation named after the bird, called Pavo (Latin for *Peacock*), visible from the Southern Hemisphere. Saraswati, the Hindu goddess of wisdom and the arts, is accompanied by a peacock, and the multi-headed god Murugan would ride on the back of a peacock, accompanied by his wives **(bottom, previous page)**. The Vedic god of war, Subramanja, likewise has a peacock as his preferred mount.

In some countries, however, the feathered 'eyes' are a symbol of the *Evil Eye,* and the birds are believed to be ill-omens. The Greeks believed that these 'eyes' were those of the slain multi-eyed giant Argos. The Persian royal throne was known as the *'Peacock Throne'* and peacocks also have associations with the thrones of both the Buddhist character Amitabha, and the Hindu god Indra. The bird may also be shown as an escort of Krishna.

Early Christians hiding in the catacombs of Rome painted peacocks, as it was believed that the bird's body did not rot after death, and so became an emblem of eternal life and the Resurrection; a 3-4th century Roman or Byzantine mosaic depicting a peacock is shown here **(top)**. Peacocks are sometimes portrayed drinking from a chalice, the motif of eternal life. The bird is closely associated with the Virgin Mary, who took over the mantle of Juno and Hera as *'Queen of Heaven'*. The 'eyes' of the tail are also symbolic of the 'all-seeing' God and his Church. But the bird has also been a symbol of vanity, pride and arrogance, because of its strutting as it shows off its plumage. A fine example of the peacock in Christian art is shown here **(second image)**, in the Basilica of Notre-Dame de la Grade, Marseille, France.

Cockerel/Rooster

Cockerels are often associated with the dawn and with the Sun, and was a bird dedicated to Apollo. In Romano-Celtic traditions, the cockerel represented Mercury (another solar deity) as shown on a relief from Gloucester (Green 1992, p. 58), and the example here **(left)** is a Roman artifact found at nearby Corinium (Cirencester); Mercury was a popular god in the Cotswold area.

The Roman fertility god Priapus is sometimes represented by a cockerel and it was thus used as an erotic symbol, although the bird was also a symbol for Aesculapius, the Roman god of healing and medicine. In China and Japan, the birds are sacred with many positive attributes and are allowed to roam free around Shinto temples. The cockerel is one of the Chinese zodiac years, and many scenes of the Buddha also show the bird. The Hindu war god Karthikeya is sometimes depicted with a cockerel, due to its fighting attributes. The Cockatrice (or Basilisk) was one of the deadliest of Christian medieval beasts, with the head, wattles and feet of a cock **(left)**, but with the tail of a serpent

118

or dragon. It was symbolic of the Devil, but was also used in heraldry to repel one's enemies.

Because of its combative spirit, the cockerel was a symbol for the warriors of the Goths and the Gauls, and the bird is depicted on Celtic coinage. Later, it was adopted as the emblem of France, as it was said to hover (along with the eagle of victory) over the souls of fallen French soldiers. Throughout the ages, the cockerel has been offered up as a sacrifice to the gods, such as in honour of Brighid at Imbolc festivals, and the Greeks also spilt the bird's blood on the foundation stones of new buildings. Some cultures have even used cock fighting as a form of divination.

In Islam, the bird was seen by Mohammed in the First Heaven, as it crowed, *'There is no God but Allah'.* The cockerel is mentioned in various Hebrew texts, generally comparing people to the *'gallantry of cocks'.* Some ancient Hebrew images (dated 7th century BC) show the cockerel within the Star of David hexagram, and the Hebrew word *geber* means both *'man'* and *'cock'.* There are, however, some negative attributes associated with the bird, such as in many African cultures, which associate the cockerel with occult knowledge and witchcraft. The bird can also symbolise arrogance and conceit, hence the phrase *'cocky'.* It is a cockerel that is most often seen perched on weather vanes, symbolising watchfulness against 'evil', which may be blown in by the wind from any of the four directions.

As well his *'Keys to Heaven'*, the cockerel is one of the other symbols of St Peter **(right)**, due to his three denials before the cock crowed, as foretold by Jesus (John 13:38). Many early Christian sarcophagi have been found with the cockerel or cockfight emblems on them, symbolic of St Peter and his desired victory over death. Some cockerels were even depicted with haloes around their heads, as in this example **(top)** held in the Vatican, dated c. 600AD; the bird has also been found inscribed on vessels from the catacombs of Rome. St Augustine later described cockerels as being endowed with much reason, and Pope Gregory I regarded the bird to be a, *'most suitable emblem of Christianity'.*

I apologise that I have not been able to include all animals and birds that have mythological associations, but my brief was to include the creatures that most commonly made the crossover into Christian iconography. So keep an eye open for animal carvings and images in windows when you walk around churches and cathedrals. The choir area is often a good place to look, as animals may be carved in wood, especially on the misericords or seats.

Because of the wealth of symbolism and meanings, and the universal nature of reverence of both serpents and dragons, we shall now look at these creatures in more depth in the succeeding two chapters.

24. The Power of the Serpent

The image of the serpent or snake is well represented in prehistory, and was also universally widespread throughout historical times; arguably no other animal is so deeply rooted in the mythology of Man, and it is still a powerful and revered icon today. The meanings attached to serpents are diverse and multi-layered, and can represent high esoteric wisdom, even enlightenment, as well as healing, primeval life-force, sexual potency, and the destructive and creative forces of the Universe.

Serpents have frequently been associated with the Goddess and Mother Earth, probably due to them residing underground, within the earth, especially in caves, so often associated with the Underworld of the Earth Goddess. They have become associated

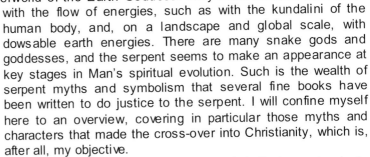

with the flow of energies, such as with the kundalini of the human body, and, on a landscape and global scale, with dowsable earth energies. There are many snake gods and goddesses, and the serpent seems to make an appearance at key stages in Man's spiritual evolution. Such is the wealth of serpent myths and symbolism that several fine books have been written to do justice to the serpent. I will confine myself here to an overview, covering in particular those myths and characters that made the cross-over into Christianity, which is, after all, my objective.

Thousands of years ago, shamans took hallucinogenic plants to achieve trance states, and it is possible that the origins of serpent cults could have been from the ingestion of snake venom concoctions, taken in order to induce similar altered states. Today, some of the indigenous tribes of the Americas allow a snake to bite them, and if they survive the ordeal it is considered that it is because they have gained sufficient insight and wisdom.

The multi-headed Hindu god Murugan would ride on the back of a peacock, which is sometimes shown stepping on a snake **(image p. 117)**. Vishnu, the Hindu creator god, is often seated on the coils of a huge snake as he floats on the comic waters. In Indian mythology, the Nāga are divine water-serpents **(top)**, and in Hindu alchemy *nagayuna* seeks to help the body's energies to conserve the *elixir of life* during one's journey towards self-realisation. Sometimes images depict both male and female Nāga, representing the balance of the yin and yang forces of Nature **(image p. 222)**. In Buddhist tradition, Buddha is shielded by Mucalinda, a multi-headed Nāga, as he meditates **(left)**, and many multi-headed serpents are depicted at Angkor Wat, in Cambodia. Serpents have been associated with *kundalini*, the Eastern concept that currents of energy, called chi or ki, flow through the human body.

The serpent is one of the days of the Aztec farming calendar, and the god Quetzalcoatl was the Aztec bird/serpent deity. This double-headed serpent **(right)** is an exquisite Aztec relic kept in the British Museum, comprising a snake with two heads, covered in turquoise, and which is thought to represent Quetzalcoatl.

At the Maya temple at Chichen Itza, Mexico, the head of a plumed/ feathered serpent Kukulcan rests at the base of a pyramid; at each equinox the Sun casts a shadow so as to create the body of a snake running down the entire side of the pyramid **(right)**. Recent work (Burke and Halberg 2005) has scientifically shown that seeds placed on some Mesoamerican pyramids increased their size and rate of growth, suggesting that this led to increased crop production. The authors note the Mayan and Aztec association between serpents and fertility, and suggest that this fecundity aspect may have been the *primary* reason cultures engaged in pyramid construction. They also suggest similar

reasons for the erection of the Egyptian pyramids. In Egyptian mythology, *Mother of Creation,* Per-Uatchet or Wadjet Isis, was also a serpent, in this case a Cobra. Buto was an Egyptian snake goddess, also depicted as a cobra, and her image on the headwear of Pharaohs ensured protection from their enemies; four golden cobras, inlaid with lapis lazuli, adorn the throne of Tutankhamun. The Asp was a particular attribute of Isis, the goddess of life and healing, and the god Thoth was also known as the *'Serpent of Wisdom'* (Gardiner and Osborn, 2005).

The iconic Minoan *Snake Goddess* brandishes a snake in each hand **(right)**, probably invoking her role as a source of deep wisdom and fertility. The ouroboros of Egyptian and Greek tradition was a mythic serpent which swallowed its own tail, thus forming a circle, symbolic of the eternal cycles of destruction and regeneration of Nature; the imagery may also have been inspired by the circuit of the Milky Way around the sky.

The Orphic Egg had a snake coiled around it, which the Greeks used as a symbol for their view that the world was protected by a cosmic serpent **(image p. 68)**. This relates

121

to Zervan, the Mithraic god of time, whose body was part lion/part man, and who was entwined by the coils of the cosmic serpent. The Greek god Medea, granddaughter of the Sun god Helios, rode a chariot pulled by snakes **(image p. 76)**. The Goddess cult at Delphi was symbolically dissipated when Python, the female snake, was killed by the arrows by Apollo; this may be referring to the ascendancy of male gods over the preceding Snake Goddess cults. Medusa was a female Gorgon with hair made of living snakes, said to be the guardian of ancient mystical secrets; a Gorgon was placed on one of the most prominent points at the Temple of Artemis at Corfu. Some Roman myths say that Bacchus was born a serpent.

No less than four constellations are related to serpents. The classical god Ophiuchus ('Serpent Handler') is represented by the constellation of the same name; two other groups of stars, Serpens Caput and Serpens Cauda, are also named after snakes; and the constellation of Hydra comes from the multi-headed serpent defeated by Heracles/Hercules (Knight 2013, p. 121). The *Year of the Snake* is one of the twelve animals of the Chinese zodiac.

To Germanic, Norse and Celtic races, the serpent is often associated with wisdom and authority, but also with divine retribution. A flood would ensue should Jormangand, or, Jormungandr, the serpent undermining the Tree of Life (Yggdrasil), be roused from slumber; this serpent, also known as Midgard, was also an ouroboros that encircled the world in the ocean's abyss, biting its own tail, and in one myth Thor battles with this mighty beast. The serpent appears on the famous Gundestrup Cauldron **(image p. 49),** associated with the Celtic god Cernunnos. The goddess Ceridwen had a vehicle drawn by serpents.

In African myths, the *Rainbow Snake* links the heavens and the earth, and in Australian Aborigine mythology the *Rainbow Serpent* is a main player in Creation myths, images of which appear on rock art going back 8,000 years **(below left)**. This ancestor of the Dreamtime is the creator spirit, responsible for fertility and the rains, and is capable of bringing about floods on those who break natural laws.

Several serpent myths feature in Native American mythology, and surely one of the most enigmatic North American archaeological wonders is the Great Serpent Mound, Ohio **(below right)**. The mound is 1,348ft (411m) long and has the head of the snake, which is either eating or disgorging an egg; this head/egg aligns with the midsummer sunset. We have seen elsewhere, with the Orphic Egg, this association between a serpent and an egg **(image p. 68)**. Recent research suggests that the Amerindians may have placed seeds on the mound to be energized, potentially increasing crop production (Burke and Harlberg 2005). Estimates vary as to the mound's age, but current theories suggest it originated 500-1070AD.

 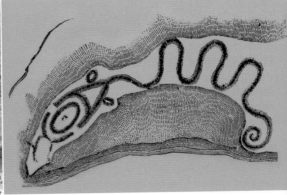

Caduceus

Carvings of the Sumerian god Ningizzida, or Ningishzida, depict him as a serpent with a human head, but also as two entwined serpents, a double-helix, seen as here on a 21st century BC libation vase, one of the oldest known examples of a caduceus - snakes entwined around a central shaft **(right)**.

Serpents have a long history linked with healing. In Greek myths, the god Aesculapius, son of Apollo, could turn himself into a snake to procure healing and even bring back the dead. He often carries a staff with one snake **(centre)**, which is also the emblem of Hygeria, his daughter, who was also gifted with healing. A similar sigil, this time with two snakes, is associated with both Hermes and Mercury, and which may also bear wings on top of the rod, as in this example from France **(bottom)**. This originated from a myth in which Mercury intervened in a fight between two snakes, which confirms him as a figure who conducts souls between worlds, as well as a messenger of the gods. Both the Aesculapian and the Mercurial staffs have been used as symbols of the medical profession, and may sometimes be seen at the entrances to hospitals.

Perhaps the origins of the serpent-capped caduceus go right back to prehistoric shamanic cave rituals, depicted on rock and cave art. Shamans today still get a snake to bite the end of a staff to extract its psychoactive venom, that they may drink it.

Earth Energies and the Caduceus

The double-helix/two-serpent emblem also mirrors the serpent-like earth energies that dowsers have found flowing, caduceus-like, along several long distance alignments, such as the Belinus Line (Biltcliffe and Hoare, 2012), the St Michael Line (Miller and Broadhurst, 1989), and the Apollo/Athena Line (Broadhurst and Miller, 2000). A global energy pattern, known as the Rainbow Serpent, flows around the entire planet, passing through major sacred sites. All of these examples consist of a flow of female, yin energy, and a yang or masculine current. These can be compared with the flows of energy around the human body, as already mentioned.

In terms of dowsable energies, on several occasions I have personally found serpent imagery associated with spiralling energy nodes, most of which were in churches. In the church at Stoke Trister, Somerset, I dowsed energies that spiralled in a node directly above carvings on a floor monument displaying two coiled serpents **(image p. 82)**, whilst at Crediton church, Devon, the two energy flows or 'serpents' of the St Michael Line cross paths right next to a column on which two serpents are carved **(right)**. This implies that either the builders of the church knew of these energies, or that the energies have gravitated to their present localities because of the symbolism; either offers intriguing prospects. These interactions of yin and yang energies flowing across the landscape are complemented by ancient images of twinned-polarity deities, such as the twinned Näga, a

123

common image seen across Asia **(image p 222)**. I have had the privilege to visit Gosforth, Cumbria, where a 9-10th century Anglo-Saxon cross depicts the god Heimdallr accompanied by two serpents, each with interwoven, caduceus-like bodies.

The Christian Serpent

It comes as no surprise to me that the serpent, being such a major player in ancient mythology, was assimilated into the Hebrew-Christian tradition. The Naassenes (*nass* meaning *'snake'*) were a Christian Gnostic sect dating from around 100AD, who revered the snake in the form of the Sumerian serpent deity Enku, seeing it as the one who introduced the Tree of Knowledge to Adam and Eve. Tanith, the Phoenician fertility goddess, is associated with serpents, linking her with Lilith and with Adam and Eve and the serpent of the Tree of Life **(image p. 56)**. Sumerian seals relating the Gilgamesh epic, dating to at least 3500BC, show the serpent guarding the Tree of Life, and demonstrate the connection it had with eternity and the collective unconscious; some scenes show a female offering a male figure fruit from the tree, later to be retold, of course, in the Book of Genesis with Adam and Eve, as portrayed here by Michelangelo **(top)**. But the serpent of wisdom has now been relegated to a creature that tempts Eve into ungodly practices. This serpent, however, is one of only two animals in the Bible gifted with speech, Balaam's ass being the other, and it is not until the Book of Revelations, near the end of the Bible, that the serpent is directly identified with the Devil/Satan.

In Exodus 4: 3-4, we read how Moses laid down his staff or rod, at which point it turned into a serpent. Later (in Exodus 7: 10-12), the Rod of Aaron was transformed into a snake, again showing the association of serpents with high magic. It is this same rod, being used in a similar role to a wand, which is used in releasing water from a rock, and which parts the Red Sea. Moses also raised a pillar or pole with a bronze snake, the Brazen Serpent, upon it **(centre)**, similar to the symbol the Greeks used for Aesculapius; the serpent here is clearly a device for carrying out God's will, for Moses and the faithful had to look at the serpent to be saved as Yahweh (God) sent seraphim (*'fiery serpents'*) to punish the sinful. It is interesting that the Aztec serpent god Quetzalcoatl also carried a staff and some Mexican art shows him *'raising the serpents'*, like Moses. *'Leviathan the serpent'* is mentioned in Isaiah 27:1, and Hebrew reverence for the serpent is echoed by the *Flying Serpent*, the emblem of Israeli Paratroopers.

There is little doubt that early Christian sects revered the serpent. The Gnostics venerated Sophia, who was known of as, *'The light of the serpent'* (Gardiner and Osborn 2005, p. 202-3). Gnostic mysticism sees the ouroboros **(bottom)**, the snake that bites or is eating its own tail, as a symbol of the cycles of time and Nature, of eternity; it

124

can be seen in many churches, and is one of the emblems of the Theosophical Society. The cross-over between serpents and dragons is demonstrated with the many images of dragons biting at their own tails.

The caduceus of the old healing gods was metamorphosed into an icon of St Luke, the Christian patron saint of healing, seen here at Grittleton, Wiltshire **(right)**; compare this with the images of Aesculapius and Mercury on page 123. Both St Paul and St John the Divine both survived encounters with snakes, and are sometimes portrayed with them. St John holding the chalice containing a 'winged serpent' or dragon **(image p. 130 & front cover)** symbolises the chalice containing poison from which John drank to confirm his faith, although in esoteric terms it represents enlightenment, as the serpent of knowledge rises from the Grail, the chalice of rebirth.

I find it fascinating that the title given to Jesus, the *'Nazarene'*, comes from the Hebrew *nacash*, meaning *'serpent'*, and implies that he is the messenger of wisdom. The shedding of its skin has led to snakes being associated with *'rebirth'*, either in this life in the shamanic sense, or through attaining everlasting life in some Otherworld; a parallel can be made between the Resurrection of Jesus and that of a snake shedding its skin; Jesus arose from the cave having shed his physical body. This has led to the creature being associated, perhaps inevitably, with the Holy Grail, which also had to power to rebirth and rejuvenate.

The serpent is sometimes shown below the feet of the Virgin Mary, as a symbol that she was absent of *'sexual sin'* **(image p. 190)**, and Jesus can be depicted trampling a snake underfoot **(centre)**, symbolising his triumph over sin and the Devil. To Gnostics, however, this represents the *serpent of wisdom*, and the esoteric knowledge that Jesus attained.

The legend that St Patrick ordered all the snakes to leave Ireland in the 5th century, as shown here in a chapel at Glastonbury Abbey **(right)**, could in fact be a memory of the saint cleansing the lands of serpent cults. In medieval times the snake generally became synonymous with evil and was associated with the Devil, as was the Leviathan, the sea serpent. Finally, in Christian folklore, a snake is also associated with the Christian hermit St Simeon Stylites (390-459AD), representing the demonic temptations of the saint. Ironically, various parts of the animal continued to be used for healing and medicine, and they are to this day.

Legend has it that fossil ammonites are troublesome snakes that were miraculously turned to stone by St Hilda, the Saxon Abbess of Whitby, and these fossils were hence known as, *'snake stones'*. This, however, is merely a continuance of a long tradition of the serpent representing the duel expressions of both good and evil. Carl Jung thought the snake to be symbolic of the polarities of *'evil and wisdom'* because it represented the huge gulf between humankind's conscious and subconscious states (Jung 1964).

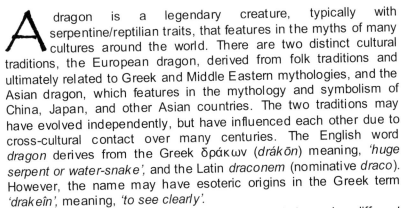

25. Here Be Dragons

A dragon is a legendary creature, typically with serpentine/reptilian traits, that features in the myths of many cultures around the world. There are two distinct cultural traditions, the European dragon, derived from folk traditions and ultimately related to Greek and Middle Eastern mythologies, and the Asian dragon, which features in the mythology and symbolism of China, Japan, and other Asian countries. The two traditions may have evolved independently, but have influenced each other due to cross-cultural contact over many centuries. The English word *dragon* derives from the Greek δράκων (*drákōn*) meaning, *'huge serpent or water-snake',* and the Latin *draconem* (nominative *draco*). However, the name may have esoteric origins in the Greek term *'drakeîn',* meaning, *'to see clearly'.*

Although dragons occur in countless global legends, different cultures have varying stories about *'monsters'* that have been grouped together under the generic dragon. The morphology of a dragon usually resembles that of a four-legged reptile, but in antiquity, dragons were mostly envisaged as legless serpents. Since the Middle Ages the common depiction has been with legs, resembling a lizard. Dragons are usually shown today as a huge, fire-breathing reptile, often with bat-like wings. A dragon with wings but only a single pair of legs is known as a Wyvern.

Dragons are often held to be of major spiritual significance in various religions and cultures around the world. They have a strong association, along with the serpent, with the Tree of Life and fecundity **(top)**. In many Asian traditions, dragons were, and in some cultures still are, revered as representatives of the primordial forces of Nature and the Universe, and can be associated with longevity and wisdom, often said to be wiser than humans. They are commonly said to possess magic or other supernatural powers, and dwell in an underground lair or cave, sometimes guarding *'buried treasure'.* They are often linked to water, such as the sea, wells and rain, and are often thought to reside in rivers. Some prehistoric structures, notably Dragon Hill, Uffington, have associations with dragons; the White Horse of Uffington **(left and image p. 13)** may have originally been a white dragon (Dragon Hill is visible in the middle distance). Many natural features, especially

126

conical hills, often possess dragon folklore, as do caves and bodies of water (see Whitlock 1983 for a good overview of dragon folklore). The serpentine ridge of the Isle of Wight may have been a vital element as to why the island was regarded as an ancient sacred place (Biltcliffe and Hoare, 2012).

They are many theories as to what animals may have inspired dragon myths, such Komodo Dragons, crocodiles, alligators, whale skeletons, fossil dinosaur bones, as well as large animals which, although now extinct, were alive during Man's early evolution. Esoterically, the dragon symbolises the potent force of Nature and its energies, and some traditions believe that dragons still exist as ethereal entities, in Otherworldly dimensions.

The image of a dragon as a monstrous opponent, to be overcome by a hero or deity, has its roots in the traditions of the ancient Near East, including Hebrew, Hittite and Mesopotamian mythology. In the Epic of Gilgamesh, a fire-breathing beast called Humbaba is described as a dragon, with Gilgamesh playing the part of dragon-slayer. The great *'Dragon Queen'* of Mesopotamia was Tiamat, the *'Mother of all living things'*, the female elemental spirit that pervaded the Cosmos, shown here on a monument at Ninevah **(right)**. The Egyptian serpent-dragon Apep pursued the Sun across the sky, and every night battled with Seth, champion of the solar god Ra.

In Ancient Greece, the first record of a *'dragon'* is in Homer's *Iliad,* where Agamemnon is described as having a blue dragon motif on his sword belt, and an emblem of a three-headed dragon on his breast plate. Cadmus fought the Ismenian dragon (which guarded the sacred spring of Ares) in a legendary story from Greek lore dating to at least 560BC. Greek dragons, as shown here **(right)** on a mosaic, commonly had a role of protecting important objects or places. For example, the Colchian dragon guarded the Golden Fleece, and the Nemean dragon protected the sacred groves of Zeus. In another myth, Greek hero Heracles famously defeated the multi-headed Hydra, a dragon-like water monster. In 217 AD, Flavius Philostratus discussed dragons in India, and according to a collection of books by Claudius Aelianus, called *On Animals*, Ethiopia was inhabited by a dragon that hunted elephants, and could grow to 180 feet (55 m).

Depictions of the Chinese dragon, seen here in Edinburgh Museum **(right)**, can be found in artifacts from the Shang and Zhou dynasties, some on Bronze Age pottery dating to at least 16th century BC. They are positively associated with the fertilizing rain, and one Chinese archaeologist believes that the Chinese word for dragon is an onomatopoeia of the sound of thunder; in fact a dragon embellishes the flag of Bhutan, whose name of *Druk Yul* means, *'Land of the Thunder Dragon'.* The dragon is the highest-ranking animal in the hierarchy of the Chinese zodiac, and is said to be the luckiest sign. It was strongly associated with the Emperor, and hence with power and

sovereignty. Emperors believed they were descended from the *Yellow Emperor*, who had the head of a human and the body of a dragon. The Chinese also believed that solar eclipses were caused by dragons eating the Sun **(image p. 133)**. Today, the Chinese dragon is an important element of the street theatre during the Chinese New Year celebrations, as featured in this magnificent float in New York, USA **(left)**.

Sometime after the 9th century AD, Japan adopted the Chinese dragon through the spread of Buddhism, and local myths amalgamated with imported stories from China, Korea and India. Like other Asian varieties, Japanese dragons are water deities associated with rainfall, and are typically depicted as large, serpentine creatures; a three-clawed variety was the symbol of the Mikado, the Japanese Emperors.

Draco (the *dragon*) is a sinuous northern constellation that curves around the North Pole, and at times has hosted the celestial pole; the star Thuban was the pole star c. 4500 years ago. Because of their inclination, the orbits of planets cross the path of the Sun, the ecliptic, twice every orbit. These points are called the ascending and descending nodes, but in medieval astronomy they were the *'dragon's head'* and *'dragon's tail'*.

Russian dragons are usually multi-headed **(left)**, often in multiples of three, and some have Turkish names (such as Tugarin Zmeyevich), probably symbolising their loathing of the Mongols and other nomadic races invading from the Russian steppes. One myth has a hero, Dobrynya Nikitch, rescuing a damson in distress from a dragon, like the Christian dragon-slayers. Accordingly, St George slaying a dragon (symbolising evil) is represented on the Moscow coat of arms.

In the Indian Vedas, Vritra could be both dragon-like and a Näga (serpent), as the personification of drought and the enemy of Indra. The Persian hero Rostam slew a dragon, and the beasts were often depicted upon Persian banners of war; in Middle Persia there was a dragon called Dahāg or Bēvar-Asp, mentioned in Zoroastrian scriptures, which was mostly malevolent, like several other dragon-like beasts. Zahhāk was one such creature in Iranian and Arabian myths, the name meaning, *'having ten sins'*.

Dragon effigies were carved on the prows of Viking long ships **(left)**, as a symbol of protection, sovereign power and fearlessness. The famous royal helmet of Sutton Hoo is a Pagan relic from the 7th century, and features dragon symbolism (Hodges 2008). In Germanic legends, dragon blood had the power to render skin or armour invincible when bathed in it, and in the Anglo-Saxon saga *Beowulf*, the blood of the dragon has acidic qualities, enabling it to eat through metal.

In the same saga we are informed that, '... *the dragon shall be in the tumuli, old, rich in treasures'.* But is this literal treasure - or knowledge? In medieval legend and literary fiction, the blood of a slain dragon could be either beneficent or poisonous.

Under Christianity, European dragons have usually been seen as malevolent, as on this bench-end at Crowcombe, Somerset **(centre)**, whereas pre-Christian dragons, such as Y Ddraig Goch, the red dragon of Wales, were regarded as benevolent. In Welsh mythology, after a long battle (which Welsh King Vortigern witnesses) a red dragon defeats a white dragon; Merlin explains to Vortigern that the red dragon symbolised the British, and the white dragon the Saxons – thus foretelling the ultimate defeat of the Saxons by the English. Henry VII adopted the red dragon and the Griffin (a 'dragon' with the body of a lion, and the head, wings and talons of an eagle). The symbol of the City of London is a dragon **(top)**, from a legend that one lived in the River Thames guarding the city.

The Dacian Draco was a standard ensign featuring a dragon on a tall pole, named from the ancient Dacians of the Carpathian Mountains. It was adopted by the Greeks and Romans as an aid to archers as it indicated wind direction and strength, as well as providing visual intimidation on the battlefield. Dragon relics start to appear in Britain with the coming of the Romans, who had them emblazoned on their standards.

Later, the Britons made the dragon their battle symbol against the invading Saxons. Arthur Pendragon means *'head of the dragon'* or *'chief dragon',* and he was associated with the red dragon. Arthur also has associations with the White Horse of Uffington, which may have originally been fashioned as a dragon; this hill figure, and the adjacent Dragon Hill, had alignments with the constellation Draco in prehistory (Biltcliffe and Hoare, 2012, p. 127-30).

Dragons feature on heraldry and symbolise a defender who is strong, protective and brave; dragon banners were used by King Harold of Wessex at the Battle of Hastings, and are shown on the Bayeux tapestry; later, Henry III, Henry VIII and Elizabeth I also used dragon symbolism.

The Wyvern is a two-legged, winged beast which has dragon-like attributes and became a popular heraldic emblem, representing vigilance.

In Jewish/Biblical texts, the first mention of a serpent/dragon-like creature is in Job (26:13), and Isaiah (27:1). This is identified in Genesis 1:21 as Leviathan, from the Hebrew word *Taninim: '... and God created the great sea-monsters'.* The Book of Isaiah, the Book of Job, and Psalm 89, all describe a sea-demon called Rahab, and in Isaiah 51:9 this is equated with a dragon or monster. The building that once was the synagogue at Merthyr Tydfil, in South Wales, features a dragon on its gothic front gable.

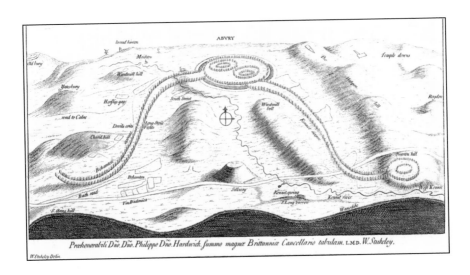

Prœhonorabili Dño. Dño. Philippo Dño. Hardwick. summo magnæ Britanniæ Cancellario tabulam. L.M.D. W. Stukeley.

W. Stukeley Delin.

Dragon Lines

Dowsers speak of earth energies as *'dragon lines'* or *'dragon currents'*, which are associated with some of the world's famous ley lines. In ancient China, these *lung mei* forces were seen as dragon energies, and only the palaces and tombs of their Emperors were allowed to be built on these *'dragon paths'*. One of the pioneering initiatives of the British earth mysteries movement was called the *Dragon Project*, an investigation into the energies and light phenomena at sacred sites. The landscape energies of the Belinus Line (Biltcliffe and Hoare 2012) pass through the Uffington White Horse and the adjacent Dragon Hill – surely the horse was originally a dragon. In the 18th century, antiquarian William Stukeley described the sacred sites of the Avebury area as a *Druidic Temple,* perceiving that a landscape dragon **(above)** was laid out by the purposeful position of certain sacred sites, and which he termed *Dracontia*. I think it is significant that two dragons (representing the two caduceus-like energy currents of the St Michael Line) are portrayed on the Norman font at Avebury **(bottom, previous page)**. These two serpentine flows are often seen as *'earth dragons'* (Miller and Broadhurst 1989).

Dragon folklore speaks of dragons flying from one hill to another, or one sacred site to another, and this may be a distant memory of the flow of earth energies between these places (Knight 1998, p. 20). Perhaps the quote from *Beowulf,* above, is not referring to monetary treasure or gold, but rather the ethereal forces experienced at such ancient sites.

London was known as *Dragon City* (Thorley ed. 2012), and Peter Dawkins has recently proposed a *'Chakric Dragon Temple'*, which can be overlaid on the plan of Celtic-Romano London, and which determines the flows of earth energies (Thorley ed. 2012, p. 38-43). Work on the Dorset landscape and its sacred sites by the author (Knight 1996) and Michael Hodges (Hodges 2008) has shown that certain alignments of sacred sites and natural features have dragon associations, such as local folklore or place names. I have found that many of the winged dragons on the outside of churches **(centre, previous page)**, look along such alignments towards the next sacred site; I have termed these *'ley gazers'*,

Christianity and the Dragon Slayers

Dragons generally tend to be benevolent in the East, and malevolent in the West, and this is due largely to Christianity's relationship with the creature. In the Bible, dragons and serpents are interchangeable, both being symbols of both religious and political opposition to God, and therefore to all good Christian folk. To the Church, the dragon epitomised the *'old ways'* of Paganism, and therefore the creature needed to be demonised. Christian myths were the primary influence in ensuring that the dragon became an adversarial symbol, representing the Devil, evil, turmoil and bestiality. Dragons appear in medieval mumming plays, representing these very facets, although perhaps many British dragon stories are allegories, illustrating friction between the local Pagan peasantry and the Church. To me, the mask of the Padstow 'Obby 'Os **(image p. 25)** resembles a dragon as much as a horse. The bad press of dragons was perpetuated by their association with any unexplained and fearful natural phenomena, such as comets, earthquakes, or eclipses of the Sun. For instance, an account from 1113 from Christchurch, Dorset, speaks of the town being consumed by fire, the blame for which was directed at a fire-breathing dragon that came out of the sea (Hodges 2008).

As well as being depicted as a serpent, the ouroboros may also be portrayed as a dragon biting its own tail, as shown in this fine example from Sherborne Abbey, Dorset **(bottom)**.

St John the Divine holds a chalice with either a dragon or serpent emerging from it **(front cover)**; the beautiful example here is from South Molton, Devon **(previous page)**. John was challenged to drink a cup of poison by the goddess Diana at Ephesus. He did so, but was unharmed. Clearly the dragon here portrayed evil and the Goddess, whom the Church was also looking to usurp.

Legend has it that St George was a knight who saved a Pagan town, and their princess, from being terrorized by a dragon. The townsfolk were so grateful that they converted to Christianity. Such bravery in defence of the helpless appealed to Christian ethics, and in the 14th century he was made patron saint of England; much later he was even used in WWI recruitment posters. George is commonly shown slaying a dragon **(top & p. 97)**, which came to personify evil, sin and the Devil, and medieval mumming plays also involved him slaying the beast. History tells us that George was a senior officer in the Roman army of Emperor Diocletian, and yet complained about the harsh treatment of

Christians. As a result of his dissention was beheaded; St George's Day, April 23, is the anniversary of his martyrdom in 303AD.

Many places are associated with St George's dragon-slaying exploits, including Dragon Hill **(image p. 126)**; a patch of bare ground on top of the hill, where the grass never grows, is supposed to mark where the dragon's blood was spilled. Images of St George slaying the dragon **(title page & previous page)** can be distinguished from those of St Michael doing similar by the fact that George generally lacks wings (although I have found a few exceptions), whereas Michael is always winged.

St Michael the Archangel smiting a dragon (representing the Devil and evil) is a common image encountered in churches, as shown here at Stoke St Michael, Somerset **(bottom image, previous page)**. The icon is based on a passage in the Book of Revelations, where Satan takes the form of a dragon. Michael is the champion of God as he sweeps aside all the evils that the Devil lays before him. St Michael's origins, however, lie back in Babylonian myths **(top image p. 127)**, with Michael now substituting the god Marduk, and the Devil having replaced the goddess dragon-queen Tiamat. St Michael also replaced the god Lugh, and churches dedicated to the saint replaced hilltop places of the old gods **(images p. 18 & 32)**, typified by several such examples along the St Michael Line in England.

Medieval legends tell of St Margaret of Antioch, a 4th century saint. She was apparently swallowed by dragon, which represented the Devil. The cross she wore expanded so much in his mouth that the beast regurgitated her unharmed. The Knights Templar revered her as a saint, and she is often shown killing, standing on, or riding on the back of a dragon **(top)**. These tales are retellings of the dragon's links with the divine feminine and the earth energies of the land; I actually found this engaging, ancient-looking, bare-breasted she-dragon adorning the pulpit in the church at Cheriton Bishop, Devon **(left)**.

St Perpertua was a 3rd century woman who was martyred by the Romans. Her symbol is a gold dragon and a silver ladder, due a vision she had in prison in which she escaped captivity via a ladder guarded by a dragon that did her no harm.

The griffin has sometimes been used as a symbol for Jesus' nature, combining the *'lion of earth'* to his divinity as *'eagle in the sky'*. The dragon is occasionally shown as a symbol of the Resurrection, such as on a medieval crozier held in the British Museum, which shows the Agnus Dei lamb (Jesus) held within the looped neck of a dragon.

The Gnostic Dragon

Dragons often dwelt underground, germinating the creative forces of Nature. This is demonstrated around the base of the famous Apprentice Pillar at Rosslyn Chapel **(image p. 57)**. Here, eight intertwined dragons demonstrate the close relationship between the Tree of Life and the beast; out of their mouths issue vines, demonstrating the primal, creative forces once associated with dragons. In alchemy, two dragons often represent the union of the white queen (mercury) and the red king (sulphur) to produce the Philosopher's Stone, the Elixir of Life, and enlightenment. Dragons feature in many ancient initiation mysteries, and perhaps the *'buried treasure'* which so many dragons guarded was really an allegory for landscape energies, hidden wisdom and Gnosis. Is this what the image St John the Divine **(below left)** is really telling us, as the dragon/serpent of Gnosis rises from the Grail of rejuvenation and rebirth?

The dragon epitomises the psychological barrier to the acquisition of self-change, the *'riches'* of our inner psyche; this is the eternal conflict of opposites, which, ultimately, dragon-slaying and twinned dragons symbolise, as shown in this 17th century alchemical illustration **(bottom, previous page)**. On a personal level, the dragon has guided me to deeper mysteries of my own landscapes, both external and internal.

Dragons, it would seem, were once held as stewards and keepers of secret esoteric knowledge, guardians of the Grail, as well as symbols of the fertility and vitality of the land. To ancient cultures, the dragon was everywhere, part of all of creation, there to guide and teach Mankind, to remind us of our higher nature, our spiritual birthright.

Left: St John the Divine with a dragon rising from a chalice, Horsington, Dorset.
Right: a dragon impressively carved from a pumpkin.

Above: a sequence taken by the author at the eclipse of sun, March 20, 2015.
People once believed a dragon was trying to devour the sun.

26. Plants and Nature's Bounty

Mankind has had a long and imperative relationship with the Plant Kingdom. And this bond has not been just a connection born of the necessity for plants as a commodity and foodstuff, but has also been in relation to Man's spirituality and mythologies. Plants have provided us with both the concept and imagery of the seasonal cycles of life, and of Divine benevolence.

Countless worldwide festivals are pinned by the annual background cycle of the sowing, growing, harvesting, and retreat of vegetation, as I demonstrated in Chapter 6. In Chapter 14, we looked at the Tree of Life, the mythical tree of the Creation myths of so many cultures, including those of the Garden of Eden and Yggdrasil, the Norse Axis Mundi. In Chapter 15, I described in detail how the inherent spirits and deities of plants became the Green Man, the foliated male or female imagery that reminds us of the soul of Nature, a life force that cannot be tamed. I have also touched upon the sacred geometry inherent in Nature, including plant growth, which follows the Fibonacci Sequence **(image p. 7)**.

Many stories concerning plants are well known, such as the Hanging Gardens of Babylon, Jesus in the Garden of Gethsemane, and the Glastonbury Holy Thorn. But this is not the place for me to deal with *all* the imagery associated with plants, which would in fact be a near impossible task and a book in itself. Instead I must confine myself to those plants which are most strongly associated with Church symbolism, in keeping with my overall brief.

Agriculture
The change from hunter-gatherer to farmer was one of the most crucial transformations that Mankind has ever undertaken; the consequences have altered, quite literally, the face of the planet. It was not, in fact, hunter-gatherers but farmers who were the Neolithic colonialists, venturing into new areas out of necessity; they had herds to graze, and had larger families, whose offspring would ultimately need their own land (Knight 2011, p. 16). People were now anchored to one place, which led to a new spiritual relationship with one area of the landscape, on which they were almost completely dependent.

The symbol of wheat-sheaves, and the goddesses of wheat and other grains, first make their appearance in the Neolithic (Baring and Cashford, p. 68-9), incorporated in ceremonies of crop sowing and the subsequent harvest. A relationship also developed between the fertility of women and the fecundity of the land (which was almost exclusively personified as a goddess). The Greek deity Demeter, and the Roman Ceres, was the *'Grain Mother'*, earth goddess of the harvest and ploughed fields **(image p. 28)**. Ceres, in fact, gave us the word *cereal,* and Persephone, her daughter, was the *'Corn Maiden'*. Compare the image of Ceres to the Christian figure shown here from Grittleton, Wiltshire **(image previous page)**, who carries a bundle of wheat on her back, as is surrounded by the fruits of the earth; even today we still speak of *'Mother Earth'*.

Corn or maize features in the Creation myths of the Aztecs and Maya. Such was Man's increasing need to grow crops that it has been suggested that some of the world's pyramids, and indeed some European temples and tombs, were built to augment and enhance the growing potential of grain seeds into which they were temporarily deposited (Burke and Harlberg 2005).

In Christian art, wheat represents bountifulness, the sheaf being symbolic of thanksgiving and which is still involved in festivals today, such as the Straw Bear Festival in Whittlesey **(top)**, Cambridgeshire, the Rush-bearing Festival in Sowerby, West Yorkshire, and every Harvest Festival **(images p. 27)**.

Cornucopia

The Cornucopia, or *Horn of Plenty*, is the mythical receptacle that could not be emptied, and which represented bountiful harvests and the generosity of the gods. It was also symbolic of maternal nourishment and love, of good fortune, hospitality, abundance and prosperity. It originated from the classical myth in which Zeus (or Jupiter) broke off a horn of the Goat Amaltheia as it sucked the god; subsequently, the horn provided a limitless supply of food and drink. Abundantia **(right)** personified abundance for the Romans, and was shown with fruit cascading out of the horn, as in this painting of her by Rubens. The horn is also associated with deities connected with fertility and the earth, such as Priapus, Flora, Demeter, Ceres, Dionysus, and Bacchus. The Cornucopia is the badge of office of the Steward of Freemasonry lodges, and can also be seen in churches and secular buildings, representing God's bounteousness.

Trees and Shrubs

Tales of sacred groves and trees occur in many ancient and modern cultures, and tree mythologies are universal, often associated with the Axis Mundi (Chapter 14), as well as wisdom, initiation and death/rebirth. For instance, the Egyptian myth of the god Osiris saw him placed into a wooden chest which is thrown into the Nile. The casket beached and an Acacia tree grew up around it. Isis recovered the chest and liberated Osiris from the tree, which then became an object of veneration to the local people. This story is the personification of the perpetual retreat and subsequent regeneration of nature.

Over 400 stone carvings of Ogham marks survive across Britain **(bottom)**, the largest number of which are found in Ireland, dated 4th–9th century AD. Ogham is the Celtic tree oracle, developed by Druid bards to pass on messages, as well as for use in sacred rites; some of the Norse/Anglo-Saxon runes also represent trees. Inverted trees are found in the Hindu Bhagavada-Gita and in the Jewish Kabbalah **(image p. 54)**; this has parallels with Seahenge, the Bronze Age site in Norfolk, which had an inverted Oak stump at its heart. In Islam, trees symbolise abundance and plenty.

Arguably the most dramatic Biblical event involving a tree or bush was when God spoke to Moses in the form of a *'burning bush'*, telling him that he was to lead the Israelites out of bondage (Exodus 3:2). Jesus' lineage is sometimes depicted as the *Jesse Tree,* which traces his line back to King David. Many festivals and ceremonies today revolve around the cycles of Nature in which participants don foliage, such as the Burry Man (South Queensferry), Garland Day (Castleton, Derbyshire), and various Jack-in-the-Green festivals and parades **(image p. 60)**; the one shown here is from May Day celebrations in Hastings **(left)**.

Let's look at the main trees that made it across to Christian iconography; I apologise in advance for any ancient sacred trees I have omitted, but this is because they have little or no connection with Christian symbolism.

Acacia is associated with the Egyptian Tree of Life, such as in the myth of Osiris and Isis, representing the immortal nature of the soul. Acacia was the flaming bush of the Moses story, and later, when God gave Moses instructions for building the Tabernacle, or holy shrine, he said to, *'make a table of acacia wood',* possibly meaning an altar. The Ark of the Covenant **(images p. 39)** was also to be made from acacia. The tree is a potent sigil in Freemasonry, representing endurance and purity of the soul, and as a funerary decoration symbolic of resurrection and everlasting life. It is interesting that several species of the Acacia have psychoactive elements.

Apple tree myths occur in many ancient cultures, often linked with health and immortality. Apples are an icon for peace and beauty in China, whilst they also appear in several classical myths. Greek legend says that the first apples were golden, and put under the care of three minor goddesses called the Hesperides and a dragon called Ladon, but that Hercules later stole the apples, killing the dragon in the process. Scandinavian legend says the gods rejuvenated themselves with apples from gardens in Asgard, their legendary homeland. Celts saw the apple tree as an Otherworldly doorway to the fairy realms. King Arthur is strongly associated with Avalon (Glastonbury), which means the *'apple orchard'.* Apple is one of the Celtic Ogham trees, and the Celts and Romans imposed strict penalties on anyone cutting down an apple tree. A cross section through an apple **(lower image)** reveals a five-pointed star, the pentagram, which is associated with the Earth Goddess. Apple-related wassailing rituals and parades are still carried out today (see text p. 23 and **image p. 22**).

Unfortunately, the apple has become synonymous with the temptation of Adam and Eve, the *Fall of Man.* In the Garden of Eden, as it was apparently the fruit on the Tree of Knowledge. But the Bible does not actually mention the tree species. It is interesting that the Latin word for apple is *malum,* which also has an adjective meaning of *evil.* The story of Snow White has of course linked apples with witches. But, as usual with Christian icons, apples can represent good or bad. They are a symbol of sin in the hands of Adam and Eve, but salvation when held by the Virgin Mary and Jesus (the new Adam). This 16th century painting is said to be the Virgin and Jesus under an apple tree **(right);** yet we see a woman with long reddish hair; is this in fact Mary Magdalene with *her* child; we shall return to this theme in Chapter 40.

Three apples are the symbol of St Dorothea, a martyr who died c. 304AD. The story goes that on the way to her execution a man taunted her, requesting her to send him some fruit and flowers from Paradise; when an angel later brought him three flowers and three apples he instantly converted to Christianity.

Aspen is one of Celtic Ogham trees, and was the favoured wood of Greeks and Celts for making shields, as it was both lightweight and also said to be imbued with magical protective powers. In Christian symbolism, the tree is symbolic of shame and lamentation, as it is thought to have been the wood used for Jesus' cross at the Crucifixion; legend tells us that the reason the tree appears to tremble at the slightest breeze is because of its shame.

Cherry can symbolise noble deeds in Christian art, but the juicy red fruit can also be associated with feminine sexuality, such as, *'losing one's cherry'. 'Eating cherries'* is a Chinese euphemism for sexual intercourse, whereas Japanese Samurai warriors would meditate beneath the tree.

Fig trees and their fruit have much associated mythology. When the Greek goddess Demeter travelled the land looking for her lost daughter, she was welcomed into the home of a man in Attica; she thanked him for his hospitality by gifting him the very first fig tree. The fig was a sexual symbol due to the graphic similarity between male genitalia and shape of a fig leaf, notions reinforced by the milky sap extracted from many species. The name of the fertility Sun god Dionysus means, *'friend of the fig',* and the fig also represented plenty, fertility, immortality, and femininity. The *Ruminal Fig* of Rome was the tree under which Romulus and Remus were suckled by a wolf **(image p. 99)** Prince Siddhartha attained enlightenment (becoming the Buddha) sitting beneath a Bodhi tree, a variety of fig **(below).** Fig leaves were of course the chosen attire of Adam and Eve, and because of this some scholars believe that the Tree of Knowledge may have been a fig, rather than an apple tree.

Frankincense is the tree that gifts us the aromatic resin or sap, still used during initiation and purification ceremonies. It can grow with little or no soil, such as in deserts, and is therefore a symbol of endurance and resilience. It featured in many stories from ancient cultures, such as the tale involving Venus and Sol (the Sun), in which a frankincense tree magically grows from the body of Leucothie, the deceased lover of Sol. The Assyrians believed that the phoenix would only feed on frankincense gum, which was often used in Middle Eastern ceremonies to enhance contact with the Divine. The Egyptians had many medicinal uses for it, such as treating gout and head injuries. There are 52 references to frankincense in the Bible, the most famous reference being that of the gift by the Three Magi to the infant Jesus just after his birth (Chapter 32). The valued sap runs out of the tree in tear-shaped flows, which in religious lore are known as *'Madonna's Tears'.*

Holly is another of the sacred Celtic Ogham trees. As a symbol of joy and hope, holly was carried during the Roman midwinter festival of Saturnalia, from whence we get the tradition of decorating churches and homes with holly sprigs. Holly represents the Passion of Jesus, symbol of his suffering, its spiked leaves symbolic of the crown of thorns, its red berries his blood. It is one of the candidates for the wood used for his cross, for in the song, *'The Holly and the Ivy',* the line, *'The holly bears the crown'* makes reference to this.

Laurel was an iconic symbol of truces, as well as triumph during games in ancient Rome, and it played an important part in the rituals of Rome's Vestal Virgins. It was adorned by followers of Apollo and priestesses of the Temple of Apollo at Delphi, who would chew on laurel leaves prior to giving their prophesy. Daphne, the Greek nymph, was turned into a laurel by Apollo after rejecting his love, and it is also associated with Artemis/Diana, Zeus/Jupiter and Dionysus/Bacchus. In China, it is the tree beneath which a lunar hare blends an elixir of immortality. The laurel (and its variety Bay) was adopted accordingly by the Church as a victory emblem for Jesus, as the foliage takes a long time to wilt, suggesting eternity; laurel has also been associated with chastity. I found this beautiful example of the tree **(left)** in the church at Hornblotton, Somerset.

Myrrh is the aromatic resin from some desert thorns. It was highly prized by ancient cultures and its desert locations were closely-guarded secrets; frankincense and myrrh were sometimes considered more valuable than gold, and the Greek historian Herodotus wrote that the trees producing the resin were guarded by winged serpents. It was used in ancient Egypt for embalming, and has symbolised feminine and nurturing aspects, being linked to the Earth. It was known as the *Balm of Mecca* by Arabs, and the Hebrew Bible describes its use as an incense in the Temple at Jerusalem. It was also used to anoint the Tabernacle, as well as kings and high priests. Myrrh is mentioned 156 times in the Bible, most famously as one of the gifts presented to the newborn of Jesus by the Three Magi. Some believe that it was a crown of myrrh thorns that was placed on the head of Jesus by the Romans following his conviction. The Eastern Orthodox Church uses oils scented with myrrh to perform some of its sacraments.

Oak was sacred to goddesses such as Juno and Cybele, and to nature spirits such as the Dryads. It is also associated with thunder gods of several ancient cultures, such as Zeus and the Norse god Thor, as it was the tree most struck by lightning. Successful Roman commanders were presented with wreaths of oak leaves, and the Romans made ink from oak galls. Oak is one of Celtic Ogham trees and the Roman writer Pliny described Druid ceremonies in oak groves. They associated oak with the Axis Mundi as well as wisdom, magic and male potency, and oaks were particularly revered when laden with Mistletoe (see below). Gog and Magog **(right)** are two ancient oaks at the foot of Glastonbury Tor, and said to be all that remains of a Druidic oak avenue. The Major Oak in Sherwood Forest shares folklore with Robin Hood, who has been associated with the tale of *'Gawain and the Green Knight'*, and the Pagan icon Robin Goodfellow.

Acorns and oak leaves are popular in the borders and backgrounds of stained glass windows **(right)** and in woodwork and stone, and can often form the foliage of a Green Man **(image p. 62).** The oak symbolises faith, endurance and strength, and the Bible compares people who are *'proud and lofty'* to the *'oaks of Bashan'*. In the Old Testament, King David's third son, Absalom, was killed by his enemies after being caught up in the branches of an oak. Also in the Bible, an oak was the site where Jacob buried the foreign gods (idols) of his people (Genesis 35:4); Joshua erected a stone under an oak as the first covenant of the Lord (Joshua 24: 25-7), and in Isaiah 61, the prophet calls the Israelites, *'Oaks of Righteousness'*.

According to legend, the Christianisation of Norse/Germanic tribes by St Boniface was marked by oaks being replaced by fir; in the 8th century Boniface famously destroyed Thor's Oak **(right)**, a sacred Germanic tree, building a church from its wood. Oaks are today still elements of festivals and customs, such as Oak Apple Day and Arbor Day. Folklore says that if a worm is found inside a gall on Michaelmas Day, the following year will be good, yet if a spider is found inside there will be crop shortages. This prophetic folklore harks back to the Druidic use of the oak as a tree of wisdom and divination.

Olive trees are generally a symbol of peace, success and prosperity, which goes right back to the Roman goddess Pax, who used an olive branch as a symbol of peace. Olive trees were sacred to the Greek goddess

Athena, who planted the first olive tree by a well at the Acropolis. A Greek amphora containing olive oil was given to victors of games held in honour of Athene during her annual July festival, a tradition that was carried over to the Olympic Games. Hercules/Heracles used a stake made of olive to help him smite the Cithaeron lion, and his club was said to be made from the same wood. Rather than the apple, the olive is the Islamic forbidden fruit tree in Paradise/Garden of Eden, and was one of seven plants that God promised the Israelites would find growing in the Promised Land. It was an

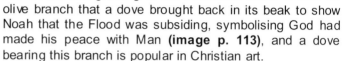

olive branch that a dove brought back in its beak to show Noah that the Flood was subsiding, symbolising God had made his peace with Man **(image p. 113)**, and a dove bearing this branch is popular in Christian art.

Palm trees were sacred to the solar god Apollo, as well as the goddesses Ishtar and Astarte. Palm leaves were a solar and triumphal symbol across the Middle East, and their fronds were an ancient processional emblem, which was adopted by Christianity for Jesus' triumphant entry into Jerusalem **(image p. 97)**, now celebrated as Palm Sunday. They symbolise a martyr's victory over death, especially that of Jesus' Resurrection. A palm may be shown with a saint to illustrate that he or she was martyred, as in this 6th century mosaic **(left)** featuring the martyred virgins of Ravenna, Italy. St Christopher's staff was also made from palm wood.

Pear trees, and their fruit, are sacred to three goddesses in Greek and Roman tradition – Aphrodite/Venus Hera/Juno, and Pomona, the Italian goddess of gardens and harvests. The pear was venerated by Russian cultures, such as the Vainakh, and in pre-Islamic Chechnya it was believed that pear trees were the abode of beneficial spirits - it was forbidden to fell them. Pears may be shown with Mary the Virgin in Renaissance and Baroque paintings, symbolising the fruit of her womb, and the fruit has also been used to symbolise Jesus' love for Mankind.

Thorn trees were seen as sacred to the Earth Goddess, linked with the hymen and weddings in ancient cultures. Blackthorn and hawthorn are two of the Celtic sacred Ogham trees. The most famous *'Holy Thorns'* are the those growing around Glastonbury **(left)**, which, unlike native varieties, blossom twice every year. Legend has it that Joseph of Arimathea came to the area following the Crucifixion and thrust his staff into the ground on Wearyall Hill, which sprouted into a thorn. A cutting from a flowering bough of one of its descendants in Glastonbury Abbey is sent to the Queen every Christmas. Thorns are symbolic of the crown of thorns with which the Roman soldiers mocked Jesus after he was condemned to death; they meant it as a parody of the crowns of roses worn by Roman emperors at festivals.

Willow was sacred to Hecate, the Greek lunar goddess, who taught the magical arts, and it was also associated with Orpheus, who carried willow branches into the Underworld. Willow is one of the Celtic Ogham trees, and images of hunter gods chopping down the tree appear on Celtic stonework at Notre Dame, Paris, and at Trier, Germany. Christian imagery links the willow with grief (Psalm 137), hence the *'weeping* *willow'.* The tree was often used for making gibbets, whilst in Scotland it was used to repel the *Evil Eye.* Willow boughs were often used to decorate churches on Palm Sunday as a substitute for the largely unavailable leaves of the palm.

Yews are the oldest living life-forms in Europe and Asia (Pakenham 1996, p. 31) and have had much mythology and folklore attached to them by Indo-European cultures, particularly concerning their longevity. They are evergreen and are generally thought of as goddess trees. They are one of the Celtic Ogham trees and some Celtic tribes took their name from the yew, such as the Iverni of Ireland. The Druids thought the yew was immortal, as no one ever sees one die, and it is said that Druids planted the yew forest on Hambledon Hill, Dorset (Knight 1998, p. 124). The gnarled barks of yews lend themselves to perceiving faces and *'spirits',* as I found here in a hollowed-out yew at Alton Barnes, Wiltshire **(top and centre)**.

When growing in churchyards, the roots of the yew are believed to absorb the souls of the dead, to be released from their branches via the winds. The tree has become a widespread symbol of immortality, sadness and mourning. Some say it was the tree used at the Crucifixion, and it therefore became associated with death around Europe. Some of the oldest yews seen in churchyards today were alive at the crossover from Paganism to Christianity, and many were allowed to survive (and even new ones planted) to placate those whose beliefs were about to be turned over.

A yew is said to have sheltered the missionary St Augustine when he came to Britain at the end of the 6th century. In the cloisters of Vreton on Brittany, one yew is said to have sprung from the staff of St Martin; the royalty of Brittany would pray beneath the tree before entering the church.

Some really ancient examples of yews that mark the takeover of old sacred sites by Christianity can be found at Knowlton Henge (Dorset), Much Marcle (Herefordshire), St Cynog (Powys), and Fortingall (Perthshire), all of which are between 2000-3000 years old. The Fortingall Yew stands at the exact centre of Scotland, and serves as the nation's Axis Mundi. The Pre-Christian yew at Wilmington, Sussex, is now accompanied by a church, but at one time it was the best place from which to view the Long Man (Knight 2013). According to Thomas Pakenham, there are around fifty yews in British churchyards that have a circumference in excess of 30ft (9m), many of which are hollowed out (Pakenham 1996).

I have spent time inside hollow yews, and I have certainly absorbed their feeling of immortality and timelessness. I personally find that time spent in a yew forest can be a profound experience, as I found in Kingley Vale, West Sussex **(right)**; you can bridge the vast gulf of time between yourself and these ancient trees of wisdom.

Say It With Flowers

Whilst flowers have inspired artists and poets over many centuries, there is also an ancient tradition of the use of flowers in religious ritual, ceremony, and healing. Flowers generally represent the culmination of the growth of nature, of its cycles, and are symbolic of aspiration, achievement and, of course, love. Some Indian gardens are based on mandalas, sacred geometrical designs, whilst many Chinese and Japanese gardens are designed to strict constraints of spiritual symbolism. The lotus is the symbol of India, and both Lakshmi **(left)** and Brahma stand on, or are seated on, lotus blossoms; in the East the lotus is generally associated with an elevation of spirit.

The *Flower of Life* **(image p. 74)** is a design incorporating sacred geometry, found at the Temple of Osiris at Abydos. It is comprised of six-petalled flowers, surrounded by circles. The design is seen across the world in sacred buildings and manuscripts, and has been called the *Genesis Pattern* (Knight and Perrott, 2008).

Across Europe, May Day (Beltaine) was traditionally a time when large shows of flowers were put on display in houses, churches, and as an adornment to maypoles, to celebrate the approach of summer **(image p. 25)**.

Let us look now at those flowers that were absorbed into Christian symbolism.

Acanthus is a type of nettle that is commonly spoken of as *'troublesome'* in the Holy Land and is probably the plant referred to in the Bible when *'nettle'* is ever featured (such as Job 30:7 and Zephaniah 2:9). The name comes from the nymph Acantha of Greek mythology, and it has been used for decoration on Greek, Roman and Christian art. Acantha was raped by Apollo but managed to scratch his face, at which point the god turned her into the plant. Acantha decoration was popular in Greek art and from the 5th century BC the plant adorned the capitals of columns.

Anemones symbolised the Holy Trinity in the early days of Church, and were later used in Crucifixion scenes; the red spots on the petals are said to be drops of blood shed by Jesus. But this probably derived from the classical legend of Adonis; on the spot where the beautiful Adonis had died, the goddess Venus made anemones grow where the earth had been stained with his blood.

Basil is said to derive its name from the terrifying Basilisk, a dragon-like creature from Greek mythology, which possessed a fatal stare; the Greeks believed basil could be used to cure someone from the stare, bite and even the breath of the beast. Others believe the name comes from the Greek *basileus,* which means *'King'*. This may have survived in a corrupted form into medieval times, when it was thought that scorpions were born from basil; African legend does speak of the plant protecting against scorpions. To the Romans, basil represented hatred, although later in Italy it became a symbol of love. Egyptians believe the plant would help open the gates of Paradise for a person passing on, and today it is placed in the mouths of the deceased to help them reach God. *'Holy Basil'* is sacred to the Indian god Vishnu, and Hindus avoid damaging the plant. Basil is said to have been growing on the original cross of the Crucifixion when found by Empress Helena, and hence it has religious significance in the Greek Orthodox Church, where it is used to sprinkle holy water. Known as St Joseph's Wort in some English counties, and it should be presented to one's sweetheart on the religious holidays of St Anthony and St John.

Carnations are symbols of love and marriage, and the scientific name comes from the Greek word *dianthus,* meaning *'heavenly or divine flower'. Carnation* is thought to have come from *coronation* or *corone,* as it was one of the flowers used in Greek ceremonial crowns. The flowers were said to have burst into flower on the day Jesus was crucified, springing up where the Virgin Mary's tears had fallen. Pink carnations hence became an emblem of a mother's undying love, an apt gift for Mother's Day.

Clover (or Trefoil) was held as sacred by the Druids, and is also the Chinese emblem of summer. To Christians it is a symbol of the Holy Trinity, due to its three leaved arrangement. St Patrick is said to have used the plant (as the shamrock), to explain the Trinity, and he is sometimes depicted holding it **(right)**. A four-leaf clover is said to be good luck because Eve carried one out of Eden, to remind her of the Paradise she had lost.

Columbine (or Aquilegia) was said to resemble five doves clustered together, or an eagle's claw (the Latin for dove is *Columba,* and eagle is *Aquila*). This association with the dove led to the flower being a symbol for the Holy Spirit until the 16th century. Each stalk has seven flowers so it has also been used to represent the *Seven Gifts of the Holy Spirit* (Isaiah 11:2).

Dandelion has been used for thousands of years as a medicinal herb and tea (described by the Chinese and Arabs), and has been associated with the Sun, due to its colour. These attributes come together with the solar god Apollo, who was also the god of healing. Dandelions have been called *'fairy clocks'* because they open and close predictably, and astrologically they are governed by Jupiter and the Sun. The plant appears in early Christian art as a symbol of the Passion of Christ, the bitter leaves symbolising Jesus' suffering.

Lilies appear as compelling symbols across the ancient world. The Egyptian Blue or Nile Lily was psychotropic, and is a common motif in Egyptian art. Lilies generally signify purity and innocence, and occur on Greek, Roman and Celtic coins. It is the symbol of the Greek goddess Hera, and her Roman equivalent Juno. Hera spilt some of her milk whilst breastfeeding Heracles (Hercules), and lilies grew where the milk fell. In China and Japan, lilies are thought to have the power to dispel grief. The flower's association with purity has led to the white lily (the *'Madonna Lily'*) being a symbol of the Virgin Mary. She is often holding the flower, seen here in this mesmerising window at Burley, Hampshire **(right)**, or else they are shown next to her; in alchemy, the white lily represents purity and because of this the lily is also associated with Archangel Gabriel from his role in the Annunciation, seen here **(centre)** in the gloomy crypt of Canterbury Cathedral.

One legend speaks of the Virgin Mary giving lilies to Clovis, the 3rd king of the Franks, at his baptism, and the lily can also be shown with Joseph, Mary's husband. Jesus gave the lily Divine approval when he spoke of the, *'lilies of the field'*, to demonstrate the virtues of denouncing wealth. The lily is also a sign of repentance, as it is said to have grown where Eve's tears fell to the ground when she was expelled from the Garden of Eden. Lilies were carved on Boaz and Jachin, two pillars at the Temple of Solomon, and Freemasons today see lilies as standing for the need for morality and modesty (Harwood 2006).

The lily is expressed in heraldry as the Fleur-de-lys (or Fleur-de-lis), which in French literally means *'lily or Iris flower'*. It is a stylised lily or iris, and its three-petalled design gives it an association with the Holy Trinity. In 800AD, the Pope gave Emperor Constantine a banner emblazoned with golden lilies on a blue background, and the French have used the Fleur-de-lys thereafter to signify the divine right to rule. It is interesting that Egyptian pharaohs cultivated lilies (which were not a native plant) as a symbol of their royal lineage. The Fleur-de-lys is also the symbol of the Priory of Sion, and was a favoured emblem of the Knights Templar; it is often shown on their tombs **(top)**, as well as being a common decoration in churches, as in these floor tiles **(left)**; part of the ceiling of Rosslyn Chapel is decorated with lilies. The Fleur-de-lys is also the chosen symbol of the Scouting Movement.

Narcissus is a symbol of joy and good luck in China, as it blooms at the Chinese New Year, and it was a flower symbolising youth to the ancient Persians. The genus is named after the character from Greek myth who, due to his vanity, ignored the beautiful nymph Echo and chose instead to look at his own reflection in a pool, shown so wonderfully in the John Waterhouse painting **(below)**. He did this for so long that he died, and the flower symbolises the youthful dead (Narcissi bloom and die early in the year). The flower's upright stem also became a symbol of faith to Muslims. This was also taken on by the Church, who turned the narcissus around from being a symbol of vanity to one of the triumph of Divine love.

Roses are said to have been created by Chloris, the Greek goddess of flowers, from the body of a beautiful nymph; her Roman equivalent was Flora, whose name describes the assemblage of plant life occurring in a particular region. Roses were sacred to Venus and Aphrodite, the goddesses of love, and to the Egyptian goddess Isis, as well as Dionysus. In Greek and Rome mythology, Harpocrates, the god of silence, finds Venus making love, and in order to bribe him to silence, Cupid/Eros (Venus' son) gives him a white rose; rose is an anagram of Eros. Roses were scattered on graves at the Roman festival of Rosaria, and emperors would wear rose crowns. Arab tradition says that the first rose was created by the rays of the rising Sun in the *Great Garden* of Persia, and in Islam the rose is sacred to Mohammed; Sufi mystics associate the rose with both pleasure and pain, due to its thorns, and the Sufi master Jilani was known as the *'Rose of Bagdad'*.

The red rose, a symbol of passion and desire, is associated with Mary Magdalene, possibly from it being a symbol of Venus; this example is from the church of Mary Magdalene, Woodborough, Wiltshire **(right)**. Mary is often dressed in red, and this and the red rose are said to represent the holy bloodline (see Chapter 40). The red rose also represents the love and spilt blood of Jesus, the five petals being symbolic of his five wounds; red roses can also symbolise the blood of other martyrs. The Rosicrucians, a Christian sect founded in the 15th century, have an emblem combining a cross and a red rose, known as the *Rosy Cross* **(centre)**; the multi-layering of the petals symbolise the stages of Rosicrucian initiation into arcane knowledge. In Freemasonry, St John's Rose symbolises love, life and illumination.

Two famous longitudinal alignments, one passing through Rosslyn Chapel, the other through Paris, are known as *Rose Lines*; roses feature in the architecture of Rosslyn Chapel, which has been dubbed the *'Temple of the Rose'*, and its ceiling is decorated with roses. The great medieval *'rose windows'* of Europe **(image p. 73)** are all based on the rose being a powerful symbol of the Sun, the wheel, love, enlightenment, and alchemy.

The *Mystic Rose* is a symbol of the Virgin Mary, who is sometimes called *'Rose of Heaven'*, symbolising her purity, and she is also called, *'the rose with no thorns'*. The *'Christmas Rose'* is linked with the Nativity.

Roses are associated with St George's Day, as the Tudor Rose is the national flower of England; Henry VII introduced it as a symbol of unity, combining the white rose of the House of York and the red rose of Lancaster. The late Princess Diana was known as *'England's Rose'*, and this plaque **(right)** occurs at her memorial in London; with some poignancy, this five petalled rose was known as the *'Rose of Venus'*, the goddess of love.

Red roses are of course associated with February 14th, St Valentine's Day. Valentinius was a 3rd century Roman martyr, who appears in local records between 460 and 544AD, and whose feast day was established in 496AD. His connection with romance is said to derive from the fact that Valentinius, who was a Roman priest, secretly married couples so that the husbands would not have to go to war. February 14ᵗʰ may have been chosen as his feast day to supersede the Pagan holiday of Lupercalia, which was held in honour of the Roman wolf deity Lupercus.

Spikenard is an aromatic essential oil derived from more than one variety of flowering plant. It is mentioned several timed in the Bible, such as in the *Song of Solomon*. It was used in temples to ease the transition between life and death, as well as in rituals of the goddesses Isis and Ishtar. The most notable use of it was when Mary Magdalene anointed Jesus **(image p. 223)**. It is recorded in the Bible that after she had anointed Jesus' feet, the whole house was filled with the aroma of the ointment, leading to some researchers suggesting that it induced a psychoactive effect. Spikenard is included the personal coat of arms of Francis, the current Pope.

Thistles were associated with the Greek god of agriculture, Ceres, who had a torch of thistle, and the plant was also linked with healing, and thought to be a powerful amulet. Adam and Eve were punished with, *'thistly ground'*, so it became associated with sin and sorrow. The white spotted Lady's Thistle is linked to the Virgin Mary, and thistles can also be shown as symbols of martyrdom.

Violets were flowers of remembrance in ancient Rome, and were also used at feasts to cool the brow. White Violets were said to grow on the graves of virgins, signifying innocence. Because of their small size, Christians see them as symbols of Jesus' humility, as well as his meek and mild nature as a youth. Violets are also symbols of the chastity of the Virgin Mary, and both Mary and Jesus may wear violet robes in scenes of the Passion; St Bernard called the Virgin Mary, *'The violet of humility'*.

Other Fruit, Nuts and Vegetables

Fruit, nuts and vegetables are usually associated with abundance and fertility. The virtues of Jesus are said to be the *Fruit of the Holy Spirit*.

Almond juice was related to semen in the ancient world, and in Mediterranean cultures the tree was a symbol for spring, as its blossoms are the first to appear. The tree originated in the Middle East and is mentioned ten times in the Bible, usually symbolising divine approval and favour. In the Moses story, he puts the twelve staffs of his potential successors in front of the Ark of the Covenant. In the morning, the staff or rod of Aaron had miraculously sprouted almond blossoms **(left)**, showing that he was to be the next leader of the Israelites (Numbers 17: 1-8). Almond has been a symbol for the Virgin Mary, due to the womblike/vulva shape of the nut, and may be used as imagery for the *Virgin Birth*.

Beans were used to ward off evil spirits in Japan, were love charms in India, and Native Americans even held bean festivals in honor of them being symbols of fecundity. Greek philosopher Pythagoras thought that the souls of the dead resided inside beans, and the Romans believed that misfortune would follow if spirits of the dead pelted your house with beans during the night! There is an ancient belief that ghosts and spirits resided in bean fields; as a consequence, it was also thought that a person could be immune from the evils of a witch if they spat out a bean at her! Christians used to made baked bean cakes for the feast of Epiphany, or the Twelfth Night.

146

Grapevines often decorate the edges of church windows and stonework, and yet the origin of the imagery is ancient. Vines are symbols of the Roman god Bacchus, the god of the vine and wine, and his Greek equivalent Dionysus, who are both associated with sex, passion and fertility. Bacchus is shown here with grapes on a cameo glass from Italy, dated 1st century AD **(right)**. Grapes represented the Promised Land to the Israelites and many Old Testament references attest to the importance of this crop in the Middle East; it became a symbol of abundance and wealth. Its strong association with Jesus derives from when he said to his followers, *'I am the vine, you are the branches'.* This connection is sometimes shown in the Green Man, who may issue grapevines **(top image, p. 59)**. It is also linked to the Eucharist of the Last Supper, as wine represents the blood of Jesus.

Peaches originated in China (Tao is the Chinese word for *peach*), and the Chinese thought them to be their sacred Tree of Life, as well as symbolic of immortality and springtime; it was said to be the wood from which miraculous bows were made. The peach is one of the *Three Blessed Fruits* of Buddhism, and to Christians it represents truth, virginity, and virtue - it may be shown in the hands of Jesus as a youth.

Pomegranates were left in Egyptian tombs as food for the dead on their journey to the Afterlife, and they were also employed as a cure for tapeworm. In classical mythology, the goddess Persephone, daughter of Zeus, ate four pomegranate seeds in the Underworld, which symbolised the winter time of the year, one month for each seed; when she reappeared it triggered the spring and the rebirth of the Sun. Persephone holding a pomegranate is captured in this famous painting by Rossetti **(right)**. Christians see the fruit as symbolising bountifulness and the hope of resurrection.

In Hebrew tradition, there were said to be 613 seeds in a pomegranate, which is the number of commandments in the Jewish Torah. To the Israelites, it symbolised the wisdom of its people and the Promised Land, and in the Islamic Qur'an, the fruit is said to be one of the gifts of Allah. Christianity has taken on the Persephone association, seeing it as a symbol of the Resurrection. In some scenes the infant Jesus holds the fruit.

Strawberries were associated with the Norse goddess of love, Freya, as well as Frigga, Odin's wife, who takes the spirits of children to the Afterlife by hiding them in strawberries. The fruit is connected with Aphrodite and Adonis as a plant of fertility and love. This led to an association with the Virgin Mary, representing her righteousness, and the fruitfulness of her spirit. Strawberry leaves are trifoliate, and so also represent the Holy Trinity.

147

Other Plants

Mistletoe was linked by the Anglo-Saxons to Freya, the goddess of love. In Norse mythology, Loki tricked the blind god Hodur into murdering Balder with an arrow made of mistletoe. The plant was sacred to the Druids, who used to collect it from sacred oaks **(left)** by means of a golden sickle on the sixth night of the Moon following midwinter; it was made into an elixir to cure fertility and as an antidote for any poison. Sprigs would then be distributed for people to put over their doorways as a protection against evil and thunder and lightning.

Kissing under the mistletoe derives from a Greek myth in which the plant once offended the gods, and was condemned to gaze forever at couples as they kissed beneath it. Druids also thought the juice to be the sperm of the gods, and it was used as an aphrodisiac. Mistletoe in berry **(left)** was associated with marriage rites, and with the festival of Saturnalia, due to its association with fertility. The festival was held over the midwinter, which was probably the origin of it being related to Christmas today. When Christianity came to Western Europe some tried to ban its use in churches, without success, probably due to the insistence of its parishioners. York Minster used to hold a special winter *Mistletoe Service*, where wrong-doers came to be pardoned for any sinful shenanigans.

Ivy represents eternal life and immortality due to its evergreen nature, as well as fidelity because of the way it clings to its host. It was sacred to the Greek god Dionysus, and his Roman counterpart Bacchus, who would be depicted with a crown of ivy and carry a staff entwined by the plant. Ivy is seen in churches as a decorative motif on stonework and in the borders of stained glass windows.

Bulrushes and Reeds. The story of the infant Moses being retrieved from the Nile **(bottom)** in a basket made of bulrushes (Exodus 2:1-10) ensured that the plant became a Christian sign of hope and salvation to the faithful (Job 8:11), and shows God's power to nurture and sustain. But the Moses story is simply a retelling of more ancient stories. In Roman mythology, Romulus and Remus were left in a vessel in the Tiber; the Sumerian king Sargon I was left in a basket in the Euphrates, and the god Horus was floated on an ark made of papyrus. Papyrus is of course associated with the Egyptians, as it was an excellent writing medium. Their huge temple columns were often abstractions of papyrus **(third image)**, and images of the plant feature in countless tomb and temple art. Bulrushes (also known as Cattails) appear in Native American myths, and the Mexican Kickappo Indians associated the plant with water serpents and would make offerings to the *Snake People* before gathering it. The pan pipes of the god Pan were made of reeds, which were also a purification plant to the Celts. Reed is symbolic of Christ's Passion, as a sponge soaked in vinegar was hung on the end of a length of reed to reach Jesus' mouth during his Crucifixion. It may also appear as a symbol of John the Baptist, due to his river baptisms.

Biblical Tripping?

In *'The Sacred Mushroom and the Cross'* (Allegro 1970), archaeologist John Allegro controversially expounds his theory that the roots of Christianity lay in fertility cults which would partake in such practices as ingesting *'visionary'*, psychoactive, plants to help

them connect with God, just as cultures had done for thousands of years. Allegro advocates that the Essenes and other early Christian groups used mind-altering plants to achieve ecstasy, and that these Judaic-Christian traditions were cultic expressions of Man's endless pursuit to discover power and knowledge – by any means available. He uses the example of a 13th century image of Adam and Eve in the Garden of Eden, depicted in a fresco at Plaincourault Abbey, France **(right)**; the figures stand either side of the Tree of Life, which, in this instance, does look like a huge version of the *'magic mushroom'*, Amanita muscuria.

In the Book of Exodus, God guides the Israelites out of bondage and intervenes en route to the Promised Land by instructing them to go and collect *'manna'*. This had to be done first thing in the morning, that very time before desert mushrooms shrivel under the hot Sun. Manna has never been identified, but some scholars believe it is a small, round desert mushroom; Moses said manna was the *'bread of the Lord'*, which is very similar to the Aztec name for the psychoactive psilocybe mushroom, *'flesh of the gods'*. Both the Old and New Testament contain descriptions of people entering a shamanic, trance-like state to witness *'visions'*, which is later repeated with Christian saints, and one has to ask as to what helped them enter these ethereal, dream-like states. Had Moses ingested mushrooms (manna) before his visionary journey up Mount Sinai to *envision* the Ten Commandments?

A window in Chartres Cathedral, dedicated to St Eustace, has several mushroom-like plants in the scene. Jesus is accompanied by red-capped mushrooms in a window at Notre Dame de Laon, France **(bottom)**. Another stained glass image at Laon shows a knight next to large, spotted mushrooms. Were the Knights Templar trying to tell us something? Some claim that the Eucharist of the Last Supper included the ingestion of psychoactive plants. St Peter's water miracle is portrayed on a Christian sarcophagus in the National Museum in Rome, and yet the image also depicts a mushroom-like plant on which two men are chewing!

The images on this page come from perhaps my favourite church window in terms of plant decoration. It depicts Jesus as the *Light of the World,* and is in St Mary's Church at Mortehoe, Devon. The window depicts ivy, the thornless Holy Thorn, holly, bramble and other plants, as well as the thorny crown on his head. It not only demonstrates the artistry of the stained glass window craftsman, but also serves as an acknowledgement of how plants have always been essential to Mankind, and not just from the point of view of a food or medicinal resource, but also as a constant and indispensible element of our spirituality.

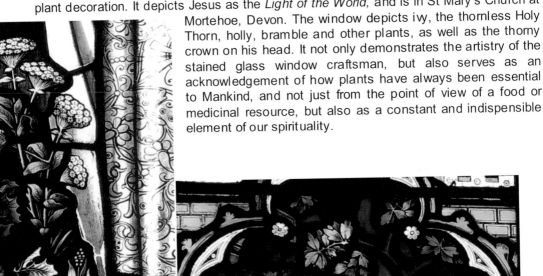

27. The Gates of Paradise

Of all the symbols that man has devised to represent transition, the gateway or door is the archetypal image of an entrance to another realm, a threshold to a different place or a new state of being. It is a liminal place, where we venture from the known to the unknown, and has inevitably become associated with death and rebirth. These entrances may be guarded, and may be open or locked, sometimes requiring a key or password, or admission requires a test to be completed – a quest no less. Gateways are symbols of initiation, and offer the promise of greater wisdom or a state of bliss. Modern tales, such as the *'Lion, the Witch and the Wardrobe'*, *'Alice in Wonderland'*, *'Lord of the Rings'*, and *'The Hobbit'*, all include secret entrances, which are negotiated through either solving a code, or perhaps by merely following intuition or curiosity; *'Open Sesame!'* is the magical phrase that had to be uttered to open the hidden entrance to the cave in *'Ali Baba and the Forty Thieves'*. This may have derived from Babylonian magical practices using sesame oil.

In ancient Egypt, the solar god Ra passed through twelve gates during his nightly passage through the Underworld, symbolising of the twelve hours of darkness. A common depiction in Egyptian art is the god Osiris standing on a boat, beckoning the deceased to board the vessel and travel with him through gates to the Otherworld. The Colossi of Memnon **(right)** are two 18m (59ft) high statutes of the Egyptian King Amenhotep III, which once stood at the entrance to his mortuary temple – the king's place of passage to the Otherworld.

Like the entrances to caves, the portals of Neolithic chambered tombs were liminal places through which the bones of the dead had to pass. But they were also where the living would enter to contact the ancestors. As if to set the scene, the entrance to Newgrange is guarded by a huge megalith decorated with spirals **(image p. 79)**. I have already detailed my opinions on how the entrance of West Kennet Long Barrow, Wiltshire, is a portal to another realm (Knight 2011), through which one can enter the otherworldly world of the prehistoric shaman. Just like caves, chambered tombs are places where we can 'journey' to states of being beyond that which we normally experience. As I enter the long barrow **(right)** I cross over to a holy space - both physically and spiritually.

The skies have been thought to contain entrances to Otherworldy realms (Collins 2006 and Gilbert 2005). In my book on the Cerne Giant (Knight 2013), I explain how

both the Great Rift in Cygnus, and a place above the extended arm of Orion (Osiris to the Egyptians), were seen as entrances, or *Star Gates*, to the realms of the dead, and how both of these areas once aligned with the Cerne Giant. In the Roman depiction of Mithras found at Walbrook, in London **(image p. 41)**, the god stands encircled by zodiacal imagery, as if slaying the bull at the gateway of initiation. The Romans would sometimes depict a deceased person as standing in front of a door which would be ajar, as if waiting for the gods to receive them. Romans also had minor deities watching over doorways into buildings; holly wreaths on the doors of homes at Christmas are a remnant of this, as holly was once seen as a protective spirit. The two-faced god Janus **(image p. 44)** was the ultimate guardian of doorways and gates, watching all who enter and exit; Romans adopted Janus as their sigil for the New Year, as he looks both back and forward in time, and from whom January is named. In Viking mythology, the Otherworld realm of Valhalla was sometimes depicted as a doorway or an arched gate, as shown in this carved stone from Sweden **(top)**.

Chinese and Babylonian temples were guarded by huge lions or lion-men, and in Greek myth a three-headed dog named Cerberus safeguarded the gates of Hades. A cave mouth at Chalcatzingo, in Mexico, has a huge beast carved around it, symbolising the passage from this world to another; this is also the case at the entrance of Gao Gajah, a sacred cave on Bali **(second image)**. In Hindu tradition, a holy gateway may also take the form of a monster's mouth, into which one must enter. The Mycenae *Lion Gate*, in Greece, is named after the two sculptured beasts that appear above the entrance **(image p. 55)**.

Equally symbolic are the profound entrances into Stonehenge, formed by the trilithons **(left)**; when I pass through these Neolithic portals I know I am entering a sacred place, in every sense of the word. In Japan, open arches known as *torii* mark the entrances to Shinto shrines and temples, symbolising the point where one passes from the mundane world into the sacred; the example shown here is the beautiful Akino Miyajima Torii **(left)**. These are echoed by the magnificent entrances to classical temples, and to their descendants, the great Gothic cathedrals of Europe; impressive doorways signify one is about to enter the house of God. One shown here is the beautifully crafted doorway of the church at Kilpeck, Herefordshire **(bottom right, next page)**, which equals anything at Rosslyn Chapel in my opinion; the Green Man, dragons, serpents, an ouroboros, and astrological signs are all here, plus a figure wearing a Phrygian cap, like that on the Walbrook carving, an ancient sign of initiation derived from the cult of Mithras.

Later, these grand portals were mirrored in secular buildings, to represent wealth, power and knowledge; the entrance to the Natural History Museum, London, must be one of the finest modern examples. Gateways were also used to symbolise victory and imperial might, such as the Arc de Triomphe in Paris and Marble Arch in London. In Freemasonry, twin columns known as Boaz and Jachin feature in rituals of the First and Second Degrees. They are named after those that stood at the entrance to King Solomon's Temple in Jerusalem.

Where water issues from underground, such as at Bath **(image p. 47)**, the sacred, life-sustaining waters were seen to emerge from the vulva of the Earth Goddess. The woman's yoni itself has been seen as a sacred gateway by many cultures; in Hebrew, the word for *door* is *daleth* which also means *'womb'*, the gateway through which all humans must pass. The Celts thought lakes were entrances to the Otherworld; the Lady of the Lake gifting Excalibur is a famous Arthurian myth.

Moses created a *'gateway'* as such when he parted the waters of the Red Sea for the Israelites, just as the Egyptian army approached. St Peter is often depicted holding the keys to the Gates of Heaven **(right)**, and is sometimes shown about to unlock those proverbial *Pearly Gates* **(below left)**; this imagery comes from when Jesus said to Peter, *'I will give you the keys to the Kingdom of Heaven'* (Matthew 16:19). The Church later adopted keys as symbols of its authority, proof that it had the blessing of God. The term *Pearly Gates* actually occurs in Revelations 21:1-27, when we are told that in the New Jerusalem or Paradise, *'the twelve gates were twelve pearls, each gate being made from a single pearl'.* You may recall that the Egyptian Sun god Ra had to go through twelve gates in order to be *'reborn''* at the next sunrise – what a coincidence! It is interesting that keys had once been as symbol of Janus, the transitional god of the Romans.

Doors are symbolic of transition, a passage from one world or state of being to another. The door has particular relevance to Christianity because of Jesus' words, *'I stand at the door and knock. If anyone hears my voice and opens the door, I will come in...'* (Revelations 3:20), and the passage, *'... knock and the door will be opened to you'* (Luke 11:9). Jesus can be seen knocking on the door at Mortehoe, Devon **(image p. 150)**.

153

28. The Flood

The concept of an all consuming deluge that destroys most or all of Mankind is one of the most convincing pieces of evidence that Christianity adopted myths that were already universal and ancient by the time of Jesus. Water represents cleansing, emotions and the flow of life; it can signify both abundance and, in the case of the flood, destruction and divine retribution. It the case of flood narratives, water is the means by which deities seek to bring about a realignment of spiritual and natural laws when humanity has upset the equilibrium, in order to bring about a renewal.

The Aborigines of Western Australia tell of the Dreamtime flood, which inundated the land and killed everyone except a girl and a boy, who were saved by grabbing the tail of a kangaroo that took them to higher ground. Several African myths speak of floods, one telling of how a deluge changed humans into monkeys and lizards.

In Indian Hindu mythology, texts such as the 'Satapatha Brahmana' (written c. 700-300BC) tell of how the god Vishnu, in his avatar of the fish-god Matsyavatara, warns the first man, Manu, of an impending great flood, advising him to build a gigantic boat. As the waters subside, the god led the vessel to the shore **(below)**. Irish legend tells how the first people to arrive in Ireland were led by Cessair, daughter of Noah's son Bith, who was told by Noah to go to the western edge of the world in order to escape the impending Flood. Chinese traditions also tell of *Great Floods,* but these are usually natural disasters, as opposed to divine punishment. They usually involve heroes attempting to mitigate the disaster, leading eventually to the betterment of Mankind. In the mythology of the Hopi of North America, *Spider Grandmother* makes boats from reeds in which to save righteous people from a great deluge. Pre-Columbian Aztec myth speaks of how a human couple survived the flood by hiding in a hollow vessel, but when the smoke from their fire reached the gods they were turned into dogs or vultures, depending on the account. It is said that the reason Machu Picchu, in Peru, was built on such an elevated locality in the Andes was so the Inca could escape the reaches of a great flood.

The famous classical legend of a deluge is of course that of Atlantis, the locality of which people are seeking to this day. This land was written of by the Greek Plato in 360BC, although many historians and philosophers now regard his story to have been intended as an allegory of Plato's idealised state of Athens. His story ends with the Atlanteans falling out of favour with the gods and being consumed by the waters of the Atlantic Ocean. Some researchers, however, have mused that the demise of Atlantis may have lead to the founding of the Mayan and Aztec civilisations by survivors.

Others speculate that Plato's account could be a distant memory of the eruption of Thera in the 17th or 16th century BC, and of the subsequent tsunami that devastated the Minoan civilisation. Others believe that the flooding of the Black Sea by the waters of the Mediterranean c. 5,600BC may be the catalyst for the Atlantis story. Greek mythology also tells how the god Zeus was angered that humans were always warring and punished them with a flood; Prometheus found out about the plan and instructed Deukalion to build an ark.

In one account of the Babylonian *Epic of Gilgamesh* (c. 700BC), a wise man tells Gilgamesh of a flood that will last seven days. Instructed by the god Ea, Uta-Napishtim (or Utnapashtim) built a ship for his family, servants and animals **(top)**, and rode out the storm, which lasted for six days (the duration God took to create the Universe in the Bible). The ship eventually came to rest on Mount Nisir, and Uta-Napishtim released a dove and a swallow to search for more dry land. The god Enlil acknowledged his efforts by granting him and his wife immortality. This is mirrored by the Sumerian flood myth, where it is Enki who warns Ziusudra. Based on his reading of the dimensions of the ark on an ancient Babylonian tablet, Prof Irving Finkel, of the British Museum, was overseer of a reconstruction. His ark was, in effect, more like a huge coracle than the traditional, elongated, ship-like structure.

In Genesis, we are told that Noah was a descendant of Seth, Adam and Eve's third son. God (Yahweh) apparently decided to destroy the world due to mankind's wicked ways, but saw Noah as a virtuous man and told him to build a huge vessel for himself, his family and a male and female of every bird and animal. It rained for 40 days and 40 nights, until all the land was inundated. After 150 days the waters began to subside, and the ark came to rest on top of Mount Ararat. Noah sent out a dove (as did Uta-Napishtim in the Babylonian flood myth), which returned with a fresh olive branch in its beak, indicating to Noah the floods were receding, as shown here in Canterbury Cathedral **(second image, and image p. 113)**. Noah often holds a miniature ark, such as here at St Cross, Winchester **(right)**.

It is interesting that in Greek mythology, a dove with an olive branch is a symbol of Athena, as her attribute of the renewal of life. The duration of the flood is linked to ancient associations with the number 40, such as the Roman belief that the dead took 40 days to pass over; Babylonian astronomers believed that the 40 days when the Pleiades were not visible in the sky marked a period of storms and floods; in Egyptian myths, Osiris disappeared for 40 days; and Moses conversed with

God on Mount Sinai for 40 days and 40 nights. It is also interesting that in the Babylonian flood epic, Uta-Napishtim was rewarded with immortality, and that Noah also seems to have been similarly bestowed by God, as he lived to be over 600 years old! He is shown here giving thanks to Yahweh in a beautifully crafted window **(bottom)** in the Holy Trinity Cathedral, Addis Ababa, Ethiopia. The rainbow, seen at the start and end of this chapter, is mentioned by God in his address to Noah, telling him that the flood will subside, '... *when the bow is seen in the clouds'.*

What *is* missing in the Biblical version of the flood is the Goddess. In the Sumerian and Babylonian versions, Earth goddesses Ishtar and Inanna lament the demise of the human race, who they themselves had created. The only relic of the Goddess in the Noah version is the dove, an emblem of the divine feminine (see p. 110).

Noah's ark became a symbol of the Church saving Mankind from the destruction of the world; The Noah story is also told in the Qur'an, where he is known as Nûh, who Muslims regard as an important prophet. Jesus was also to use the concept of a salvation vessel on the Sea of Galilee. This is of course mirrored by several ancient myths, such as Osiris taking the dead to the otherworld on a boat down the Nile, and the Ferryman story of Greek Mythology.

We must also remember how, in Exodus, God made the waters of the Red Sea consume the Pharaohs' army in the Moses story; yet another example of God using water as a purgative.

I find myths of The Flood to be remarkably universal, recurrent and similar. With climate change, it makes me wonder if, in hundreds of years time, people will be relating stories about our sunken lands and rising sea levels; it may well turn out that one man's global warming is another man's divine retribution!

29. Sacred Waters

Water has played an imperative role in Man's spiritual practices and myths for thousands of years. Water has unique qualities, possessing the ability to transform its shape into any vessel into which it is poured, and can transmute from a liquid to a solid, as well as to vapour. The mysterious appearance of morning dewdrops on spider's webs must have caused wonder when observed thousands of years ago, just as it does today **(right)**. Water is essential to life on Earth, thus connecting all living things on the planet, and yet it can also be associated with death and purging. Evidence of water symbolism has been found on many artifacts dating right back to 6000BC, and water cults existed in all the major civilisations, from Greece to Egypt, from Babylon to Rome. Seas and rivers are symbolic of rites of passage and transformation, and primordial waters feature in many Creation myths (see chapter 13); countless legends also tell of how water will be part of future destructions of the Earth (French 2012).

In ceremonial magic, the water element is incorporated into the Golden Dawn system; the archangel of water is St Gabriel, and in the *Supreme Invoking Ritual* water is one of the points of the pentagram. In sacred geometry, the feminine symbolism of water, the yin principle, is defined by the inverted triangle, which resembles a chalice or the pubic triangle **(right)**. In a hexagram, one of the basic forms in sacred geometry, the yin triangle balances the upward-pointing yang triangle **(image p. 168)**. Some Islamic mosques have their floors inlaid with blue tiles, to represent water as the source of life; this is displayed in spectacular style at the Shah Mosque at Isfahan, Iran, where the floors, walls and ceilings are all iridescent blue **(right)**.

Water is associated with the emotions, intuition and psychic abilities, and is linked with the subconscious. In Hindu tradition, water is connected with intuition and emotions and is linked with Chandra (the Moon) and Shakra (Venus). Astrologically, Pisces, Cancer and Scorpio are water signs. We have been in the Piscean Age since the time of Jesus, which is said to be an age of monotheism and the fish, which will end, or has ended depending on various interpretations, sometime between 1989 and 2680AD.

To Pagan cultures, water often symbolised the Earth Mother, through whom life was assured, and the waters at springs and cave mouths rose from her womb, purifying and regenerating all those who drank of the healing elixir. Perhaps the reflective qualities of the waters of a calm lake led to their association with the Underworld. Many divinities were born from water, and the Greeks would annually wash statues of their gods with water to purify them. Ritual bathing was carried out by many ancient cultures, and was the forerunner of Christian Baptism. Egyptian art often depicted Osiris on a boat, carrying people on their journey to eternity **(image p. 40)**.

The ancient Chinese science of geomancy is known as Feng Shui, which literally means, *'wind and water'*. When considering the location for a new building, the effects of the mountain (yang) energies and the water (yin) energies are taken into account. Places where waters flow gently in wide meanders are considered to be where *Chi* energy is favourable. In Chinese folklore, baby dragons hatch from eggs on hillsides next to running water. In Taoism, water represents intelligence and wisdom, flexibility and pliancy, after water's ability to find its way around obstacles.

The Sea

The sea is formless and full of potential and regeneration, and yet can be destructive and the abode of monsters and other hidden perils. The Greek god Poseidon (the Roman god Neptune) was ruler of the oceans, and was a god to be feared as he had the power to whip up storms and powerful waves with his trident; the image here **(top)** is Neptune at a fountain in Berlin, Germany. Jason and Argonauts went on their quest across the sea on a ship called the Argo.

In Norse myth, the seas were said to be the blood of the giant Ymir, and it is interesting that God used Moses' staff to turn the waters of the Nile to blood (Exodus 7:19). Viking ship burials involved the deceased being set adrift onto the sea in a long ship, which would then be set alight with flaming arrows.

Egyptians believed that boats carried the souls of the dead to the Otherworld, and King Arthur was also taken on a boat, called Pridwen, on his final journey to Avalon, the Underworld, shown here in a 19th century painting **(left)**.

Sometimes mythical islands lie across the seas, such as Avalon, as well as Utopia, Thomas More's legendary land. The Fortunate Isles, or Isles of the Blessed, feature in Greek and Celtic mythology, and were a place where heroes and other favoured mortals were received by the gods, to live in Paradise. Holy Islands around the world, such as Lindisfarne, the Isle of Man, the Isle of Wight, Iona, and St Michael's Mount, offer a watery separation from the outside world. Britain itself was once regarded as a holy island of myth and magic (Biltcliffe 2009).

158

Rivers

Rivers are symbolic of life and regeneration, the flow of time, and the span of a human life from their source (our birth) to where they meet the sea (our death). Rivers feature in countless myths from across the world; the Celts, for instance, called river mists the *'Dragon's Breath'*. Buddha sat under a tree next to a river to attain enlightenment. The Styx was a river in Greek mythology that was the boundary between the Earth and the Underworld or Hades, and the souls of the dead were carried across by Charon, the ferryman, as shown in this 19th century painting **(bottom image, previous page)**. The

Nile, Ganges and the Euphrates all made possible the rise of civilisations that were able to flourish along their banks; Mesopotamia literally means *'land of two rivers'*, referring to the Euphrates and Tigris. These rivers, along with the River Araxes and the Greater Zab, are the *'four rivers of paradise'* of Genesis, and are thought to have determined the locality of the Garden of Eden (Collins, 2014, p. 234-5). The Mesopotamian river deity was Enki (or Ea), whom you may recall told Uta-Napishtim to build an ark to survive the forthcoming deluge; Ea means, *'House of the Water'*. He is shown here with rivers flowing into him **(right)**.

In England, the River Kennet in Wiltshire has a close relationship with many sacred sites, such as Silbury Hill, and at Stonehenge an earthen avenue goes from the monument down to the River Avon. Newgrange, Ireland's premier Neolithic chambered tomb, is located next to the River Boyne, and huge boulders were collected from the river on which to carve spirals and other motifs **(images p. 79 & 170)**. According to Yuri Leitch, three Somerset rivers, the Parrett, Cary and the Brue, help define the Glastonbury Zodiac (Leitch ed, 2013).

Waterfalls were often seen as the abode of otherworldy creatures and spirits. According the Chinese mythology, a *Dragon's Gate* is located at the top of a waterfall, for if a carp makes it up the waterfall it will be turned into a dragon; this proverb is used to encourage people not to give up. Classical and Celtic legends also include waterfalls, and it is easy to see how these dynamic and inspirational places were woven into cultural heritage. I regularly visit the White Lady waterfall at Lydford, on the edge of Dartmoor; as I experience the natural combination of raw power and beauty, I cannot help but be uplifted **(right)**. Another such empowering place is St Nectan's Glen, Cornwall **(image p. 198)**, where the waters cascade through a perforated rock – the yoni of the Earth Goddess.

The Great Serpent Mound of Ohio **(image p. 122)** was built by the Native Americans right next to a river called Brush Creek. In ancient Egypt, sluice gates were periodically opened to let in the waters of the Nile so as to completely surround the Sphinx.

The names of rivers often reflect ancient deities. The Seine comes from the goddess Sequanna; the Dee is from Deva (*'goddess'*); the Bride in Dorset derives from the Celtic goddess Bridget/Brighid, and the River Thames comes from Tamesa or Tamesis, referring to a feminine water deity; the River Lea, also in London, is Lugh's River. The

Ganges is revered as the goddess Ganga; pilgrims take water from its source and transport it around 3000km (c.1860 miles) to pour as a libation over a phallic-shaped lingam at Ramesvara, India, in doing so uniting the fertilising male (Shiva) with the divine feminine (water from the source). The Greeks had many water deities, some of which gave their names to rivers, such as the Achelous. Just as rivers had their own deities, smaller streams and pools were also the realm of water nymphs, some of which could bestow the gift of prophecy. The Romans carried on this tradition, and water nymphs often accompanied superior deities such as Jupiter, Diana and Ceres.

Hindu, Buddhist, Islamic and Jewish traditions tell of four rivers flowing in the four directions, and this was later adopted by Christianity as the *'four rivers of salvation'* – spirit, sustenance, enlightenment, and death.

Lakes and Pools

Many myths are associated with enclosed water, which was often the abode of female enchantresses, dragons, fairies or nymphs, and hidden beasts, such as at Loch Ness. Lakes were entrances to the Underworld, and Iron Age water burials testify that fenland and peat bogs were seen as liminal places where the souls of the dead could be released. Will-o-the-wisp lights may be seen over marshes and bogs at night, which have been regarded as ghosts, fairies, serpents, witches and other supernatural beings; they are known as Pixie Lights in the West Country. The River Lea (*Lugh's River*) rises from springs at Waulid's Bank, a Neolithic site where tradition says Lugh took the waters to receive his divine powers (Thorley, 2012). The Padstow 'Obby 'Oss used to pause at Treator Pool, where the 'Oss showered onlookers with its waters for good luck, echoing ancient purification rites.

Narcissus was the vain character from Greek myth who ignored the beautiful nymph Echo, choosing instead to look at his own reflection in a pool **(image p. 144)**. He did this for so long that he died. Merlin ordered a pool to be drained of water, revealing two

opposing dragons, one red dragon the other white (p. 129), by which he foretold the outcome of the wars with the Saxons. In Arthurian mythology, the Lady of the Lake rises from the waters, gifting the magical sword Excalibur **(left)**, which can be compared to the Greek goddess Aphrodite, who in similar manner rose from a lake. Lake Titicaca, in Peru, was a pilgrimage destination for the Inca, for they believed that Viracocha, the creator god, emerged from its sacred waters.

In the vast Karnac temple complex at Thebes, the Egyptians created two lakes, one in the precinct of Amun-Ra, the Sun god, the other a crescent-shaped expanse in the precinct of Mut, the Earth Goddess. These lakes are thought to represent the primal waters of the Creation, and of the Underworld. When I visited Karnac, I noticed how the buildings were reflected in the clear, still waters **(left)**; the obelisks appeared to be reaching down into the Underworld, the phallus of Osiris literally penetrating the moistness of the Earth Mother. This association between water and the Afterlife is expressed in the waters next to the Taj Mahal mausoleum, at Agra, India.

The Dead Sea is in reality a land-locked lake, seen as

a sacred place that is mentioned several times in the Bible; it was the home of the Gnostic Essenes, who left behind the Dead Sea Scrolls in nearby caves; the Biblical town of Jericho is not far distant from its waters; also close by is Masada, the mountain top site of the last Jewish stronghold that was eventually captured by the Romans after its inhabitants committed suicide; and, finally, John the Baptist was imprisoned in a fort next to the Dead Sea prior to his execution. With its high saline levels, the Dead Sea is portrayed in Hebrew tradition as a spiritual wasteland, and the sinful cities of Sodom and Gomorrah are said to have been on its shores.

The Pool of Bethesda is located in the Muslim Quarter of Jerusalem, and is associated with healing. Records of it date back to the 8th century BC, and it is mentioned in the Old Testament. It was used by both Jews and Romans, and is supposed to be where Jesus cured a lame man. It has been suggested that this story may have been to Christianise a place used by the cult of Aesculapius, which was associated with curative wells; Aesculapius was also accredited with the title *'Saviour'.*

In terms of earth mysteries, Alfred Watkins thought ponds to be useful ley markers, as their reflected light would be visible from long distances. Dowsers across the world have found a strong association between dowsable earth energies and underground water, and for hundreds of years, perhaps even thousands, people have dowsed to locate hidden water beneath their feet. Earth mysteries researchers have found that many of the world's major sacred sites, such as Avebury, are sited over huge natural aquifers, and that these underground reservoirs influence what is experienced at sacred sites on the landscape above.

Springs and Wells

Places where water emerges from underground have long been held as magical portals, often with guardian fairies and nymphs in attendance, as water issues from within the body of the Earth Goddess. They were often ancient places of prophecy and of healing, and some developed into major temple complexes, as at Bath. At the beautiful spring at Sta Cristina on Sardinia **(right)**, which I have had the privilege to visit, the waters issue at the bottom of a flight of prehistoric steps. The famous Greek oracle centre of Delphi is located in a cave by the source of the Castalian Fountain or Spring, which still flows; those coming to consult the oracle would first wash their hair in the waters. The geometric centre of the Holy land is thought to be at a place called Jacob's Well, and there was a well associated with a Druidic sacred grove on the Isle of Wight (Biltcliffe and Hoare, 2012). The Norse god Odin gave up one of his eyes to drink from the *Fountain of Knowledge* that flowed under Yggdrasil, the Tree of Life. Irish myth speaks of the *Salmon of Wisdom* residing at the Seghias, an Otherworldy well, which if caught and eaten would bestow a person with bardic powers.

At one time there were over 2000 holy wells in England and 1200 in Wales (Bord and Bord 1986); Holy Well and Holywell are both recurring place names around Britain. I have previously covered Dorset's water-related sacred sites and folklore in another book (Knight 1998, p. 98-119). Bath was one of several places of Roman water worship **(image p. 47)**, where hundreds of tons of votive offerings were deposited in the waters,

which were sacred to the goddess Sulis/Minerva **(image p. 14)**; the modern ritual of dropping a coin in a wishing well derives from such ancient votive practices.

A decree by Pope Gregory in 595AD was particularly directed at Britain, as the Venerable Bede recounts: *'The temples of the idols in that nation ought not be destroyed, but only the idols in them. Let holy water be made and sprinkled in said temples, and let altars be erected, and relics placed'*. Old Pagan practices were hidden behind a Christian façade, as wells and springs were rededicated to Christian saints and used to baptise converts (Bord and Bord 1986 for more details). Right up to the 12th century decrees were being issued by a frustrated Church that sought to ban tenacious survivals of water worship. Well dressing still continues today in many places, and mirrors ancient Pagan rites at water sources.

Many wells are re-dedicated to the Virgin Mary (there are 70 in Scotland and 76 in Wales), which are either dedicated to her by name, or are simply *'Lady's Well'*. Many of these are the rebranding of springs once sacred to local water goddesses, and St Catherine is a common dedication as a result. Where there was no holy well, baptism moved into the church, in the form of the font. As the Church's grip tightened, old sacred wells and springs were relegated, sadly, to mere water resources.

Water from Chalice Well, Glastonbury, is said to be stained red **(top)** by the blood of Jesus, brought there in the Holy Grail by Joseph of Arimathea. Pagans see this red colouration of the waters, which is caused by a high iron content, as the *'Red waters of birth and menstruation',* flowing from the vulva of the Goddess (Jones 1994). At a Wishing Well on Alderley Edge, Cheshire, water drips down a rock face into a stone trough, and carved into the rock above is the phrase, *'Drink of this and take thy fill for the water falls by the wizards will';* legend says that King Arthur and his knights sleep in a local cave.

Churches that are sited on or next to wells and springs demonstrate how Pagan sacred places were taken over, such as here at Frome, Somerset **(centre)**, where one finds the church behind the issuing spring. Ancient water sources are situated (or were formerly) under cathedrals at Winchester, Canterbury, Ely, Salisbury, Wells, Exeter and York. Under Winchester Cathedral the crypt occasionally floods, enabling Antony Gormley's beautiful sculpture to be reflected in the waters **(left)**.

At countless other sites, water issues out of the earth inside churchyards, or close by, and which, ironically, enabled well worship to continue. Four of my favourite examples of sacred springs adjacent to churches are at Bodmin, Box, Frome and Cerne

Abbas. Many wells became famous for their curative waters, such as at Bath, Hotwells in Bristol, and Buxton in Derbyshire. Some became places of pilgrimage, famously at Holywell in Flintshire, Little Walsingham in Norfolk, and Lourdes in France (see below).

Ritual Bathing and Baptism

Baptism is the Christian sacrament of admission and adoption, whereby a candidate is immersed in water, either in a baptismal pool, bath or river. The word comes from the Greek *baptisma,* a term for ritual washing. Baptism has similarities to *Tvilah*, a Jewish purification rite involving immersion in water, which is actually a requirement for conversion to Judaism. John the Baptist, a forerunner to Jesus, baptised in rivers, and his baptism of Jesus, shown here at Exeter Cathedral, Devon **(top)**, is of course the most famous baptism, and one which I shall return to later. It is recorded that early Christians were baptised naked, although this practice had lapsed by the second century AD. Christening is the name given to infant baptism, the earliest record of which also goes back to the 2nd century AD.

Ritual bathing was carried out by ancient Greeks, and is also still carried today out by Jews, Muslims and Hindis. At Varanasi, India, stone landings and steps enable pilgrims to bathe in the Ganges, which is said to cleanse them of the karma of previous lives.

Holy water is used for the cleansing of evil and sin, and is mentioned several times in the Bible. For instance, in Ezekiel 36:25, one can read, *'I will sprinkle clean water on you, and you shall be clean from all your filthiness, and from all your idols I will cleanse you'.* Today, the sprinkling of holy water on a victim seems obligatory in any exorcism.

Fonts (from the Latin *fontis,* meaning *'fountain/spring')* are usually placed near the rear of the church, often close to the door, and any water used in font rituals has to be blessed beforehand. Fonts are fascinating monuments, as they are often adorned with Pagan images, especially the older Saxon and Norman fonts. Some fine examples can be found around Britain, such as in the church at Lostwithiel in Cornwall, which has a grotesque head bearing a spiral on its forehead, at the point of the *'third eye'* in the Eastern chakra system **(image p. 81)**. The font at Avebury portrays two dragons **(image p. 129)**, whilst in the church at Lewannick, Cornwall, the font is carved with a labyrinth, a pentagram and a spiral **(image p. 85)**. The ancient font at Toller Fratrum, Dorset, is adorned with half human/half animal figures **(bottom)**, including some severed human heads! (see Knight 1998, p. 50, Knight & Power 2000, p. 32).

A piscina (Latin for *'fish pond')* is a shallow basin placed near the altar or in the vestry of a church and used for washing communion vessels, the disposal of used baptismal waters and oils, or else for ritual ablution. Stoups of holy water are often placed near the entrances of churches, especially those of the Roman Catholic faith, into which entrants dip their fingers and make the sign of the cross. It is a descendant of Jewish practices of ritual washing as one enters a synagogue.

Water Miracles

There is plenty of miraculous folklore associated with watery places. Merlin is said to have cured himself of his madness by drinking the curative waters from a spring that magically appeared out of the ground. Also in Arthurian myth, water can possess miraculous powers of regeneration if drunk from the Holy Grail.

An interesting example of the adoption of Pagan mythology can be seen in the act of creating water where none previously existed. Mithras, the bull-slaying Roman god who had been adopted from the Persians and the Greeks, is depicted in some sculptures as emerging from a rock, his so-called *Water Miracle*, in which he is rises from the earth like a spring. Some carvings incorporated a hole for a fountain, whilst one had the mask of a

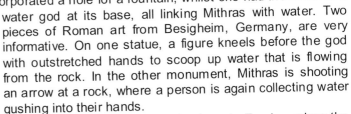

water god at its base, all linking Mithras with water. Two pieces of Roman art from Besigheim, Germany, are very informative. On one statue, a figure kneels before the god with outstretched hands to scoop up water that is flowing from the rock. In the other monument, Mithras is shooting an arrow at a rock, where a person is again collecting water gushing into their hands.

With this in mind, it is interesting how, in Exodus, when the Israelites cannot find water in the desert, Moses is told by God if he strikes a rock with his staff water will gush out; he does as instructed and water duly appears (Exodus 17:5-6), as shown here at Hornblotton church, Somerset **(top)**. It is interesting that the Moses and Persian Mithras miracles may have originated round about the same time, and I believe that the Hebrew version involving Moses is almost certainly a corruption of the Mithras story. To these two water-gushing exploits we can add the tale of St Augustine. When the missionary saint arrived in Cerne Abbas, Dorset (site of the Cerne Giant), he was originally sent packing by the locals. On his return, it is said that he struck the ground with his staff, at which point the waters of a *'crystal clear fountain of water'* sprang up from the earth, which he used to baptise converts (Knight 2013). Even though it has been known as St Augustine's Well ever since, I somehow suspect that the waters may have been flowing prior to the arrival of the saint!

St Christopher (whose name means *'Christ bearer'*) was a hermit martyred in the 3rd century. He famously carried a small child on his shoulders across a swollen river **(left)**, remarking how heavy the child was (the example here is in Cologne Cathedral). The infant then revealed himself as, *'Christ your king'*, and vanished. It is fascinating that this story parallels that of Greek hero Jason, of the Argonaut legends. He carried an elderly woman across a raging river, also remarking how heavy she was for an elder, at which point she identified herself as the goddess Hera.

Moses and his God famously parted the waters of the Red Sea **(left)**, or possibly the *Reed Sea,* which subsequently submerged the pursuing Egyptian army; this is the portend of the concept of salvation by baptismal water.

Some other saints have been involved in watery miracles;

St Barry banished a serpent or dragon from a mountain into Lough Lagan, and the holy well there is said to have sprung up where his knee touched the earth. At St Teilo's Well, at LIndeilo Llydarth, Pembroke, the waters were curative if drunk from the actual skull of St Teilo, a 6th century saint. This is the legacy of a long connection between head cults and water. A vision of the Virgin Mary, *Our Lady of Lourdes*, was claimed to have been seen at a spring by St Bernadette (then a 14 year old peasant girl) in 1858, and since then miraculous healings have been reported when the faithful have either bathed in the spring, or else drank its curative pure waters.

Walking on water is one of the miracles performed by Jesus: *'And in the fourth watch of the night he came to them, walking on the sea'* (Matthew 14:22-34). The story goes that the disciples were fishing on the Sea of Galilee and were fearful after the waters became stormy. Jesus appeared walking on the waters, as seen here at Crediton, Devon **(right)**; he then boarded the boat, at which point the storm subsided. St Peter also emulated Jesus by briefly walking on the waters until his faith wavered; he began to sink until Jesus held out a hand to him. However, walking on the sea is an ancient theme. In Babylonia, Tammuz ('*Lord of the Net'*) appeared from the waters to teach of his wisdom. In Greek and Roman tradition, Poseidon and Neptune, respectively, travelled over the sea in a chariot. Poseidon's son, Orion, was gifted the ability to walk on water. In another Roman myth, it is Neptune who stills the winds and calms the waters of the sea. Buddhist monk Huang-po also walked on water when he found his way barred by a river.

It may be useful to remind ourselves of the number of Jesus' miracles that are fish or water-related: Jesus changed water into wine at a wedding in Cana (which, by the way, the Roman god Mithras and Dionysus are both accredited with doing, as we shall see in more detail later); the disciples caught a net full of fish when told to cast it on the other side of the boat; the miracle of the five loaves and two fishes; the fish and temple tax miracle, whereby Jesus tells someone to open the mouth of a fish as it will contain coins by which to pay their taxes; as already detailed, Jesus walks on water and calms the storm on the Sea of Galilee; and after the Resurrection Jesus again appears to the disciples on the waters, and ensures they land another good catch. Clearly, Neptune and Poseidon, the ancient deities of the seas, had been replaced by a new 'water god'.

The concept that Jesus and his disciples were *'fishers of men'* also has its origins back in ancient Egypt; the god Osiris would collect the souls of the dead and sail down the Nile to the Underworld **(image p. 40)**. The passage of the Sun god Ra each night was portrayed as the god journeying on a river boat **(below)**. Both Osiris and Ra were solar deities that were destined to be replaced by Jesus, so it was inevitable that he would be involved in miracles involving boats and water.

30. Triangles
and the Star of David

Triangles can be readily observed in Nature, such as shark's teeth and their the fins, individual wings of moths and butterflies **(left)**, flower petals, leaves, the growth of stalactites and stalagmites, various mammalian ears, and the profile of many trees, mountain peaks and volcanoes. Mount Fuji is Japan's highest mountain and is sacred to both Shinto and Buddhist faiths, who believe it is a physical manifestation of deities, and its classic triangular shape is unmistakable **(second image)**. Glastonbury Tor is also triangular, be it with softened edges, when viewed from certain directions.

Triangles are fundamental to the very act of creation, and of the essence of being. As opposed to swinging between polarities, the third element of a triangle introduces stability (French 2012, p. 34-41). Cuneiform is one of the earliest forms of writing and features triangular elements, as shown in this Sumerian example from 26th century BC **(bottom)**; the name cuneiform literally means, *'wedge-shaped'*. The number three is sacred in most ancient cultures, and continues to be so in many religions today; the Egyptian trinity was Osiris, Isis and Horus. Triple-headed gods are frequent in ancient cultures, such as Brahman (Hindu) and Apedemak (Nubian). Over twenty examples been found attributed to the Celtic Gauls, so clearly triplism played a major role in the lives of the Celts (Green 1989). The concept of a Triple Goddess is also very ancient, as we will see below when it was adopted by Christianity. There is even a constellation called Triangulum, which was known to Greek, Roman and Arab astronomers, and is configured by three main stars.

Several small spherical stones bearing geometrical symbols have been found at Neolithic sites in Scotland, and have been interpreted as representing the *Platonic Solids,* even though they were fashioned a thousand years before the Greek mathematician (Critchlow 2007). I had the pleasure of seeing some of them in the National Museum of Scotland, Edinburgh **(image p. 80)**, and some of these are inscribed with triangular divisions.

I have already demonstrated that the inverted triangle

represents water **(image p. 157)**, as well as the divine feminine, the pubic mound, the yoni, and receptivity; various Neolithic cultures used this sigil to represent women and the divine feminine **(images p. 199 & 220)**. The upward-pointing equilateral triangle represents the male principle, along with fire, the phallus, fire, ascent, the heart and royalty. The Hittites associated this upward-pointing triangle with kingship and health, and the Maya thought this symbolised the shape of the corn as it broke through the earth, representing fertility and the male principle. Several Neolithic megaliths in Ireland are carved with triangles, most notably at Newgrange, Dowth and Knowth, all in the Boyne Valley (Brennan 1994). On Malta, Klaus Albrecht found several triangles incorporated into the plans of Neolithic temples, such as at Hagar Qim and Kordin (Albrecht 2001).

It has been noted for some time that stone circles and chambered tombs may comprise a combination of tall, pillar-like stones, which symbolise the masculine principle, and triangular stones, sometimes displaying holes and depressions, which are thought to be symbolic of the feminine principle (Meaden 1991). I have found this arrangement across Europe, such as at West Kennet Long Barrow, Avebury and Brittany (Knight 2011).

Pyramids are perhaps the most spectacular examples of the triangle. The square base symbolises the plane of the earth, whilst the four upwardly-pointing triangular sides meet at a fifth point, representing ether – the fifth element. A pyramid reaches up to the heavens, the apex of which symbolises Mankind's striving to reach the gods on high. Pyramid construction reached magnificent and colossal proportions in ancient Egypt on the Giza Plateau **(below left)**, but they also feature in spectacular monuments in Meso-America. The controversial Bosnian Pyramids are at the very least amazing triangular-shaped hills, such as the '*Sun Pyramid*' shown here **(below right)**. Britain's most impressive pyramid, Silbury Hill, is roughly triangular in profile, but here the top is truncated with a flat platform **(images p. 32 & p. 70)**.

The *Dragon's Eye* is an ancient Germanic symbol, consisting of an isosceles triangle pointing downwards, in the centre of which are three more triangles which come to a single point. Triple triangles are associated with the Goddess and the Nine Muses.

The very act of surveying the land is known as *triangulation*, in which *three* points and three lines are required to position an object accurately. Chris Street has proposed many triangular and hexagonal alignments across the London landscape (Street 2000 and 2010), and other landscape triangles have also been proposed (Heath and Michell 2004). The Golden Section or Golden Triangle is one of the basic foundations of sacred geometry, comprising an isosceles triangle with angles of 72º, 72º and 36º (totalling

180°). In a five-pointed pentagram, each corner of the figure is a Golden Triangle. This triangle is involved in many sacred sites around the world; Gary Biltcliffe, for instance, found churches on Portland to be located so as to form triangles (Biltcliffe 2009, p. 73-4). Elsewhere, I have previously described how the Golden Triangle can be overlaid onto West Kennet Long Barrow **(bottom left),** so as to enclose its chambers (Knight 2011). Across the world, other authors, such as Henry Lincoln, Nicholas Mann and Michael Poynder for example, have found churches that mark the points of hexagrams. Surveyor Alexander Thom controversially declared that sacred geometry, including the triangle, could be found in most stone circles he surveyed (Thom 1967).

The Greeks and Romans used triangles on their friezes as decorative art, so it is of no surprise that Christianity adopted this motif. This is also true of the hexagram, the so called Star of David, which is a common icon in churches. Hexagrams and hexagons

are created by combining the two yin and yang triangles, which then represents balance of Universal forces. This form can be seen in Nature, in the shape of the honeycombs of bees **(image p. 7)**, in flowers such as the Iris and Daffodil, and in snowflakes. This divinely-proportioned figure was used in the design of many ancient temples, as well as in Knights Templar buildings. The hexagram is also known as the Seal of Solomon and is a pre-eminent symbol of Judaism and Israel. The beautiful example shown here **(left)** is in a London synagogue. But the hexagram is an extremely ancient symbol which has been found in India, Egypt, China, and elsewhere. I have dealt at depth with the hexagram in my book about the Wessex Astrum, the huge landscape figure involving Stonehenge, Avebury and Glastonbury (Knight and Perrott, 2008), as shown on page 74. Hexagrams can be overlaid over a plan of Stonehenge (op cit. p. 20 and 56). Sometimes a roughly conical/triangular hill can be enhanced by the erection of a church on its summit, as shown here at Mont St Michel **(below right)**.

Jackie Queally has proposed that the dimensions of Rosslyn Chapel are configured by triangles, determined by the position of its key features (Queally 2007). At Rushton House, Northamptonshire, stands Triangular Lodge **(below centre)**, an amazing three-sided building, built in the 16th century by Sir Thomas Tresham, whose family tree goes back to the Grand Prior of the Knights Hospitallers. He apparently had an obsession with the Holy Trinity. Each wall is 33ft (10m) long and each floor is hexagonal in design.

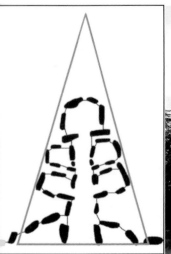

Occult symbolism and sacred geometry is evident throughout the building, including several exterior triangles.

The Church of Mary Magdalene at Rennes-le-Château, France, has a spectacular triangular tympanum over the doorway.

In Freemasonry, the triangle is formed out of the three Hebrew characters meaning *Hes - 'the sum of three'*, symbolic of the name of Yahweh, or God. Pyramids and hexagrams are recurring themes in Masonic and Hebrew ritual and imagery **(right)**, and I have shown how the Holy Trinity can be represented by a triangle, such as the imagery of triple hares and fish **(images p. 24, 101 & 108)**. This connection with the Holy Trinity is the main reason so many triangles are seen in churches. Trinity triangles are always equilateral, representing the equality of the three main players they symbolise (Taylor 2003).

We have already seen the *'Eye of God'* inside a triangle on the Great Seal of the USA, as seen on the dollar bill **(image p. 34)**, Freemasons know this as the *'Eye of Providence'*, a reminder to them that the Great Architect of the Universe observes their actions, first illustrated in Freemasonry literature in 1797. The all-seeing eye within a triangle shown here is at a Jewish cemetery in Poland **(right)**. This eye/triangle motif is a frequent depiction in secular and Christian art, and I found this fine example in the church at Kings Nympton, Devon, directly above a golden cross **(right)**.

Some types of Christian cross, such as the Maltese cross, the Patée Formée, and the Patée Fitched, are formed by triangles converging in the centre (see Chapter 39).

The power of the triangle and the pyramid has been replicated today in the form of the four glass pyramids at the Louvre Museum in Paris **(below)**, which were famously featured in Dan Brown's novel *'The Da Vinci Code'*. The pyramids consist of hundreds of triangular glass panes, and the water around the largest pyramid is integral to the total effect, as the upward (yang) pyramid produces a downward (yin) pyramid in the reflection, resulting in the imagery of balance; beneath this pyramid, two smaller ones interact in the foyer.

31. The Triple Goddess Reinvented

The concept of a sacred feminine trinity goes back at least 12,000 years to a stone relief in the Angles-sur-l'Anglin caves, France, which shows three adjacent female figures exposing their vulvas. The Romans and Greeks also depicted feminine trinities, as did the Anglo-Saxons, Norse and Celts. A typical interpretation is that they represent a three-fold Goddess, each one being an aspect of the cycles of Nature. They can also signify the waxing, full, and waning phases of the Moon, and in turn have been taken to symbolise the phases of a woman's life. The first aspect is virgin/maiden/spring; next is the mother/summer/fertility/sexuality phase, and finally the crone/autumn/winter/death aspect, although there are variations on this theme. I have already looked at the concept of feminine trinity in the form of the triple spirals and triangles at Newgrange **(left & image p. 79)** in the previous chapter, and in other ancient cultures these are primarily associated with female deities.

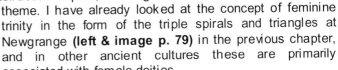

In the *'Greek Magical Papyri',* a Greco-Roman body of work found in Egypt, dated 2nd - 5th century AD, the Goddess is spoken of as, *'triple-sounding, triple-headed, triple-voiced and triple-faced'.* In Greek mythology, the Fates or Moirai were three in number, and were said to control the thread of life of all mortals: Clotho spun the thread, Lachesis measured the thread and allotted a certain amount to each person, and Atropos was the eventual cutter of the thread of life. The wife of Zeus, Hera, was worshipped as the triple deity Stymphalus – child, bride and widow. Apollo's habitual companions were the Muses, and although their number varied, those worshipped at Mount Helicon and Delhi were three in number.

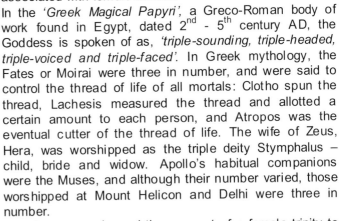

The Romans embraced the concept of a female trinity to represent the Goddess, these being Diana, Ceres and Hecate. Rome also worshipped the moon in the three deities of Luna, Diana and Proserpina. Triplicate female figures, called Matres (*'mothers'*) and Matronae (*'matrons'*) were venerated around NW Europe between 1st and 5th century AD. At Ancaster, Lincolnshire, a Roman carving of three *'Mother Goddesses'* was found, each one bearing food. At a Roman spring in Cirencester, another image of the *'Three Matres'* was unearthed, depicting two women holding produce and a third holding a baby **(bottom)**; another relief from the temple complex at

Bath also shows three female figures, the centre one of which again carries an infant. On Hadrian's Wall, one shrine revealed a frieze showing three females, thought to be the triplication of the goddess Coventina.

In Hindu tradition, the three aspects of the Goddess are Parvati, Durga and Kali, whilst in Mesopotamia she was Inanna, Ishtar and Astarte.

The Valkyries of Norse and Germanic mythologies often appeared in groups of three or nine; their role was to transport fallen warriors to the gates of Valhalla **(right)**. To the ancient Welsh, the *Cauldron of Regeneration* was associated with Branwen, who was described as one of the, *'three matriarchs of the Island'.* The Celts of Ireland had three eponymous goddesses, known as Ériu, Banbha and Fódla. The triple aspect of Brigit was also worshipped, as well as the three *Warrior Mothers*, the Mórrigna and the Machas (Green 1992, p. 170); a typical Celtic triple goddess from Burgundy, France, is illustrated here **(right)**.

The triple Goddess tradition was continued by Anglo-Saxons with the *Wyrd Sisters*, who were supposed to use giant looms on which to weave the destinies of people, spinning their fate in the form of webs; these were the Northern European equivalent of the Greek Fates. Shakespeare based the three witches of *Macbeth* on these characters, and it is interesting that the Greek Fates were thought to be elderly and ugly women, which became the archetypal image of witches. As late as 1577, Holished's *'Chronicles'* speaks of three women appearing in woods, *'... in strange and wild apparel, resembling creatures of elder wood'* (Knight 1998, p. 181).

The Christian Triple Goddess

It was imperative that this omnipresent triple aspect of the goddess was absorbed into Church symbolism. Windows showing three female figures bearing the names Faith, Hope, and Charity are common across Christendom. The origins of this imagery lie back in ancient Greece with the three female *Charites* or *Graces,* who were later associated with the goddess of wisdom. This was carried into Roman tradition, and a dedicated feast day was held annually on August 1st – on the ancient festival of Lughnassad. In Christian tradition, Faith, Hope and Charity are reported to be three 2nd century virgin saints, the daughters of Sophia, whose name means *wisdom;* in some Christian art all four are depicted **(right)**. The three sisters were martyred in Rome, and their burial place later became a place of Christian pilgrimage. It is interesting that the virgins' mother was Sophia, the namesake of the ancient Goddess of wisdom, who was a principal figure of veneration by Gnostics such as the Knights Templar. I find it interesting that the mother, sister and 'companion' of Jesus are all called Mary; this threefold association suggests a memory of the triple goddess.

In modern Christian art, such as in stained glass windows, Faith (Latin: Fides) often holds a cross or a Bible, or has serpents around her, Charity (Caritas) may be depicted

holding or comforting children and have a flame emanating from her hand, and Hope (Spes) often holds an anchor or a lamp. The three are as seen here in a fine window at Christchurch Cathedral, Oxford **(above, left)**.

Windows dedicated to Mercy, Justice and Humility can also be seen in churches. This phrase comes from the Bible (Micah 6:8), which in the King James Version says, *'... and what doth the Lord require of thee, but to do justly, and to love mercy, and to walk humbly with thy God'.* The window here **(above, right)** is at Andover, Hampshire, and is typical of the imagery. On the left, Mercy is shown as a woman holding a pardon in her hand; the centre lady is Justice, who holds the archetypal sword and scales of justice, just as St Michael is depicted **(image p. 38)**; the lady on the right has her hands crossed and eyes closed, representing humility.

One of the *Three Mary's* of the Church, the Virgin Mother, was the daughter of St Anne. The name of this matriarch is interesting, as it originated as Anu, the ancient Sumerian

goddess, who became Ana, Anann or Anu in Irish mythology. It is notable that three is usually the number of women described as attending the Crucifixion; Matthew says it was Mary Magdalene, Mary mother of James and Joseph, and the mother of the sons of Zebedee; Mark says the ladies were Mary Magdalene, Mary the Mother, and Salome; John attests that it was Mary, Mother of Jesus, Mary Magdalene, and Mary of Clopas, sister of Mary the mother. The three ladies again represent the triple aspect of the Goddess, and of women – the Virgin Mary, the Mother (Mary Magdalene, who was pregnant or had just given birth to Jesus' child), and an elder.

It is three women who the visit to the tomb of Jesus after the Crucifixion to anoint his body **(left)**, shown here at Charminster, Dorset. Although the apostles vary slightly as to the details, one character is always present, and that is Mary Magdalene, to whom we shall return in some detail later, and who, in my opinion, played a more prominent role in the life of Jesus than we have been led to believe.

172

32. Triple Gods and the Three Magi

The concept of a male trinity, either as gods or heroes, is an ancient one. In Hinduism, the three gods Brahma, Vishnu and Shiva are known as the Trimuri, the *'three forms'*. In Sumerian tradition, the gods Anu, Enlil and Ea constitute the trinity of *'Great Gods'*. The Egyptian *'Hymn to Amun'* states that, *'All gods are three'*, referring to the primal deities of Amun, Ra and Ptah. In Rome, the highest trinity was that of Jupiter, Neptune and Pluto, although in ancient Rome the *Archaic Triad* comprised Jupiter, Mars and Quirinus. The most powerful triad of the Norse gods was Odin, Thor and Freyr, who are shown together in this 12th century tapestry from Sweden **(right)**; the one-eyed figure on the left is Odin. Male triads were important to the Celts, such as the three craftsmen, Goibhniu, Luchta and Creidhne (Green 1992, p. 170). A Romano-British stone relief from Cirencester shows three male hooded figures, known as the *'genius cucullatus'*, who were featured elsewhere in Europe. At Housesteads, on Hadrian's Wall, a Roman arch shows the god Mars accompanied by two male companions.

And, of course, the Christian Holy Trinity is an extension of these ancient forerunners, as are the *Three Wise Men*. In Arthurian myth, the ancient triad is played out in the form of the questing younger man/warrior (Galahad), the king (Arthur) and the wise man (Merlin). The Welsh Triads speak of Nudd as one of the, *'three generous heroes of the Isle of Britain'*. In Taoist tradition, the *Three Pure Ones* are the highest male gods **(right)**. The idea of three central male characters forming a trinity is widespread and has continued into modern times, such as with *'The Three Musketeers'*.

The Magi

Matthew's Gospel tells the story of how the *Holy Family* was visited by three Magi during the Nativity, and who have been traditionally described as, *'three wise men from the East'*, often regarded as kings or astrologers (Matthew does not call them kings). The event was seen to fulfill a prophecy that, *'... all kings shall fall down before him'* (Psalms 72:11), and they were the first non-Jews to recognise the significance of the birth of Jesus. Matthew also says that they visited Jesus and his mother in a house, and it is possible that they in fact made their visit up to two years after the Nativity (Taylor 2003,

p. 61); Jesus is often shown considerably older than a newborn in many depictions of the Magi's visitation. The gifts of gold, myrrh and frankincense have confirmed to most scholars that the Magi were three in number, and were even named in the Western Christian Church as Gaspar (or Casper), a Persian scholar, Melchior, an Indian wise man, and Balthazar, an Arab scholar. As the names do not appear until the 8th century, these may have been mere inventions to demonstrate how representatives from *all* races and creeds had bowed down to the *'Messiah'*.

The term Magi comes to the Bible via the Greek *magos ('magician')* as described in the original Greek text of Matthew's Gospel, and other translations speak of the men being astrologers. Magi is the pleural of Magus, and Chambers Dictionary defines Magus as, *'An ancient Persian priest or member of a priestly class; an Eastern magician; a sorcerer'.* Records going back to the 6th century BC speak of *'Magus'*, and Christian Byzantine art usually depicts the Magi in Persian clothing. Magus and Magi have given us *magic* and *magician*.

It has also been suggested that the story of the Magi may have been adopted from a contemporary account of the life of the Roman Emperor Nero (Picknett and Prince 1997); three separate Roman writers recorded how Tiridates I, who was the King of Armenia and was a Zoroastrian priest, visited Nero in 66AD. He was accompanied by his three sons, who were also Zoroastrians (the religion of these Magi). They came to worship Nero as a god, according to Roman propaganda at least, with Tiridates declaring, *'I have come to you my god to pay homage as I do to Mithras'.* The account ends by recording that they returned home via a different route than whence they came, which is exactly what the Biblical Magi did! It is interesting that in this very early Christian depiction of the Adoration of the Magi, found in the catacombs of Rome **(top)**, the Magi are wearing the *Phrygian Cap* of the god Mithras, which was also used by cult adherents. Compare this to the cap worn by the god, shown previously **(image p. 41)**.

The age of the Magi story has recently been put under scrutiny by Dead Sea Scrolls historian Dr Hugh Schonfield, who says that the legend was used earlier in the same century, not in reference to the birth of Jesus, however, but to the birth of his older cousin John the Baptist (Wallace-Murphy 2005, p. 60-1).

The Magi were probably members of the Zoroastrian mystery cult of Mithraism, most likely from a priest/astrologer/shamanic class. It is interesting that the old Chinese word for *'court magician'* is *Mag,* and that the Chinese character for that word is a cross with splayed ends, like the Maltese Cross used by Gnostics such as the Knights Templar.

The three Magi were paying their respects to a new soul whom they knew was to be exceptional. Jesus' Gnostic credentials had preceded him, for his coming had been foretold by earlier prophecies. These three wise souls were from cultures where the God and Goddess were both equally venerated – they were Pagan in every sense of the word. The Church would have us believe that they came and bowed down to Jesus as subservients, but I believe they were acknowledging the arrival of a fellow *'old soul'* – a

person who they knew was to push Gnostic practice and metaphysics to where it had not been for an era. We also know that Eastern Pagan spirituality had a profound effect on early esoteric Christianity – they had so much in common after all. It has been demonstrated that there was a strong Persian influence in the Holy Land at the time of Jesus' birth, including some Persian mystery schools; the Persians were in dispute with the Roman Empire, so this could explain why the Magi came in search of someone whom they believed could deliver them from the Romanised line of Herod (Gilbert 2005, p. 91). Perhaps they were acting like the emissaries who periodically go around the world in search of the next Dalai Lama (op cit. p. 92).

The Jesus story and the number three comes full circle when we consider the following: Jesus practiced a 3 year ministry; three people died on the cross at the Crucifixion; this was followed by 3 days of interment in the tomb; three women come to anoint his body; his Resurrection was on the 3rd day.

Over the years, I have noticed that in many depictions of the Magi one of the characters often appears much younger, and often is effeminate in appearance. Was one of the Magi a woman? Did the Freemasons, and the Knights Templar before them, leave us a clue as to the true gender of one of the *'Wise Men'.* Look at the standing figure on the left in the first example **(top)**; then also look at the figure at the rear of the next image **(right)**, who has a feminine face with prominent cheek bones, and wears a heart-shaped earring. This latter example is a fine window at Dorchester, Dorset, and I have also detailed here the relevant area **(right)**. It could be argued that this person is holding the reins of a Camel and could therefore be a servant, but that would then mean that there are only have *two* Magi present in the scene, which is not the case – all three Magi are shown in this one frame.

From whence these three people came, the kingdoms of Sumeria and Persia, the goddess was held in as much veneration as the gods, as were women, and the religious practices of these lands were not administered by just priests, but by

175

priestesses too. It is interesting that in the Old Testament saga of love between King Solomon and the Queen of Sheba, the queen gifted Solomon, *'precious stones, spices and incense'*. Were the acts of the Magi at the Nativity their acknowledgment that they regarded Jesus as a king? Or did Christian propaganda use the King Solomon/Sheba story to help elevate Jesus to the status of a king? One of my favourite depictions of the Adoration of the Magi is this beautifully crafted work by Edward Burne-Jones, dated 1904: as before, one of the figures, this time on the far right, is decidedly feminine in appearance **(below right)**.

In many cultures, the three belt stars in the constellation Orion were said to represent the three magi; some have suggested that alignments of these stars with ancient sites, such as the Sphinx and the Giza pyramids, heralded the dawn of a new age, as did, it could be argued, the arrival of the Magi in Bethlehem (Bauval and Hancock 1996).

Sometimes three male figures are shown in Christian art, representing Faith, Courage and Devotion, shown here at Malmesbury Abbey, Wiltshire **(below left)**. When I look at such Christian depictions, I ponder how, thousands of years ago, ancient people would look with great devotion at *their* triad of male gods, hoping, like their Christian counterparts, that the virtues of the gods would be conferred on them.

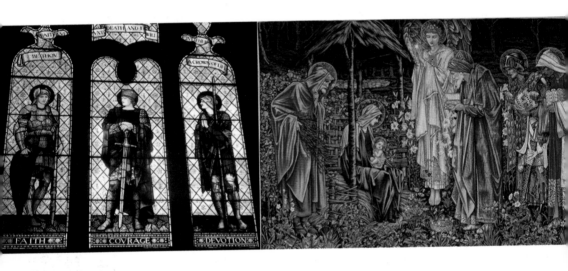

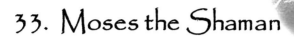

33. Moses the Shaman

I n Chapters 2 and 3, I looked at how a shamanic world view had been the backbone of ancient spiritualities, and how people viewed their world, and the Afterlife, very differently from today. How we see our lives and our place in the Universe has always been about perception, as archaeologist Christopher Tilley implied: *'What space is depends on who is experiencing it'* (Tilley 1994). I have already shown how many of the Biblical stories echo ancient myths, often telling of a hero who must endure a journey, a separation from his people – a shamanic quest no less.

Shamans are intermediaries between this three dimensional world (with its cycles of birth, life, and death) and the *'Otherworld'*, the realm of nature spirits, totem animals, the gods, and the ancestors. For thousands of years, shamans have entered trance states and *'journeyed'* to these other dimensions to bring back information of use to their

people, including knowledge of healing. By undertaking trance journeying, a shaman can contact the dead, which can be a powerful recourse. The shaman is the guardian of esoteric knowledge, sacred power, and arcane wisdom, the person who knows, and can interpret, the cycles of Nature and the workings of the heavens, including the changing faces of the Moon, and the progress of the Sun across the sky; he is in direct contact with the inner workings of the cosmos. The Druids were the wisemen/shamans of the Celts, as imagined here by William Stukeley **(right, and top image p. 148)**.

One of the practices used by shamans around the world today is to attain an altered state by means of the ingestion of mind-altering substances, such as *'magic mushrooms'*. Speaking of the Neolithic, archaeologist Mike Pitts states, *'It seems we are justified in hypothesising that altered states were indeed a component of some ceremonies...'* (Pitts 2000, p. 236). I have discussed at length the shamanic associations with West Kennet Long Barrow (Knight 2011), and have hopefully proven beyond doubt that this chambered monument was intended for use by the living, as much as it was by the dead; where better to contact the ancestors than in the presence of their mortal remains?

I have already mentioned some controversial theories suggesting that the roots of Christianity lay in fertility cults, whose adherents would partake in such practices as ingesting *'visionary'* psychoactive plants to help them connect with God (see p. 149-50). Just as cultures had done for thousands of years, the Essenes and other early Judaic-Christian cults may have used mind-altering plants to achieve *ecstasy*, a direct route by which to commune with God.

Moses is a revered prophet in Jewish, Christian and Islamic traditions. The Book of Exodus tells of how Moses led the Israelites from captivity in Egypt to the Promised

Land, a significant event in all three religions. The earliest surviving literary reference to Moses comes from Hecataeus of Abdera, dated 4th century BC, whilst several Greek historians also tell of the prophet's exploits. Moses' wisdom was held in such high regard by the Greeks that Plato was called, *'The Greek Moses'*. The story of the Exodus is dramatic, with miracles at every turn, as this aged, wise, Druidic-like figure dramatically plugs into his metaphysical powers; in fact, the usual depictions of Moses show him sporting a long, white beard, and his time spent as a hermit, are characteristics that seem to fit the stereotypical Druid/shaman archetype. Many see Moses as a Gnostic, the bringer of the *old laws*, the baton of which was taken up by Jesus, the bringer of the new; Jesus was known by some as the *New Moses*.

Born a Hebrew, the newborn Moses was rescued from the bulrushes by a member of the Egyptian royalty **(image p. 148)**, and was raised the son of the Pharaoh. Even his rescue from the Nile has parallels with Isis' resurrection of Osiris, and similar tales occur in Babylonian myths. When Moses was a child he went through an initiation by putting hot coals in his mouth, which left him with a speech impediment, and at times it was

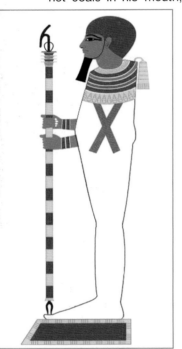

Aaron, who was his birth brother and a priest, who would speak on his behalf (Exodus 4: 10-16). This puts Moses well and truly in the category of shamanic *'wounded healer'*.

Sifting through Egyptian records, scholars have identified two possible candidates who could be Moses – Prince Tuthmoses and a royal steward called Kamose, both of whom contain elements of Moses' name. Kamose appears in Egyptian writings around 1470BC, as a young boy adopted by the Princess Thermuthis, the Greek version of the name Termut (Phillips 2002). Alternatively, Moses may be the Tuthmose spoken of around a century later, and who was the son of Amonhotep III. This person became a priest at the temple of Ra, but was disgraced and disappears from Egyptian records around 1363BC. A Jewish historian, Artapanus of Alexandria, writing in the 2nd century BC, states that Moses taught the Egyptians the value of the oxen, which led to the consecration of the beast, giving rise to the cult of Apis. As a gifted young adult, Moses built Hermopolis, and taught his people the spiritual attributes of the Ibis. Artapanus also describes how, after the Exodus, all the temples of Isis thereafter housed a rod, in remembrance of Moses' miracles; rods are often carried by Egyptian gods, such as Ptah **(left)**, as a sigil of their authority. Moses was to use his to great effect, as we shall soon see. It was also Moses who seems to have trail-blazed the concept of the one God, one that encompassed all that is. Sigmund Freud believed that because of his monotheistic viewpoint, the young Moses may have held the same beliefs as Akhenaten, the heretical Pharaoh.

So Moses, aka Kamose or Prince Tuthmoses, was raised to adulthood in Pharaoh's household, and would therefore have been involved in all the learning that the Egyptian, and therefore Pagan, mystery schools had to offer – Osiris, Isis, and all the ancient Egyptian myths would have been familiar to him. He may have been a priest to Tuthmosis III around 1470BC, who was dismissed from office around 1460BC (Phillips 2002, p. 129). Moses apparently killed an Egyptian slave master and fled across the Red Sea to Midian, where God is said to have spoken to him through a burning bush, telling him to go back to Egypt and lead the Israelites out of bondage.

In the Book of Exodus, Moses takes himself off into the desert, and also ascends mountains; this practice of taking oneself away from one's people is common in many shamanic traditions; sleep, water and food deprivation can take a shaman to the edge of madness, in order for him to obtain his Gnosis – the experiential knowledge of ultimate Truth. Moses felt compelled to trek up Mount Sinai **(image p. 31)**, a huge granite mountain in Egypt sacred to Jews, Christians and Muslims. He was on a shamanic vision quest (perhaps spending time in a cavern there known as *Moses' Cave*), and *'received from God'* the Ten Commandments. This was possibly achieved during a dream sleep, a well known practice amongst ancient and contemporary shamans. Moses later saw the Promised Land from another isolated high place, Mount Pisgah. The takeover of Pagan high places is evident in the original version of *'The Song of Moses'*, which was found in a cave at Qumran, near the Dead Sea; it speaks of *gods*, pleural: *'Rejoice, O heavens, with him; and do obeisance to him, ye gods'*. This was later changed to *'angels of God'*.

In the Bible, one of the most dramatic events is when God speaks to Moses in the form of the *'burning bush'*, telling him that he was to lead the Israelites out of bondage (Exodus 3:2). After God spoke, the prophet asked to whom he was speaking, to which came the reply, *'I am who I am'* (Exodus 4:14). One of the basic tenets of Gnosticism is the *'I AM'*, whereby the participant sees God within themselves – everyone is divine! It is to Moses that God then reveals his name to humanity – *Yahweh* or *Jehovah*. As an Egyptian prince, Moses had been trained in Egyptian mystery school practices for 40 years, and when the bush apparently *'speaks'* to him, Moses is instantly aware than something profound is afoot; he shows no fear, but simply says, *'I am here'*. He was totally present in the Gnostic *I AM*, as the culmination of his vision quest unfolds. The

burning bush episode is shown here at Frome church, Somerset **(above)**, and it is interesting how the Virgin Mary and Jesus are shown in the bush, giving the latter the authority of God; the link between Moses and Jesus will be discussed soon.

Professor Benny Shanon, of the University of Jerusalem, has recently put forward his theory (in the periodical *Time and Mind*) that Moses was under the intentional influence of mind-altering, psychoactive plants during his visions of the Burning Bush and the Ten Commandments. One early version of the Bible says Moses saw, *'a red burning plant'*, and scholars have identified this plant as the thorn acacia, which is associated with the Egyptian Tree of Life; in the myths of Osiris and Isis it represents the immortal nature of the soul. This plant contains a number of alkaloids that have hallucinogenic effects on humans, and Prof Shanon believes that concoctions of acacia bark yield similar affects to those experienced in the Americas by the ingestion of Ayahuasca; acacia is traditionally used in Bedouin and Arab medicine. The tree is frequently mentioned in the Bible, particularly in the Moses story, and incense made from it was burnt at the altar of the Ark of the Covenant. Shanon gives further Biblical examples of entheogens (mind-altering plants used in religious rites).

The Ark of Covenant **(images p. 39)**, made to house the tablets of the Ten Commandments, was also constructed of acacia wood and overlaid with pure gold, and Moses was also told to, *'make a table of acacia wood'*, possibly meaning an altar; acacia was also the wood of the staff or rod of Moses. Moses later asks the twelve contenders to be his successor to leave their staffs in front of the Ark of the Covenant; in the morning the staff or rod of Aaron miraculously sprouted blossoms that produced almonds **(image p. 146)**, showing that it was he who was to lead the Israelites (Numbers 17: 1-8). This tale reminds me of how Joseph of Arimathea planted his thorn staff into the ground at Glastonbury, whereupon it sprouted leaves (in the New Testament, the staff of Joseph also miraculously blossomed, showing he was the one chosen to marry the Virgin Mary). Moses, the shaman prophet, clearly had a close relationship with acacia, which was regarded as a sacred plant.

Later on, Moses is again associated with another mind-altering plant. God guides the Israelites out of bondage to the Promised Land, but intervenes en route, through Moses, by instructing them to go and collect 'manna'. This had to be done first thing in the morning, the very time before most desert mushrooms shrivel and die under the Sun. Some scholars believe manna to be a small psychoactive desert mushroom; Moses said manna was the *'bread of the Lord'*, which is similar to the Aztec description of the psychoactive psilocybe mushroom – *'flesh of the gods'.* Both the Old and New Testaments contain descriptions of people entering a trance-like state to witness *'visions'*, which is repeated with later Christian saints, and one has to ask what helped them enter these ethereal states. Had Moses ingested psychoactive plants before or during his visionary journeys on Mount Sinai?

Regarding Moses the magician, let us backtrack to a few Biblical events in Egypt. After the Pharaoh refuses to release his people from captivity, Moses, on the instructions of Yahweh, uses his hands or his staff in Gandalf-like manner to cause ten plagues to fall upon Egypt, such as plagues of various insects and frogs, illness amongst livestock, a hail storm, a darkness for three days, the death of the firstborn of the Egyptians, and the turning of the waters of the Nile into blood (Exodus 7-10). It is interesting that it was contact with the *magical staff* of Moses that turned the waters to blood (Exodus 7:19). In the Book of Revelations, angels likewise turn the seas red with blood.

Yet, even in the very midst of all these catastrophic events, the Egyptians apparently remembered Moses as one of their own and still held him in high regard: *'The man Moses was still very great in the land of Egypt, in the sight of the Pharaoh's servants, and in the sight of the people'* (Exodus 11:3). Was this because he was already a famed priest/magician, someone who was so powerful as to be revered and feared?

The event involving the deaths of the first born children became known as the Passover, as the Israelite children were spared because the blood of a male lamb was marked on their doors. It is interesting that the Passover event took place at midnight, the

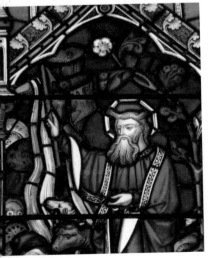

'bewitching hour' (Exodus 12:29). This story was later to be retold in the Passover events that lead up to the Crucifixion (Jesus being the new sacrificial lamb). All the events that befell the Egyptians have precedents in the stories of gods and goddesses in many cultures, and there are also myths of shaman-like witches and wizards producing changes in the weather when called for.

Throughout history, staffs were often more than mere walking aids, and even today a ceremonial staff or sceptre represents authority and sovereignty; in Freemasonry, a long stave with a metal tip is used in rituals. The staff of Moses was used in a role similar to a wand, such as when he released water from the Rock of Horeb **(left)**, and parted the waters of the Red Sea. In Exodus 4: 3-4, we read how Moses lay down his staff or rod, at which point it turned into a serpent. It was at the Burning Bush that God acknowledges Moses' ability to use a magical staff by imbuing it with even more power: *'And thou shalt take this rod in thine hand, where with thou shalt do signs'* (Exodus 4:17). Later, in Exodus 7: 10-12, the staff was again turned into a snake, showing the association of serpents with high magic. Joseph of Arimathea also had a magical staff, as did St Christopher, who was gifted a staff by the child Jesus, which flowered the next day. In Greek tradition, a staff with an entwined serpent was a symbol of Aesculapius, who had a magical staff similar to the caduceus of Hermes and Mercury **(images p. 123)**. The Long Man of Wilmington, the Sussex chalk figure, appears to hold two staffs. Many Egyptian gods and pharaohs are often depicted holding a staff or rod – Moses would have been well aware of the magical potential of such an item. I believe that Moses can be regarded as a wise, Gandalf-like shaman/magician.

The serpent is clearly a device for doing God's will, as Moses and the faithful had to look at this image to be saved when Yahweh (God) sent seraphim (*'fiery serpents'*) to punish the sinful. Moses also raised a pillar or pole adorned with a bronze snake, the Brazen Serpent **(top & image p. 124)**. It is interesting that the Aztec serpent god Quetzalcoatl also carried a staff and some paintings show the god *'raising the serpents'*. The role that serpents played in the beliefs, symbolism and magic of ancient cultures cannot be over emphasized, as I detailed in Chapter 24, and serpents are mentioned throughout the Old Testament.

Moses famously parted the waters of the Red Sea for the Israelites **(image p. 164 & below)**, although it has recently been suggested that this may have been the *Reed Sea,* referring to the Nile Delta. Once his people were across, one wave of Moses' staff subsequently caused the waters to submerge the pursuing Egyptian army, which introduced the concept of salvation by water. Scientists have recently tried to explain this chain of events by linking it to a drawback of water as the sea retreats prior to a tsunami. Others say that the Lake of Tanis was the *Reed Sea,* due to the proliferation of papyrus in it, and that a drought may have led to the waters subsiding, allowing the Israelites to cross. One passage in the Bible just before the Red Sea episode suggests that the Israelites had ground to a halt due to the local vegetation, such as a deltaic marsh: *'They were entangled in the land'* (Exodus 14:3).

Just before Moses parted the waters, pillars of both cloud and fire (i.e. tornados or twisters), kept the Egyptian army at bay; was this more weather manipulation by our wizard Moses? During the Exodus it is notable that Moses took the bones of Joseph with him; ancestor worship in the presence of their bones is one of the key tenets of shamanism. And another telling line occurs soon after, which speaks of Miriam, the sister of Moses, being a *'prophetess',* suggesting that she was a priestess/seer.

Moses is often shown carrying two stone tablets, seen here at St John's, Glastonbury **(right)**, onto which are inscribed the Ten Commandments **(also images p. 31, 34)**. When Moses descended from the mountain with the tablets, the people said his face was radiant and that he had horns; this is thought to have derived from the descriptive translation in the Latin 'Vulgate' Bible as the

term *cornuta*, meaning *'made horned'* (Exodus 34:29). This is why Moses is often shown with horns or rays coming out of the top of his head, such as here in Rosslyn Chapel **(bottom)**. However, writer J Stephen Lang has looked back at the original translations and says these texts say that Moses was, *'giving off horn-like rays'*. Was his aura so connected with spirit that it became visible to others?

Elements of Moses' vision quest, which culminated in the Ten Commandments **(left),** may have been Egyptian in origin; Egyptian myths say that Osiris disappeared for 40 days, which is the number of days in which Moses conversed with God on Mount Sinai. Did Moses choose this period of time because he so closely associated himself with Osiris? This Egyptian legacy is so clearly brought into focus when we look at this extract from Spell 125 of the Egyptian *'Book of the Dead',* which was a proclamation by the deceased on how they had lived their life, or at least how others regarded them as having lived it; here lies the real origins of the Ten Commandments:

'I have done no falsehood.
I have not robbed.
I have not committed perjury.
I have not sexually misconducted myself.
I have done no wrong.
I have not reviled God.
I am not over wealthy.
I have not blasphemed God.
I have not killed men'.

We should also bear in mind that a parallel story was being told in Sumeria, wherein the god Shamash gifted Hammurabi, *'... a tablet of Laws',* whilst seated on a throne up a mountain!

Moses had other visions, such as the *'four winged messengers of God'* (Phillips 2002) which later influenced the use of winged animals to represent three of the gospel writers, Matthew, Mark and Luke **(images p. 88 and 89).** God told Moses to partake in several sacrifices, including that of a bull and a sheep, whose blood was poured over an altar (a very ancient, shamanic practice). In the well known Moses myth, the Israelites made and worshipped a golden calf in his absence, suggesting that, up until that point, bull worship was still acceptable.

As I have already commented, when the Israelites cannot find water in the desert, Moses is told by God that if he hits a rock with his staff, water will come gushing out; he does as he is instructed and the water appears (Exodus 17:5-6), as seen at Hornblotton church, Somerset, and St Cross, Winchester **(images p. 164 & 180).** It is interesting that the Moses and Persian Mithras miracles may have originated at about the same time, and I believe that the Hebrew version is a retelling of the Mithras story. To these two water-gushing exploits we can add the tale of St Augustine in Cerne Abbas in Dorset, where it is said he struck the ground with his staff, at which point the waters of a *'crystal clear fountain of water'* sprang up (Knight 2013).

After 40 years of wandering the wilderness, the Israelites reached their ancestral home in Canaan. Moses' scouts brought back two bunches of grapes, said to represent the bounty of the land, which Moses had these erected on poles, to represent fruitfulness. The Bible tells of the death of Moses on Mount Nebo aged 120, from where he had seen the Israelites cross over to their new lands. Moses died alone (Deuteronomy 34), and God is said to have buried him in a valley in the land of Maob. A rock-cut cave was located in the area in 1839, and when a shrine within the cave was excavated it was found to contain a staff on which were carved Egyptian hieroglyphs and the head of a cobra. This is now on display in Birmingham Museum, and I recently viewed it for myself **(bottom)**; the hieroglyphics on the staff **(inset)** identify the owner as *'Tuthmoses'* or *'Tuthmosis'* (Phillips 2002, p. 236). Is this the illustrious staff of Moses, which by some miracle has made its way to the sacred Isle of Albion?

Some believe that the prophets Moses, Elijah and Jesus are one and the same incarnating soul, such are their similarities. It is interesting that the prophet Elijah (c. 660-800BC), like Moses, also brought a pillar of fire down from the sky, produced manna for his people, struck a body of water, dividing it, and travelled 40 days and 40 nights to reach Mount Horeb; Elijah is the only other Biblical character to ascend the

mountain). Here God speaks to him in a cave (1 Kings 19:9) – is this *'Moses' Cave'*, to which he was returning in later incarnation?

This is reinforced by the passage in the New Testament describing the Transfiguration (Luke 9:28-36), an incident prior to the arrival of Jesus in Jerusalem. Jesus goes up a mountain to pray with three of his disciples, Peter, James and John. Jesus' is then seen to glow with a white radiance (his light body becomes visible), at which point both Moses and Elijah appear next to him, as shown here at St James, Avebury **(right – also see image p. 213)**. Christians see this as a sign that Jesus should be regarded as at least equal to these great prophets, a sign of his future greatness. But I wonder as to the real meaning behind the story. Was Jesus shape-shifting (a shamanic practice) into of two of his previous lives?

I will end by recommending Graham Phillips' excellent book, *The Moses Legacy* (Phillips 2002), which is an invaluable guide to researching the life and times of the Moses the shaman.

34. The Holy Grail

T oday, the expression *Holy Grail* is often used to describe some goal that would appear beyond our grasp, something elusive or unobtainable. Yet for seekers of wisdom, the Grail is a guiding archetype that has the potential to help the soul achieve a state of Gnosis, an inner path back to Source – back to Divinity. The Grail as a physical object is said to be a chalice or some other form of vessel, or a stone, a womb, or a head; it may evoke the archetypal divine feminine, or be the inspiration and goal of some form of *'Quest'*. It is interesting that most Grail legends were written down in the 12th and 13th century, the very period when Gnostic orders such as the Knights Templar and the Cathars were at their zenith; the Cathars were in fact known as the *'Church of the Grail'*. It is not my intention here to take more than a cursory look at Grail legends, for the subject is complex and multilayered, and many excellent books, as well as a sprinkling of questionable ones, have already been written on the subject, some of which I will refer to. And I shall deal with the theory that the Grail may actually be a holy bloodline in a later chapter, when I look at Mary Magdalene. As elsewhere in this book, my intention is primarily to show that the Holy Grail mythos, like so many other Christian stories, owes much to ancient roots.

Possibly the oldest concept of a vessel of rebirth and regeneration comes from the Sumerians in the form of the prestigious *'Great Stone Bowl of Uda',* which was inscribed with a list of the first Sumerian dynasty. One name on it was Gin or Gan, which means, *'to make abundant or increase'* (Gardiner and Osborn 2005, p. 224-5). From Persian mythologies come tales of the *Cup of Jamshid* **(top)**, a goblet used for divination, which was long possessed by rulers of ancient Persia and was said to be filled with the elixir of immortality. It was subject to many Persian poems and stories, and the success of the Persian Empire was attributed to having it in their possession.

In Greek mythology, Psyche was a beautiful princess of whom Venus was jealous. Venus ordered Psyche to go into the Underworld to obtain a golden box, the contents of which would restore the fading looks of the goddess, and yet it was Psyche who peered into the box, as depicted in this painting by John Waterhouse **(left)**. Circe is the Greek goddess of magic and sorcery, who had an infinite knowledge of potions and herbs. In Homer's *Odyssey*, she turned some of Ulysses' crew into swine when they drank a potion from her magical cup, aided by a wave of her magic wand; John Waterhouse again presents the scene as Ulysses confronts the goddess, who holds out the magic cup to him **(right)**. The Greek virgin goddess of youth, Hebe, was responsible for dispensing to the gods the rejuvenating ambrosia, the *'food of the gods'*, which she did from a magical chalice. The Greek *Grain Goddess* Demeter possessed the cornucopia, a magical horn of plenty that represented the bountiful gifts of the earth, and which never emptied **(p. 135)**.

Stories of magical cauldrons appear in Native American, African, and Asian mythology. Quan Yin (or Kwan Yin) is the East Asian goddess of mercy and compassion, motherhood and sea-farers, who is particularly revered by Buddhists, and by Taoists of China. She is often depicted holding a small jar, which contains the so-called *'sweet dew'*, the waters of compassion.

But it was the ancient races of Europe that had the biggest influence in the development of the Grail mythos. The great Celtic hero Bran had a magical cauldron, which could restore the dead to life, but which was unfortunately used to regenerate adversarial Irish armies. Also in Irish myth, a sea deity called Manannan mac Lir rewarded one Irish king with a magic cup, which would break if three lies were uttered over it, but would be restored to wholeness should three truths be spoken.

The Knights Templar originated with the Normans, whose ancestors were the Vikings; a wondrous Iron Age bowl called the Gundestrup Cauldron **(centre)** was unearthed in Jutland, Denmark, and was a sacred vessel to one such Northern European tribe. One image on the cauldron shows a vessel into which a man is being lowered by a giant or god **(right)**, possibly representing the magical cauldron of Bran, or the local equivalent. The Norse had a tradition of a magical vessel called the *Odhrerir Cauldron*, which contained the blood of the Kvasir, a wise man, and which was coveted by the god Odin himself; if drank from, it had the power to bestow the gift of poetry and ancient occult knowledge. Another Norse myth tells how Loki, the shape-shifting god, went into the Underworld to steal a magic vessel, the *Cup of Jonar*, from a giantess.

The recurring *Cauldron of Rebirth* theme features in several Celtic tales. The enchantress Ceridwen is spoken of in medieval Welsh tales from the 12th century, such as in the *'Tale of Taliesin'*, where it is written that she had a magical cauldron called Awen, which could bestow poetic inspiration and wisdom; modern Pagans regard her as the goddess of rebirth and transformation. In Welsh Arthurian tales, Arthur journeys into the Underworld, Annwyn, to retrieve a magical cauldron which offers the seeker an inexhaustible source of food, and which is possibly the origins of the Arthurian Grail Quest myths. Arthur is a common image seen in churches, as he represents virtue and chivalry, and he also fought to defend Christian Britain against the

Pagan Saxon invaders. In the well known Grail legends, King Arthur and his knights famously go off questing for the lost chalice, in the hope of restoring health to Arthur and the land. The Culdees (8th century Scottish monks), had a legend of a lost cup containing the blood of Jesus that could only be found by a chaste knight partaking a quest for its recovery. I happened upon this little-known window **(left)** at Longbridge Deverill, Wiltshire, in which Arthur kneels before an angel who holds the Grail aloft; the words below read, *'Here is the Vision King Arthur longed for to see'.*

The myth that Joseph of Arimathea brought the Grail to Glastonbury is equally enduring and compelling. This has birthed a debate as to whether the Grail is the cup used at the Last Supper, or Jesus' blood and sweat collected by Joseph in two jars at the Crucifixion **(left)**, or whether it was indeed Mary Magdalene, brought to Glastonbury under Joseph's care. In the last case, the Grail is the womb of the Magdalene, which gave birth to the bloodline of Jesus; Old French for Holy Grail is *'san greal'*, whilst the very similar *'sang real'*, means *'royal blood'*, as is famously revealed in Dan Brown's bestseller *The Da Vinci Code*. It is perhaps relevant that neither a chalice nor the term *'holy grail'* appear in any of the earlier Christian accounts of the Last Supper, although clearly a receptacle of some kind would have been used for the Eucharist wine.

Several chalices and other containers have been advocated as being the actual vessel used at the Last Supper. The earliest record of the survival of the chalice was that of Arculf, a 7th century Anglo-Saxon pilgrim, who described seeing it in a chapel near Jerusalem. Today, there are various cups claimed to be this chalice, three notable examples (all in Spain) being at Galicia, at Valencia Cathedral (recorded from 262AD), and a third in the Basilica of San Isidoro, Leon. The bejeweled Leon chalice **(left)** has been carbon-dated between 200BC and 100AD, making it arguably the strongest candidate.

Another contender is the so-called *Marion Chalice*, a small alabaster cup into which either Joseph of Arimathea or Mary Magdalene (hence the name) collected the blood of Jesus at the Crucifixion. It was said to have been found by St Helen when she excavated the tomb of Jesus in the 4th century. It was taken to Rome, but later found its way to Britain for safekeeping when the Visigoths sacked Rome in 410AD. The cup was recorded in the 13th century as being at The White Castle at Whittington, but has not been seen since its disappearance in the late 19th century.

Others claim that the Grail cup is buried beneath Rosslyn Chapel, or at the Chalice Well, Glastonbury. Yet another interesting vessel is the *Nanteos Cup*, currently in Rhydyfelin,

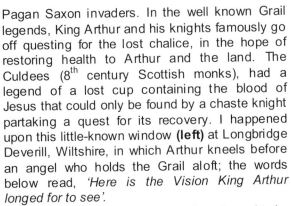

Wales, which is a medieval wooden bowl said to have been responsible for healing since the 19th century.

A chalice or cup is a common depiction in churches, and they can be associated with particular characters. As already mentioned, Joseph of Arimathea may be depicted holding a chalice, and his crest features a thorny cross overlaid with a silver chalice; St John the Divine is often holding a chalice with either a dragon or a snake within **(images p. 130 & front cover)**; St Dunstan's symbol is a golden cup on a blue background; a cup is also the motif of St Bonaventure, a 14th century Franciscan, as well as St Chrysostom, the 5th century Archbishop of Constantinople. At Rosslyn Chapel, an image of the Old Testament priest/king Melchizedek, who blessed Abraham (Genesis 14), shows him holding a chalice; here, the grail cup has been seen as, '*the receptacle for grace to pour from or into*' (Queally 2007).

But it is in the Garden of Gethsemane that we have actual references made by Jesus to a cup. In Mark 14, Jesus prays to God, and says, '*take away this cup from me*'; he repeats this in Matthew, but later adds (Matthew 27): '*O My Father, if this cup may not pass away from me, except I drink it, thy will be done*'; John's gospel does not mention the details of Jesus' prayers. Throughout the Bible, however, the cup is often used as a metaphor for an individual's fate, or the depth their spirituality, which has given rise to phrases such as, '*My cup runneth over*'. It has therefore been suggested by theologians that Jesus' reference to a cup refers to the pain, degradation and death he knows will be required of him.

It is not difficult to find images of the Garden of Gethsemane, and sometimes they show Jesus accompanied by a hand holding a cup coming out of the sky, or an angel with a cup, shown here at Andover **(centre)**. But is this cup being taken away from the prophet, or being given to him? The last window **(right)** clearly shows Jesus holding the cup whilst in meditation, achieving some realisation. To me this is depicting his attainment of Gnosis, the perception of his true metaphysical nature, the realisation that his light body/spirit will survive his death. As I outlined in my novel, *Thirteen Moons – Conversations with the Goddess*, I believe the Grail is in all of us, and it beckons us forth to a journey into the unknown. And this journey is not just into the past, into history, but is ultimately a sacred quest that will create our future. Ultimately, the Grail is all of the objects and concepts mentioned in this chapter, and more, for each and every one of them can lead us to our personal Truth. Perhaps we should ask not if a myth is historically factual, but rather is it spiritually valid, to us *individually*. I will relate more on the subject of myths as aids to personal growth towards the end of this book.

187

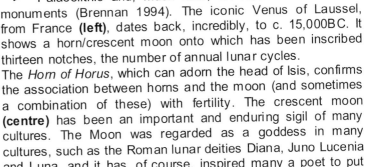

35. The Moon Goddess and the Virgin

The Moon has been venerated for thousands of years; images of it were painted in caves as far back as the Palaeolithic and, much later, on Neolithic chambered monuments (Brennan 1994). The iconic Venus of Laussel, from France **(left)**, dates back, incredibly, to c. 15,000BC. It shows a horn/crescent moon onto which has been inscribed thirteen notches, the number of annual lunar cycles.

The *Horn of Horus*, which can adorn the head of Isis, confirms the association between horns and the moon (and sometimes a combination of these) with fertility. The crescent moon **(centre)** has been an important and enduring sigil of many cultures. The Moon was regarded as a goddess in many cultures, such as the Roman lunar deities Diana, Juno Lucenia and Luna, and it has, of course, inspired many a poet to put pen to paper. The Moon creates the tides and has long illuminated Man's nocturnal hunting parties; Neolithic and Bronze Age people had a knowledge of the Moon's complicated movements through the sky, and knew why its face waxed and waned, and it seems that lunar cycles may have been as important as solar ones.

It has long been proven that many Neolithic monuments have intentional lunar alignments, most famously seen at Callanish and Ballochroy (Thom 1967), Stonehenge, and Newgrange (Brennan 1994). I have described Neolithic lunar standstill alignments at the Dorset Cursus and Maiden Castle (Knight 1998) and at West Kennet Long Barrow (Knight 2011); here I show a virtual equinox moonrise at West Kennet during the Neolithic, prior to the erection of the blocking stone **(left)**. Prof John North has suggested that chalk balls/spheres found at Windmill Hill and Stonehenge may link fertility with the Moon, as these white objects resemble both the testes and the lunar disc (North 1996, p. 543). It is interesting that *'chalk ball-like nodules'* were found in the west chamber of West Kennet Long Barrow, which the moon would periodically illuminate.

One of the most amazing prehistoric objects with celestial associations ever found is the Nebra Sky Disc, a 30cm diameter Bronze Age object unearthed near Leipzig, Germany. Dated at c. 3600 years old, it is adorned with a disc of the Sun or Moon, as well as a crescent Moon and stars **(top)**; the cluster of seven dots may represent the Pleiades. Analysis has found that the gold and tin components of this work came from Cornwall.

Because the monthly cycles of the Moon and women so closely match, the Moon has primarily (but not exclusively) been associated with the divine feminine, an association that continues to this day; *menstruation* comes from the Greek word for Moon, *mene*, and the Latin *mensis,* meaning month. The Moon thus represents cycles of renewal and rebirth, and that the polarities of life and death were cyclical. The Moon is also associated with intuition, imagination, psychic powers, dreaming, and the emotions, probably due to its ability to move the waters of the oceans.

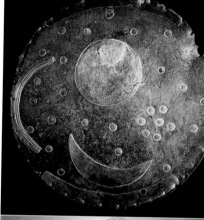

The Moon is often seen to have a triple aspect. The Crone Goddess is the *Dark of the Moon*, examples being Hecate, Kali and Heli; when new she is Artemis; and at full is Anu, Isis or Cybele. The Egyptian god Thoth is sometimes shown as a Baboon with either a solar disc or a lunar crescent on his head; another Egyptian deity, Kensu, also sports a crescent Moon headdress. The Hebrews had moon cults, for we read that they would, *'... make cakes for the queen of heaven'* (Jeremiah 7:18). Moses ascended Mount Sinai, which means *'Mountain of the Moon',* to receive his vision of the Ten Commandments.

The Moon is often associated with the fertility of the land, and folklore says to plant seeds with the growing phase, when the energy is rising, as many farmers still do today. The Greek goddess Artemis was a similar aspect to the Roman Diana, and was sometimes depicted with multiple breasts **(image p. 77)**, and is on occasion portrayed with animals and plants springing out of her body. Luna is the Roman equivalent of Selene, another Greek Moon goddess; it is thought to be her who is depicted on a pediment **(centre)** at the Roman spring complex at Bath (Bédoyère 2002, p. 23). Selene is shown here with a crescent moon on a Roman altar dated 2nd century AD, which is now in the Louvre Museum, Paris **(right)**.

As well as being the cause of tides, astrologically the Moon was also thought to affect human destiny, and was associated with both attaining insight and wisdom, a great light guiding our way, both physically and psychologically. It also had the power to affect the mind adversely (particularly when full); Hecate could equally bestow both insightful visions or induce madness. Tales of witches and werewolves are survivals of the negative association with Moon when full. The moon-gazing hare has become a popular Pagan icon; this echoes the Chinese *Festival of the Moon*, one symbol of which is the white rabbit, and the Chinese also believe that the features on the Moon's face depict a hare. Also in China, the moon is symbolic of the complete and whole family, whilst to Buddhists the moon represents beauty and serenity.

Virgin Mary – the Moon Goddess

As the Church spread its influence far and wide across the world, early missionaries must have encountered Moon goddesses at every turn. This aspect of the divine feminine clearly had to be replaced with a Christian counterpart, to fill a spiritual void, so to speak, and there could only be one candidate who could fill the vacancy – the Virgin Mary. It is said that Mary is represented by the Moon in Christian art because she is the

'reflector of the light of Christ'. The Moon of course has no light of its own, and the *'light of Christ'* is in reality an acknowledgment of how Jesus took over the role of the solar god, which I shall discuss at length soon. It is interesting that if Jesus was born on December 25 (which is in itself debatable), then presumably Mary must have been pregnant with him for the usual nine months term. Her Annunciation (when an angel told her she was to bear a child) is celebrated on March 25, which is spring, the time of the virgin/maiden aspect of the Earth Goddess.

The Moon had been associated with Sophia, the Egyptian and Greek goddess of knowledge, who was a lunar deity, the personification of wisdom and divine awareness; she was therefore absorbed by the Church in the persona of the Virgin Mary, who is also called *'Moon of the Church'*, as her wisdom was said to be perfect. Mary is frequently shown with a crescent moon, as with this example I found at St Lawrence, Malta **(left)**; as well as the moon at her feet, note the halo composed of twelve stars, one for each sign of the zodiac, confirming her celestial connection. Mary also stands on a serpent biting an apple, symbolising her chastity, for she was pure, unlike Eve.

Another common variation of the association between the Moon and Mary is when she is depicted standing on an *upturned* crescent Moon **(left, and images p. 192)**. This is an attribute of the High Priestess in a Tarot deck, who represents intuition and the power of the subconscious mind. This upturned crescent is also the sigil of the Egyptian goddess Isis, who can likewise be found standing over one. The Babylonian Moon goddess, Astarte, is sometimes depicted with a crescent moon on her head. The lunar crescent is stamped on Byzantium coins dated 341BC to celebrate, according to folklore, when the goddess Hecate saved the city from the invading Macedonians. Coyolxauhqui, the Aztec lunar goddess, is often portrayed wearing a crescent-shaped nose ring, whilst to Muslims, the crescent represents concentration, paradise and resurrection.

In Celtic and Hindu traditions, the lunar crescent can be shown in the form of a cup, which contains the elixir of immortality. Is this another reason why the Virgin Mary stands on the crescent moon, for within the vessel of her womb she carried Jesus, who was to cheat death, becoming an immortal? Another link between Mary and classical Moon goddesses of Greece and Rome is that the latter sometimes hold a lunar crescent, or wear one in their hair, both of which represents their chastity. To the

Greeks, the moon goddess Artemis was a committed virgin and famed huntress with a deadly bow, as was Diana. Minerva was another virgin Roman goddess, also associated with wisdom, magic, art and medicine; she is often depicted with her sacred attribute, the *'Owl of Minerva',* due to her links with the Moon, the night, and wisdom. The ancient Chinese lunar goddess, Ch'ang-o, is usually depicted as a beautiful young woman, with attributes similar to those of Mary.

Virgins have often been revered by ancient cultures and have even been consulted as oracles, such as the priestesses known as the Vestal Virgins, whose temple is said to be the Rome's oldest; Vesta was the Roman equivalent of Hestia, the Greek virgin goddess who made a life-long vow to remain pure. Athena was another staunchly virginal Greek goddess, who advised Odysseus on his way back from Troy, in order that he would avoid seductresses such as Circe and the Sirens. Astrea was yet another Greek virgin goddess, known as the *Celestial Virgin.* Despite the Mother and Crone aspects of the turning year, the Virgin goddess was always able to return to her pristine state, making her the *'Ever-Virgin',* a title which was shared by Ishtar, Anathita, Anath and others. This pretext was bestowed on the Virgin Mary, even though she later married and had other children. Sometimes an ancient goddess could transmute from virgin to mother/lover, such as Ishtar, and, in the case of the virgin goddesses Aphrodite and Diana, could even been associated with orgiastic feasts, conveying the combustible potential of the virgin aspect.

It is interesting that after her death and her 'Assumption' up to Heaven, Mary is known as, *'The Queen of Heaven',* which is exactly the title given to the Moon and several lunar goddesses by various ancient cultures! Mut, for instance, was the, *'Queen of the Goddesses and Lady of Heaven'* to the Egyptians, who was a virgin and sexually dimorphic, able to conceive offspring without the means of intercourse – just like Mary! In the Old Testament, the Book of Jeremiah (written around 628BC) refers to people being rebuked for burning incense and giving offerings to Asherah, the Hebrew/Canaanite *'Queen of Heaven'.*

In elevating Mary to the status of *'Virgin Bearer of Christ',* the Church suspended natural laws, thus securing the divinity of Jesus. The Egyptian goddess Mut could create life by interaction with the divine wind; was the process of conception without sexual intercourse taken on board by the Church, with the concept of the Holy Spirit, the *'Breath of God'*?

There is no Biblical account of Mary's death or her ascent to Heaven, but accounts from the 3rd-5th century written in Syriac (an Aramaic dialect still spoken in the Christian Church in Syria), clearly sought to put this right, and speak of Mary being taken up to Heaven. Interestingly, these early versions speak of Mary's body being carried up to, *'the Tree of Life',* to be united with her soul (Husain 1997, p. 124). Others state that Mary did not die at all, but instead ascended to Heaven whilst still alive; whatever the case, to all intents and purposes Mary was made divine and, like Ishtar, Isis and other goddesses before her, she became the *'Queen of Heaven;* at the service of Compline, she is addressed with, *'Hail, Queen of Heaven'.*

This powerful window of Mary is at Burley, in the New Forest **(right)**. Mary is shown in her usual white and blue

191

attire, holding her attribute, white lilies, all said to represent her purity. But I believe this colour scheme is symbolic of the waters of the world (blue) and the colour of the Moon (white); In another window I found at Godshill, Isle of White **(below left)**, note how Mary is standing not only on an upturned crescent moon, but also over the flowing waters of a stream emerging from a cave; the Moon, water and a cave – all imagery associated with the Earth Goddess; the Virgin's name, Maria, actually comes from the Latin *mare*, meaning *'sea'*. In Chapter 29, I demonstrated how water is often a symbol of the Divine Feminine.

The last example **(below right)**, is in Exeter Cathedral, Devon. Mary stands on the upturned crescent, and holds Jesus in her arms. But look at the background: the fiery rays of the Sun form the aureole behind Jesus and Mary, representing the Sun god/yang, which is balanced by the Moon goddess/yin. The image is the epitome of balance - the ancient God and Goddess have re-birthed.

Whenever I stand in front of an image of Mary standing on a lunar crescent, I acknowledge her not only as the mother of a great prophet, but also as the latest incarnation of one of Mankind's oldest figures of veneration, the Moon Goddess – Queen of Heaven.

36. The Earth Goddess and Mary the Mother

The concept of a Mother Goddess, she who births and nurtures all and represents Nature and the Earth, is a very ancient one. The Jungian scholar Erich Neumann concluded that most of the earliest prehistoric religious works of art were, '... *figures of the Great Goddess – the Palaeolithic image of Mother, before there was any Father either on earth or in heaven*' (Neumann 1972). Caves may have been seen as the womb of the Earth Mother, and their entrances her yoni **(images p. 9 & 198)**.

In Baltic regions, Saule was the mighty goddess of the Sun, as well as the goddess of childbirth. By mating with the Moon god the Earth was born, which they took turns to watch over. Twinned hills were seen as the breasts of the Great Mother, as is proven here by the very naming of the *Breasts of Aphrodite*, at Mykonos, Greece **(top)**. The author has shown examples of twinned hills elsewhere (Knight 1996 and 1998). Early figurines, such as the 24,000 year-old Venus of Willendorf, show swollen tummies and pendulous breasts, suggesting pregnancy and fertility **(images p. 12 & 13)**. Many Neolithic figurines of the Goddess have been unearthed at Malta, and at Catal Hüyük, in Turkey, one sculpture features a goddess sitting on a throne flanked by lions, dated c. 6,000BC **(right)**. Ancient depictions of the Triple Goddess often show

one figure holding an infant, representing the mother aspect **(images p. 170 & 171)**. The god Zeus and a mortal, Alceme, had a child called Heracles/Hercules, but he placed the child next to his wife Hera so he could drink of her milk and become immortal. However, he suckled so powerfully that the milk spilled across the sky, forming the stars of the Milky Way, as shown in this painting by Rubens **(right)**.

This image of the Mother Goddess holding an infant is very widespread across the ancient world, and was to be adopted by the Church to depict Mary and the child Jesus, as I shall soon demonstrate. Let us look back to see where this image came from, and how widespread.

193

A small figurine of the goddess holding a child-like bear cub on her lap, dated at 4500BC, was made by the Vinca culture of Yugoslavia. Another example of a mother and child is on a Sumerian seal, from the Akkad period, c. 2330 – 2154BC, which is accompanied by a bright star, predating the Nativity by over 2000 years! The scene is thought to represent the goddess Inanna, who gave birth to a son called 'The Shepherd'.

A beautifully crafted golden pendant, dated 1400- 1200BC, is shown here and depicts the Hittite Sun goddess Arinna with her offspring **(above left)**. Another very early image of a figure holding an infant comes from the 5th century BC, and was found at Sesklo, Greece **(above centre)**. Other images of goddesses holding a child were found on Malta, also dating to the Neolithic **(above right)**.

On a Phoenician stele found at Marash in Anatolia, a mother goddess is depicted, and on her knee stands a smaller male figure holding a falcon **(left)**, relating him to the Egyptian falcon-headed Horus.

The Great Goddess of the Hindu tradition is Shakti, whilst her mother goddess aspect is known as Mahadevi, who often holds a child in her arms. Lakshmi, the Hindu goddess of fortune, may hold an elephant (a sign of loyalty). In South America, Pachamama is the Inca Earth Mother, who was later portrayed as the Virgin Mary after the conquest by Catholic Spain; however, she is still honoured as the old fertility goddess by many aboriginal cultures.

Despite all the other early images, it is the Egyptian Goddess Isis that provides an ancient, convincing and close comparison with the Virgin Mary holding Jesus. The numerous images of Isis nursing her son, the solar god Horus, are the most relevant. Shown here is a bronze statue of Isis suckling Horus, c. 600-400BC **(image p. 197)**.

But the imagery goes back much further; a copper statue dated c.2040-1700BC also shows Isis the mother nursing Horus, the latter of which was sitting in the very place on his mother's lap that Jesus would occupy over 2000 years later. At the Temple of Seti I, Abydos, Isis is depicted with King Seti I sitting on her lap, tenderly stroking his chin, which has been dated around 1300BC **(right)**; the Earth Mother, in this case Isis, was seen to birth all living things, including pharaohs.

Prior to the Romans' advance across Italy, the Etruscan Mother Goddess was also depicted holding an infant. In Roman mythology, Tellus or Terra Mater was a goddess who protected the fecundity of the land, and also watched over marriages and children. This image **(centre)** is on the Ara Pacis Augustae in Rome, which was inaugurated in 9BC. Another Roman goddess, Cybele, was vilified by the early Christians, but one priest, called Montanus, founded a Christian sect in the 2nd century AD based on the identification of Cybele's son, Attis, with Jesus! This sect was declared heretic in the 4th century.

King Solomon himself imported the Canaanite Mother Goddess Asherah to Jerusalem c. 1000BC, as it is recorded that an image of her occupied a prime space in the Temple of Solomon for around three hundred years. There is evidence that the cult of Asherah survived until at least 621BC (Husain 1997, p. 88), and there are other Hebrew texts referring to Yahweh as female – God was once a woman!

The next image **(bottom)** is of the Jain Mother Goddess caressing a child, from the temple at Orissa, India. It is dated c. 1150-1200AD, and demonstrates the cross-fertilization of this iconic image. Krishna is also depicted suckling from the breast **(image p. 205)**.

Mary – the New Mother Goddess

Throughout the entire world, from the Nile to Mesopotamia, from Greece to India, the all-birthing and all-supporting Mother Earth Goddess was omnipresent. St Francis of Assisi clearly tuned into this when he said, '... our sister, Mother Earth, who sustains and governs us'. However, starting from around 2000 years ago it came to pass that the sole inheritor of this ancient tradition was the Virgin Mary. It looks as if the imagery of the ancient Goddess had passed directly to Mary, who was both Virgin and Mother. This may have been inspired by the spiritual needs of the people, as well as an understanding by the priests of the new religion that the long-established customs and devotion to the divine feminine had better be assimilated into Christianity, as it would surely enhance its chances of success. Mary's birth and death are not even mentioned in the Bible – she is eternal like some of the mother goddesses of old. The first images of Mary do not appear in the catacombs prior to 200AD, and less than 200 years later, in 380AD, the cults of Artemis and Isis were being repressed by Emperor Theodosius; between 400 and 500AD, the Temple of Isis at

195

Soissons, France, was rededicated to the *Blessed Virgin Mary,* and Isis (*'Mother of the Gods'*) became Mary, *'Mother of God'.* At the Parthenon in Athens, Athena's temple became a church between 500-600AD, rededicated to Mary. This transition is reflected by another early Christian heretical sect in Arabia, called the Collyridians, who worshipped the Virgin Mary as a goddess, as described by Epiphanius of Salamis as late as 375AD.

So, after thousands of years of worship, it took only 200 years for the goddess to fully metamorphose into Mary, the Virgin-Mother, who was called by some Christians *'The Great Mother of Life'.* People had needed their Divine Feminine, just as cultures had for so long, and the new religion had not disappointed them. A new Mother Goddess had been created **(left)** or, in a sense, the old one had never gone away, but was merely morphed into a new guise.

The Black Virgin

Black Virgins, or Black Madonnas, stand in crypts and on altars across Europe, usually holding her son, Jesus, on her lap. There are over 450 examples, most dated 12th-15th century. Much controversy has ensured regarding why Mary and Jesus should be depicted thus, but the answer may be provided, once again, by the ancient Earth Mother. A clue occurs in the Old Testament, when the Goddess speaks in the *Song of Songs*: *'I am black but comely, O ye daughters of Jerusalem'.* Black queens, princesses and goddesses abound in ancient texts and imagery and this too had to be assimilated into the new religion. In Apuleius' vision, Isis wears a black robe and some statues show her in this apparel. There were black adaptations of Demeter and Athena, and Cybele was also worshipped as a black stone; at Ephesus, Artemis was decidedly black **(centre and image p. 77)**.

The Chinese and Japanese earth goddess Quan Yin was depicted as a black idol at a temple at Miako in Japan (Scott 1966, p. 177), and the Hindu goddess Kali is also sometimes shown completely black.

Sites of black virgins are often found at or near ancient goddess sites, especially in France **(bottom)** and Spain at places associated with the Cathars and Mary Magdalene. Some of figures are said to have been brought back from the Holy Land by the Knights Templar and other Crusaders. In the crypt under Chartres Cathedral was formerly a shrine built around a statue of the Black Madonna, who was known as, *'Our Lady under the Earth';* the statue was destroyed in the 6th century. The oldest statue or carving of a Black Madonna in Britain is Our Lady of Hal, at Camden Town, London, although we do know that some were lost during the Dissolution of the Monasteries. The last example here is from Andover, Hampshire **(top)**.

Some believe that these black icons are associated with Mary Magdalene, a subject we shall return to later. Ultimately, the black virgin relates to the Dark of the Moon, where the old light has gone but from the depths of which new light is born, whether that light be Horus, Jesus or any number of the *'sons of the gods'*.

It is interesting that the Virgin Mary's mother is St Anne, who is thought to be the Christianisation of Ana or Anu, the Earth Mother; Black Anna, or Black Annis, is spoken of in the folklore of Leicestershire, concerning an anchorite who lived in a cave, the very birthplace or abode of goddesses and gods in countless ancient myths.

Mary is the last link of a long chain of Mother Goddess veneration, and the very fact that her Pagan *'family tree'* had not been fully acknowledged ultimately ensured her survival.

Perhaps the time is long overdue for the Divine Feminine, whether she be in the form of Mary or Isis, or simply Gaia, the Earth, to come to centre stage once more, and be acknowledged as such, rather than be portrayed as just a vehicle, a womb, for the latest edition of the Divine Son.

I will end this section with three images of the Great Mother with child: the first is from Egypt featuring Isis and Horus, dated 680BC **(below left)**; the next is from ancient Rome, depicting their portrayal of Isis and Horus **(below centre)**; the last is Christian, from the church at Bodmin, Devon **(below right)**. They say a picture tells a thousand words … need I say more.

37. The Divine Yoni and Sheela-na-gigs

In Chapter 16, I looked at how male sexual exhibitionism can be found in churches, and how it is associated with ancient gods and fertility rites. The former celebration of life in the form of the phallus was metamorphosed, in Church architecture, into warnings of the *'sins of the flesh'*, visual propaganda to ensure the illiterate masses walked the moral high road. However, in the process, the act of sexual union, central to the survival of life on this planet, was castigated and virtually demonised - spiritual castration no less.

This is equally true for the divine feminine, whose vulva and breasts had been worshipped for thousands of years, and still are in some non-Christian cultures; some examples of this veneration have been shown in previous chapters. However, vestiges of the sexual, reproductive Goddess *have* survived due to their portrayal on churches and cathedrals across Europe. This is one several ironies that have arisen as the Church preserved the very concepts it had sought to replace.

Natural places have been revered as the divine yoni. Narrow cave entrances, hollows in tree trunks, and fleshy fruit have all been seen as natural symbols of the yoni. St Nectan's Glen **(top)** is a sacred place at Tintagel, Cornwall, and I have stood in front of its powerful, cascading waterfall as its waters gushed through a perforated rock – the yoni of the Goddess. Brockley Cave, near Bristol, has an elongated yoni-like entrance **(centre)**, as does a 6ft (2m) high yoni-like feature I found at the entrance of the Ghar Dalam Caves, Malta, where the rock is even stained red **(left)**. I have already shown the Tolmen Stone, a perforated stone associated with the Druids that sits midst a Dartmoor river **(image p. 9)**.

It is not too difficult to find the origins of sheela-na-gigs amongst ancient cultures. There are over 1000 examples of Palaeolithic cave art, some dating back to 27,000BC, which have been interpreted as female genitalia – the yoni. Sometimes these were accompanied by clay pendants incorporating triangles and real seeds, the latter being a metaphor for the potential regenerative powers of both humans and vegetation.

I have already described how the aureole and the centre of the vesica piscis can be seen as the yoni, the sacred opening of the Earth Goddess. Several megaliths around the world are perforated to allow 'rebirthing' by means of passing through to the other side. Probably the most famous is at Men-an-Tol, Cornwall **(right)**, through which I have personally been re-birthed. The inverted triangle has been a symbol of the yoni of the Goddess since prehistory. Terence Meaden sees the triangle as symbolic of the divine feminine, at such places as Newgrange in Ireland (Meaden 1991).

Whenever I lead tours around Avebury, the world's largest stone circle, I point out that several of the megaliths display yoni-shaped holes, suggesting that some process of selection took place; the one shown here (stone 106) is involved in a Beltaine sunrise alignment (Meaden 1999); it has a long gash down its centre, complete with clitoris above the main, yoni-shaped crevice **(right)**. Also shown here is the fabulous, enthroned figurine *The Lady of Pazardzik* **(bottom)**, a Thracian fertility goddess from central Bulgaria, which dates back to the Neolithic, c. 4500 BC. Note the yoni, which is enclosed within a triangle, both features which are also evident on the Venus of Willendorf **(image p. 12)**.

In China, one of the names of Quan Yin, the earth mother, is *'Yoni of Yonies'* (Scott 1966, p. 176). Delphi was the Greek's greatest oracle site, sacred to the Great Mother, and named from the Greek word *delphos,* which means *'womb'.* The oracle room was underground in a fissure – the womb of the Goddess indeed.

In Hindu cultures the yoni has been the symbol of Shakti for thousands of years as the divine feminine element of Nature (the word *yoni* derives from ancient Sanskrit). The yoni mudra is a practice used to calm oneself before a meditation, where the participant makes a yoni-shaped triangle with their hands. Images of the Hindu goddesses Kali and Devi often show them on their back with legs splayed, releasing their sacred fluid, the *yoni-tattva,* the divine elixir of life, which is drunk by their adherents. The vulva or yoni is worshipped by devotees of Shakti/Kali as the *Great Womb.* A temple dedicated to the goddess Sati stands at Kamakhya, Assam, where the yoni is represented by a cleft rock face, which is kept constantly moist by an underground stream; once a year the waters flow red over the yoni (due to iron-oxides), signalling the onset of the monsoon.

Altars in India are often painted with red triangles, symbolising the menstruating yoni and the cycles of nature. In temples and ashrams, a bowl or other

receptacle representing the yoni may have a stone phallus, the lingam, placed within it, this combination being known as the linga-yoni. It represents the balance of yin and yang, the marriage of the gods, and linga-yonis are much venerated **(left)**.

The Christian Yoni

The term sheela-na-gig comes from the Irish language, probably deriving from *Sighli-na-gCioch,* meaning, *'the old hag of the breasts'* (Kelly 1996). In her book *'Archaeology of the Welsh Marshes',* S C Stanford considers sheela-na-gigs to be, *'... the portrayal of the Celtic goddess of creation and destruction. The sheela-na-gig at Kilpeck offers wordless instruction in the art of self-delivery'.*

Across Europe there are Church carvings of naked women posing in such a manner as to expose and emphasize their genitalia. These are hardly the images you would expect to find in a Christian context; so one has to ask why there are literally hundreds of images of the female sexual organ, a French example of which is shown here **(below)**. Can we dismiss them as mere whimsical creations, the product of fun and devilment by the masons? I think not. Although many appear to be comical expressions of a mason's humour, Church symbolism was strictly regulated right through medieval times, each icon representing some specific moral or Biblical concept, and every sculptured piece of stonework cost money as it employed a man's time and skill. More than this, why did so many of them survive the destruction of *'idolatrous and inappropriate'* imagery by the Puritans, especially considering that many are within easy reach and within plain sight of anyone with a puritanical mindset. Surely they cannot have survived on the grounds of artistic merit alone (Weir and Jerman 1986).

One view is that these were put onto churches by locals, who were chiefly agricultural folk, and who regarded them as representative of the old fertility gods, and obviously vital ones at that, even though the Church was stamping down on sexual practices

outside of marriage. Perhaps by bringing the fertility goddess, which is what she is, into the fabric of a church, it could now be shown that it was God that was blessing the fields, not the Earth Goddess. This is why so many images of the Green Man are to be seen in churches – it is now the Christian God that ensures fecundity, not the gods of old. However, the goddess did not go easily, for as late as the 14th century, monks of Frithelstock Abbey in Devon were rebuked for worshipping a Goddess statue, described as, *'the unchaste Diana',* at a woodland altar. It is interesting that amongst Indo-Iranian cultures a good harvest was referred to as, *'a fertile yoni'.*

Linked to this is the idea that, as fertility symbols, sheela-na-gigs have the power to repel the forces of evil, turning aside the glances of the *'Evil Eye'.* Female genitalia has for many centuries in many cultures been thought of as a powerful device for the warding off evil and, in the case of India, lightning strikes! (Bord and Bord 1982, p. 73).

Clearly, there is some archetypal force at work here in the creative mind of the stone mason and wood carver, some urge that compelled them to create carvings which were seemingly so opposed to the dogma of the time. We know there are good luck associations with many of these images, such as several whose vulva had to be touched by newly-weds for good fortune and to ensure fertility in their marriage. Lots of records exist of the yoni of sheela-na-gigs being worn smooth by people having rubbed that area over generations.

Another view is that these sexuality explicit images were placed in and around churches to remind people of the evils of sexual sin, so that they may choose the more morally acceptable path - many are said to be literally, *'ugly as sin'*. This invites comparison with the concept of Eve, who was cast naked out of Eden due to her sinful misdemeanors. This has always seemed a strange concept to me, for surely these displays would be counter-productive, serving to *remind* people of sex; would you place a huge bar of chocolate on each chair at a weight-watchers club, or set up a free bar at a meeting of Alcoholics Anonymous? I think not.

Should we even class *all* sheela-na-gigs as erotic art? Many display their genitalia by parting their legs, which would seem to be very explicitly sexual. But can the act of opening ones legs to give birth to a child be classed as eroticism, or that of a nudist lying with legs slightly splayed whilst soaking up the rays on a beach, or a gynaecological examination? Nudity in itself need not be seen to be erotic, as a judged by the thousands of nudes adorning the walls of art galleries and museums across the world. I am not saying that all sheela-na-gigs lack any sexual connotations, as some clearly do; a small number involve serpents or else have appropriately positioned phalli, or else feature the caressing of the yoni by the fingers of the sheela-na-gig herself! I am simply saying that genital exhibitionism once held a more profound meaning.

Take the example shown here on a capital in the crypt of Canterbury Cathedral, said to be a *'She-Devil'*, who is shown between two dragons **(right)**. We must be careful not to project our modern views onto objects that were created many centuries ago. What we see today as vulgar and distasteful may have had a purpose above and beyond that which we now envisage. Early Gnostic Christians saw sexuality as a celebration of the union of the God and the Goddess, and carried out ritual sexual intercourse and sacramental nudity in their churches (Freke and Gandy 2002, p. 51). There is a sheela-na-gig carved into the dark cave walls of Royston Cave **(right)**, next to a sword, and which may have been carved by the Gnostic Knights Templar, who were Christians (Beamon 2009).

I believe that these images began in the early church as symbols of fertility, to ensure the fecundity of the fields and the crops; it is interesting that concentrations of sheela-na-gigs occur in areas where the *Celtic Church* was established, such as in Ireland and in parts of France, the old Gaulish lands; there are nearly 40 sheela-na-gigs in the UK, and around 75 in Ireland (Bord and Bord 1982). Although we have no sheela-na-gigs older than c. 1000AD, that does not mean they did not once exist, for we have few Saxon churches surviving in their original state. Many of the Irish examples have come from ruins, or else on blocks of stone from

former churches. It has been noted that so many of the Irish sheela-na-gigs are, or were formerly, on the keystones of entrance arches, so they were once prominently displayed, not hidden away in some dark corner where few would see them. I think it relevant that at Tara, the Irish sacred centre of sovereignty, a sheela-na-gig is carved on a stone in the churchyard. Archaeologist Barry Cunliffe has described sheela-na-gigs in Ireland as representing, *'... the Irish Goddess of Creation'* (in *'The Celtic World'*, 1979).

I think that it was only later, around the time the great gothic cathedrals were built and many local churches were being remodelled, that the female exhibitionist figure came to represent sexual impropriety and sin. *'Images of Lust',* by Weir and Jerman (1986), is a thoroughly recommended book on the subject.

The last sheela-na-gig I illustrate here **(left)** is iconic and is, in my opinion, Britain's finest example; she is carved in all her glory on a corbel on the exterior of the church at Kilpeck, Herefordshire. As well as the ovate shape of her vulva, note how the eyes are also yoni-shaped, as are those on the French example shown on p. 200. Her alien-like eyes and gaping yoni both draw us into mysteries with which we have lost our connection; as well as being an exit, the mystical yoni can be an *entrance* to Gnosticism – that original and pure strand of Christianity. They represent a time when Gnostic Christians held women as equals, as did Jesus. Something got lost along the way.

Sheela-na-gigs often strike a strong chord today with both women and men, and are of renewed importance on many levels, being capable of offering different things to different people; they have, for example, become symbols for both Neo-Pagans and the feminist movement. The powerful creative forces of the divine feminine are again being appreciated - in full flow once more, so to speak.

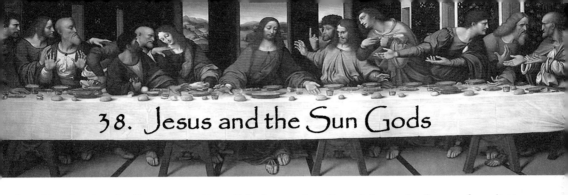

38. Jesus and the Sun Gods

I n this chapter, I will compare the attributes and myths of Jesus to those of ancient gods and heroes, as well as delve into the beliefs of the original Christians, to whom the Jesus story was employed as a means to attain Gnosis, the hidden mysteries of the soul and the inner self. Although I will touch upon it briefly, the enduring debate as to whether Jesus was an actual historical person, or a mythical character concocted for the teaching of inner mysteries, does not really fall within my remit, and I am somewhat relieved at that! Jesus and his parables certainly reveal allegories concerning spiritual initiation with much encoded philosophy and profound wisdom. But whether Jesus actually lived, or was merely a re-vamping of previous Sun god myths, is neither here nor there, for surely it is the *content* of the Jesus story that ultimately matters. The vast majority of ancient philosophers knew that myths were merely allegories by which to obtain spiritual Gnosis, that personal connection with the divine, whatever people perceive that to be; in the New Testament, Jesus himself taught that, *'Everyone when his training is complete will reach his teacher's level'* (Luke 6:40).

If we investigate the Jesus myth, as I have done, we will find many comparisons between his tradition and the myths of many ancient solar gods and other 'solar heroes'; it is soon evident that the perennial *'Sons of God'* has become the *'Son of God'*. For instance, in the Bible, Jesus is called, *'The Lion of Judah',* and I have already shown several ancient gods and heroes were associated with the lion (see p. 87 -8).

The unique characteristic of the Church is that, from the 4th century AD, Christian literalists claimed that their version of the resurrected Sun God/God Man *actually happened* – and very recently in the past. The Jesus story was written into history *as* history, as fact. However, later Gnostic orders, like the Cathars and the Knights Templar, continued to uphold the ideals and beliefs of early Christians, and their adherence to this truth would cost them dearly in the 13th and 14th century.

I have referred to Jesus only by that name throughout this book, and have not used the suffix *Christ*. This word comes from the Greek word *Christos,* meaning *'anointed',* and the Syriac *'Messiah'.* Although today he is called *Jesus Christ,* the early Christians knew him as *'Christ Jesus',* which is more of a description - *'the anointed Jesus'.* Anointing was an ancient practice, and statues of gods and goddesses, altars, and kings were anointed with water or oils as a symbol of their authority. The anointings of Jesus occurred at the start and end of his ministry, initially with water by John the Baptist, and with oils by Mary Magdalene prior to the Crucifixion. Both of these learned characters were marginalized by the Church, and the true importance of the roles they both played in the life of Jesus was nearly lost forever.

Due to recent discoveries of additional gospels in the deserts of the Middle East, we now know that the Jesus narrative of the New Testament is woefully incomplete, and that other versions, more heretical and controversial, are now available to us; the most famous *'lost gospels'* are the Dead Sea Scrolls **(image, next page)**, which probably came from the Temple library and hidden during the Jewish revolt against the Romans in 70AD (Picknett and Prince 1997, p. 303). 60% of their content is not found in the Bible, and it always did seem strange to me that this whole new batch of *authenticated*

stories concerning Jesus was not immediately added to the Bible; is that not like discovering half a dozen previously unknown Beatles albums and then not subsequently releasing them?

As the Church developed and expanded, decisions were made, at more than one Church council, as to which gospels were to be included into the Bible, and which were to be excluded, deemed too risky and dangerous for 'literalists' to stomach. More than this, the excluded writings were branded false and heretical. At the Council of Nicaea in 325AD, a majority vote by the holy fathers proclaimed Jesus to be divine - the *'Son of God'*. Jesus had been promoted to a demigod, whereas before this fateful assembly he was revered as a gifted prophet, yet a very mortal one.

In recent years many excellent publications have suggested that the historical Jesus never even existed and that his story was based on the myths of several ancient gods; two books by Tim Freke and Peter Gandy stand pre-eminent (Freke and Gandy 1999 and 2002). Many researchers also advocate that in prehistory there was a balance of the divine masculine and the divine feminine, the god and the goddess, and that the goddess element that was certainly present in early Christianity was gradually, and at times ruthlessly, erased from Church doctrine. To balance the loss of the Earth Mother, the Virgin Mary was wheeled out centre stage to give people their vanquished divine feminine. As Christianity spread, it freely attached Pagan rituals and myths in order to be more palatable to those it sought to convert; this tendency for early Christianity to meet Paganism halfway is beyond dispute, and was a very astute move by the early Church fathers.

Happy Christmas

The actual birthday of Jesus was soon forgotten by early Christians and various writers in the second and third century AD suggested such dates as December 21, January 2 or 6, March 25, April 18, 19, 21, May 20, Nov 17 and 20. In other words, no one had a clue! During his reign (270-275AD) Roman Emperor Aurelian sought to unify his people and get them to convert to Christianity as painlessly as possible, and declared that December 25 should be celebrated as the birth of the *Sol Invictus, 'the Unconquered Sun'*. In the 4th century, the winter solstice period had been decided upon for Jesus' birth, and December 25 was finally ordained as the date by Pope Julius in 350AD. This is the time after midwinter when the days can be perceived as getting longer as the Sun climbs higher in the sky – the solar god is reborn. The Romans were accustomed to celebrating the rebirth of the Sun on that date with the Festival of Saturnalia, so it was relatively easy to get this adopted as the birth of Jesus, the new demigod. The first known celebration of Christmas (*'Christ's Mass'*) was in 336AD in Rome, and by 379AD it had spread to Constantinople, although it took until 430AD to be recorded in Alexandria. The word Christmas is nowhere found in the Bible, and is not mentioned, as such, until as late as 1038, when *'Cristes Maesse'* appears in Old English. It is interesting that Jewish/Hebrew tribes celebrated midwinter as the birth of Yahweh, which *is* recorded in the Bible (John 10:22-3), known as the *'Festival of Light'*.

It must also be remembered that, in the Old Testament, Melchizedek was also born of a virgin mother, whilst John the Baptist was born to a sterile mother and, in Islam, the poet Kabir was also born of a virgin. In Chapter 36 I showed several images of how the ancient concept of Earth Mother nursing the infant solar god was taken on by the Church, metamorphosed into the Virgin Mary and Jesus.

Let us now take a look at a selection of *'dying and rising gods'*, as well as other mythical characters, who share many attributes with Jesus, and several of whom even share his birthday.

Krishna

Krishna, or Krisna, the mighty Hindu god, was presented with gold, frankincense and myrrh at his birth, which was said to be at the midwinter solstice. Krishna was born by means of divine intervention, with the supreme god Vishnu descending into the womb of Devaki, Krishna's mother; scholars debate as to whether she was a virgin or not. This statue **(right)** shows Krishna being nursed by his foster mother, Yashoda, and mirrors images of the Virgin and Mary we looked at earlier. The worship of Krishna can be traced back to the 4th century BC, and some early depictions show him as a charioteer, inviting comparison with solar gods, such as Apollo.

Helios/Aion/Sol/Apollo

The Greek god Helios/Aion, seen here **(right)** from the Temple of Athena at Liion, or Troy, was the personification of the Sun, born at the winter solstice by the goddess Kore, *'the maiden'*. Note the halo surrounding the head of Helios. In one myth, Helios uses a net to ensnare two lovers whom he seeks to punish, which of course invites comparison with Jesus' association with, *'fishers of men'*. In one Greek record, at the hour of sunset Helios climbed into a great golden cup in which he travels through the Underworld through the night, which evokes the traditions of the Grail and magical chalices. The Roman equivalent was Sol, specifically *Sol Invictus,* as scholars see him as a separate and distinct deity to Apollo, whose images were later taken on to portray Jesus **(image p. 22)**. Incidentally, Apollo is often shown with a halo **(image p. 77)**, representing the Sun, a motif that was absorbed by the Church for its own saints and divine beings One of Apollo's titles was *Chrēstos*, meaning *'good'*, which certainly invites comparison with *'Christ'*.

Tammuz/Dumuzid

Tammuz, or Dumuzid, was a Sumerian, Babylonian and Hebrew god; he gives his name to the fourth month of the Hebrew calendar, as well as the month of July in Iraq. His name means, *'Faithful and True Son'*. Tammuz originated as the Sumerian shepherd god, and later became their life-death-rebirth deity. At his winter 'death', in which the god enters his Underworld *'sheepfold',* he was widely mourned. The goddess Inanna seeks to rescue Tammuz, her husband, from the caves of the Underworld, reminding us that it was Mary Magdalene who sought out Jesus' body in the tomb after his Crucifixion. Tammuz was also known as *'god of date palms,'* and it will be recalled that palm leaves were laid in front of Jesus at his triumphant entrance into Jerusalem.

I came across this ancient Sumerian frieze **(bottom)**, on which Tammuz is seen with bunches of grapes and vines (the emblem of Jesus) which, incredibly, are in the shape of the cross! (We shall see more ancient images of the cross motif soon.) Some kings were named after Dumuzid, and one of these, Dumuzid of Kuara, was known as, *'The Fisherman'*. According to some scholars, the Church of the Nativity, in Bethlehem, is built over a cave that was originally a shrine to Tammuz, and his equivalent Adonis. Even more interesting is that scholars have found evidence that the god wore a crown of thorns and was annually sacrificed in Jerusalem, where he was known as *'The Anointed One'* and *'Saviour'*. Tammuz was also known as a healer god, and was, of course, resurrected.

Nimrod/Baal

This Sun deity, who was celebrated in Babylonia and whose birthday was December 25, was both the son and husband of the goddess Ishtar. After his death, Ishtar claimed that Nimrod would return and leave her gifts every year under an evergreen tree – on December 25; this is the true origin of the Christmas Tree! The word Yule in fact has its origins in the Babylonian/Chaldean word for *'child'* or *'infant'*. The fire festival of Baal or Bel was a great festival in Ireland held annually on December 25, and British Druids celebrated December 25 as *Nollagh* or *Noel*, seeing it as the day of earth regeneration.

Dusares

At temples at the ancient desert city of Petra, in Jordan **(left)**, the birth of a divine son called Dusares, by a virgin mother, was celebrated by the ancient Arabs. His name was Kore or Manat, and he was known as, *'The only son of the Lord'*. Worship of the god continued as late as the 9th century AD, as recorded by Muslim historians.

Mithras

Mithras was the Persian god and Roman god-man, who was held within either a tree or a rock tomb for three days, before rising at the time of the winter solstice as the *'Sol Invictus'*, a title that was transferred to Jesus **(image p. 22)**. On this Roman mosaic **(bottom)**, the god is shown emerging from a cave, which is very similar to Christian depictions of Jesus' Resurrection. The followers of Jesus walked in the footsteps of Mithraism, which was a very popular mystery cult prior to the arrival of Christianity. The early Christian Roman bishops even adopted the headwear of Mithras, the *mithra*, which became known as the mitre in later centuries. Mithraism was a serious competitor to Christianity until the 4th century when it was suppressed due to the similarity of its god to Jesus.

It was believed that Mithras was born on the night of December 24/25 around 500BC and his birth was witnessed by three shepherds and by Magi bearing gifts! His birthday was celebrated as, *'The Birthday of the Unconquered Sun'* and one of his titles was *'Light of the World'*. Like Jesus, Mithras performed many miracles during his lifetime, such as casting out demons, and he celebrated a final supper with *twelve* followers before he ascended to the gods on March 21 – the time of the Equinox and Eastertide.

206

Osiris

Osiris was the Egyptian god whose birth was also celebrated on December 25, and who died on a Friday, being reborn from a tree after three days, and was known by such titles as, *'Saviour', 'King of Kings'* and *'The Shepherd',* all of which were transferred to Jesus. Egyptian texts tell us that three wise men announced Osiris' birth, and that his followers ate wheat cakes in remembrance of him. A youthful Osiris represents the re-born Sun at midwinter, his 'Resurrection', shown here, seated, at the Temple of Horemheb **(right)**.

Horus

Horus was one of the oldest revered Sun gods of Egypt, who was miraculously conceived by his mother, Isis/Meri, who was both an earth mother and a perpetual virgin goddess. The *'Holy Trinity'* of Horus, Osiris and Isis is shown here **(right)**, on display in the Louvre, Paris; Horus is on the left. On the temple walls at Luxor are inscriptions telling of how Thoth announced the conception of Horus by the Virgin Isis, after Kneph *('Holy Spirit of Gods')* had impregnated her. Horus was born either at midwinter or December 25, at which times his birth was celebrated in the temples. Some of his titles were, *'The Son of Truth', 'Lamb of God', 'Word Made Flesh'.* Often shown with a Falcon's head, Horus was a sky god, and was considered to contain the Sun and the Moon, the Sun being his right eye, and the Moon his left. I have noted how the Sun and Moon are often shown together above images of Jesus. As I have shown previously **(image p. 197)**, the image of Horus being nursed by Isis is very similar to that of the Virgin Mary with the infant Jesus. More than this, in the 5th century AD, the Latin author Marcobius referred to the annual Egyptian celebration in which, *'a baby is laid in a manger/cradle... and is displayed for the adoration of the people'.* Epiphanius (c. 310-403AD), wrote of the Egyptians, *'At midwinter, the sun was seen as a small child',* just as Christians see Jesus at Christmas. It is relevant that many of the temples dedicated to Horus were aligned with the midwinter sunrise. The child-form of Horus was sometimes known as Sokar or Seker, who is depicted as a baby falcon or hawk, and whose festival was held on December 22. Dr Gerald Hawkins discovered an inscription in Kherouef's tomb, dated c. 1400BC, which read, *'The doors of the underworld are open, O Sokaris, sun in the sky. O reborn one'.* Horus was baptised in the River Eridanus or Larutana (Jordan) by *'Anup the Baptiser',* the equivalent of John the Baptist no less. Regarding miracles, Horus walked on water, exorcised demons and raised El-Azarus (El-Osiris) from the dead.

Dionysus/Bacchus

Dionysus was a Greek god, described as, *'Saviour',* and whose birth to a virgin mother (Persephone or Semele, depending on the version) was celebrated on December 25; he was killed and resurrected three days later. His Roman equivalent was Bacchus, who had a centre of worship in Jerusalem around the 1st century BC, where it was recorded that his flesh and blood were symbolically eaten in the form of bread and wine, known as *'ingesting the god',* just as Jesus taught the disciples to remember him by. Dionysus was the Greek god of wine and, like Jesus, vines were his symbol. At his own wedding

to Ariadne he turns water into wine, as did Jesus! Interestingly, Dionysus is the bridegroom at this event, which invites the question as to whether Jesus was also about to be betrothed to Mary Magdalene when he did his wine-making miracle; in the Bible, John the Baptist hailed Jesus as, *'the Bridegroom'* (John 3:29). In Matthew 9:15 Jesus said, *'Can the children of the bride chamber mourn, as long as the bridegroom is with them?'* The father of Dionysus was Zeus, the *'all powerful father god'*, so Dionysus was known as the *'Son of God'*, as well as *'Only Begotten Son'*, just like Jesus.

Dionysus was also depicted accompanied by 12 figures, and rode an ass in a, *'triumphal procession'*, as Jesus of course did as he entered Jerusalem **(image p. 97)**. Dionysus/Bacchus also raised the dead and restored the sight of the blind. His symbol was the lamb or ram, and he was known as, *'Young Man of the Tree'*, suggestive that he was not only a vegetation god, depicted with grapes and vines **(top, and image p. 147)**, but may also have been crucified.

The monogram 'IHS' is often seen in churches, as shown here in one I visited on Malta **(left)**, and represents the first three letters of Jesus in Greek, as well as *'Iesous hominum salvator'* (*'Jesus Saviour of Man'*) in Latin. It is said that it may also have derived from, *'In Hoc Signo'*, meaning *'In His Sign'*, which was a ritual cry at the temples of both Dionysus and Bacchus (Gardiner and Osborn 2005, p. 120-1). The emblem 'IHS' was shown on temples dedicated to both gods – and yet it is also the emblem of Jesus! This is direct evidence that the figure of Jesus usurped the old gods of wine and the vine, and I think it is wonderfully poignant that Bacchus was also known as Ichthus, *'the fish'*.

Attis

Attis was the Phrygian and Greek god of vegetation and is often depicted as a shepherd, complete with a flute and staff. He is winged in this example **(left)**, which is from 1st or 2nd century BC Tarsus, now in the Louvre, Paris. His cult began around 1250BC, and he later became a Roman solar god, worshipped from around 200BC, and was venerated at Herculaneum at the time of the eruption of Vesuvius in 79AD. Attis was born of a virgin mother, the goddess Cybele/Nana, after she was impregnated by divine intervention. Due to his act of self castration, i.e. self-sacrifice, his priests often had to be eunuchs. His birthday was celebrated on December 25, and later he was to be sacrificed, *'to bring salvation to all of mankind'*. After being crucified on a pine tree on *'Black Friday'* he descended into the Underworld for three days and on Sunday March 21 (around Easter) he arose, proclaiming a new season had begun. All this represented the cycles of vegetation, which 'dies' in winter to be reborn in the spring, at which time maypoles were erected in his honour. It is interesting that the date of the climax of Attis' festival, March

25, was also the date the early church chose for the death of Jesus. Bread was eaten by the followers of Attis, who took it to represent the god's body; sounds familiar!

Adonis

Adonis was the Greek god of beauty and desire who was a central figure in various mystery traditions from the 6th century BC. His cults were particularly developed by women, to whom he was the ever-youthful spirit of vegetation. His name derives from the Hebrew Canaanite word *adon,* meaning, *'Lord',* and the Phoenician word *adoni,* meaning *'my lord',* and he is the equivalent of the Babylonian god Tammuz. Following

his death, Adonis was reborn out of a tree, which his mother had transformed herself into; this is symbolic of the awakening of the Earth Mother, and with it vegetation, in the spring. This wonderfully evocative painting of his birth **(above)** is by Luigi Garzi (1638-1721). Adonis' birthday is on December 25, and Church father Jerome, who died in Bethlehem in 420AD, reported that a local holy cave had been consecrated to the god; this was later Christianised, possibly by the founding of the Church of the Nativity.

Hercules/Heracles

The Greeks celebrated the birth of this heroic figure on December 25. As a newborn, he was suckled by the goddess Hera, an act that made him immortal. However, he suckled so powerfully that the milk spilled across the sky, forming the Milky Way, as demonstrated in a painting by Rubens **(image p. 193)**; this depiction of mother and child, like those of Isis and Horus, is mirrored by the Virgin Mother and Child.

Hermes Kriophoros

This Greek god was known as, *'the Ram Bearer',* as were some other gods. He was protector of flocks and herds and I have already shown him on a statute c. 5-6th century BC **(image p. 91)**. His cult was very popular in Arcadia, and myths tell of how he would lead his animals to fresh water, sometimes carrying them on his shoulders. Jesus, of course, is the *'Good Shepherd'* and is often depicted carrying a lamb **(image p. 91)**. In one festival held in honour of Jupiter, the supreme god of the Roman pantheon, a white lamb was ceremonially led to the Capitoline Citadel to be sacrificed to him.

Apollonius of Tyana

Apollonius (who was named after the Sun god Apollo) was a renowned Greek philosopher and occultist (c. 4BC-100AD), who lived around the time of Jesus in the town of Tyana, in the Roman-held province of Anatolia, Asia Minor. He was such a respected figure that in 210AD Empress Julia Domna commissioned a biography of his life to be compiled. His wisdom led to the establishment of a cult in his lifetime and his followers included royalty and fellow-philosophers. Details of his life, that parallel those of Jesus, include the appearance of a *'supernatural being'* announcing his miraculous birth, the gathering of disciples around him, healing the sick, casting out demons, raising the dead, foretelling the future, teachings using parables, and execution by the Romans. He returned after his death to convince his followers he lived on in the heavenly realms (Ehrman 2012). Hundreds of statues were erected in honour of Apollonius in the 1st and

2nd century AD, as his fame as a *'Divine Man'* spread around the Mediterranean. Apollonius was a real historical figure, and Sossianus Hierocles, writing in the 3rd century AD, regarded his life and doctrine to be more valuable than that of Jesus. In one of his texts, Apollonius says that God cannot be influenced by prayers and sacrifices, but should be approached by a spiritual practice known as *'Nous'*, the intellect or understanding, which is Gnosis. Joseph Campbell regarded the stories of Jesus and Apollonius to be examples of individuals who can be compared to the divine hero stories, in his view comparable with Buddha and Krishna. It has been suggested that the life of Jesus was based on that of Apollonius, although, somewhat inevitably, Christians cast the accusation of plagiarism in the opposite direction. Scholars generally agree that both Apollonius and Jesus were born in 4BC, and that both figures visited Jerusalem, and were executed by the Romans. What I think is different about Apollonius, compared to the other *'candidates'*, who are ancient gods and demigods, is that this Greek philosopher actually lived and breathed in the Middle East, *at the time of Jesus.*

So I hope it is clear that there is little or no evidence to demonstrate that Jesus is the *reason for the season!* It is therefore gratifying to find out that in 1994 the Pope wrote that Jesus was probably not actually born on December 25 after all, and that this date was chosen due to the existing winter solstice festivals. Although this announcement caused a stir amongst some theologians, I would hazard a guess that most Christians are still not aware of this very significant admission.

Jesus the Shaman/Magician

If he was a real person, I believe we can place the historical Jesus in the role of shaman/magician, like his contemporary John the Baptist, and indeed Moses before them. Jesus' time in the desert to confront his 'inner demons' and ego (the *'Devil'*), his acts of magic *('miracles'),* his visions of events happening elsewhere, his predictions of future events, are all shamanic in nature. Jesus' raising of the dead **(top),** shown here at Taunton, his conversations with the ancestors and the spirit world *('speaking with God'),* and his belief in, and activation of, his own Resurrection after death *(metaphysical rebirth/reincarnation)* are more shamanic practices, which are still practiced today, just as they have been since the dawn of Mankind.

Regarding the miracles of Jesus, was it all hype, was he a metaphysical master, or were the early Christian Gnostics merely using old myths to teach the wonders of metaphysics and enlightenment? Healing the sick is one of the chief practices of shamans to this day, so we should not be surprised that Jesus was also active in these pursuits; his healing of the cripple at the Pool of Bethesda is shown here **(left)** in the church at Tormarton, Gloucestershire. Calming the sea and walking on water are two of the miracles performed by Jesus, and yet in prehistoric Babylonia, Tammuz (*'Lord of the Net'),* similarly appeared from the waters to teach of his wisdom. In Greek and Roman tradition, Poseidon and Neptune, respectively, travelled over the sea in a chariot, and Poseidon's son, Orion, was also gifted the ability to walk on water. In another Roman myth, it is Neptune who stills the winds and calms the waters of the sea. Buddhist monk Huang-po also walked on water when he found his way barred by a river; Jesus changed water into wine (which, by the way, the gods Mithras and Dionysus are both accredited with doing) at a wedding in Cana; the concept that Jesus and his disciples were *'fishers of men'* has its origins back in ancient Egypt, when the god Osiris would collect the souls of the dead and sail them down the River Nile to the Underworld **(image p. 40)**.

Jesus used an analogy between fishing and conversion, which included, *'I will make you fishers of men'*. This, however, was pre-dated by both Buddha and Orpheus of the Greeks, who were both known as *'Fishers of Men'*; I have already looked at ancient fish/men gods, such as Vishnu and Dagon **(images p. 107)**.

Another practice common to shamans is the ingestion of psychoactive plants, such as *'magic mushrooms'* and the like, as an aid to journeying to the spirit world. Moses and Jesus may have both carried out this ancient shamanic practice in order to, *'meet God'*; Jesus is depicted with red mushrooms in more than one window **(image p. 149)**.

And, lastly, Jesus' moment of realisation, or Gnosis, is shown with his links to the holy chalice/Grail in the Garden of Gethsemane **(images p. 187)**.

During excavations of the underwater ruins of Alexandria's ancient harbor in 2008, a team of scientists, led by renowned French marine archaeologist Franck Goddio, recovered a bowl, dating between the late 2nd century BC and the early 1st century AD **(right)**. On it is engraved what they believe could be the world's first known reference to 'Christ', providing evidence that Christianity and paganism were at times intertwined. The full engraving on the bowl reads, 'DIA CHRESTOU O GOISTAIS', which was interpreted by the excavation team to mean either, *'by Christ the magician'* or *'the magician by Christ'*. The Egyptian site also includes the now submerged island of Antirhodos, the possible site of Cleopatra's palace. The bowl is similar to ones on two early Egyptian earthenware statuettes that are thought to show soothsaying rituals. Egyptologist David Fabre concluded that, 'It should be remembered that in Alexandria, Paganism, Judaism and Christianity never evolved in isolation. All these forms of religion evolved magical practices that seduced both the humble members of the population and the most well-off classes. It was in Alexandria where new religious constructions were made to propose solutions to the problems of man, of God's world. The cults of Isis, the mysteries of Mithras, and early Christianity bear witness to this'.

John the Baptist and Jesus

John the Baptist is a very understated character in the Jesus story, and some authors have suggested that the early Gnostic Christians actually held John in a higher regard than Jesus, and that John was the centre of a well-established and popular cult. It was John who baptises Jesus at the start of his ministry **(image p. 163)**, so John was clearly of superior status to Jesus to be able to bestow such a sacred rite. John was, I believe, a fellow-shaman/magician. He was said to have been a fiery ascetic dressed in animal skins, who lived by simple means in the wilderness, shunning worldly goods and comforts. The church acknowledges that Jesus and John knew each other as children **(bottom image, previous page)**, and I believe that they may well have received similar teachings of esoteric knowledge in the mystery schools active at that time in the Middle East. John was known as *'The Great Nazar'*, similar to the title for Jesus, *'Jesus the Nazarean'*. This may not be referring to the town of Nazareth at all, but to the Gnostic term *'Nazarean'*, which means, *'to behold'* or *'envision'* (Gardiner and Osborn 2005, p. 96).

Some scholars have suggested that John the Baptist was the teacher of Jesus, his mentor no less, and that Jesus later left to start his own sect. One scholar retranslated the Biblical phrase of John, *'he that cometh after me'*, to mean, *'he that follows me'*. But the idea that Jesus was subservient to John did not sit well with the Church fathers once Jesus' status had been elevated to that of a deity. This depiction of Jesus and John the Baptist **(top)** is in the church of St Cross, Winchester **(also image p. 26)**.

It is interesting that St Gabriel announced the pregnancy of John's mother, Elizabeth, in much the same way as the Virgin Mary's pregnancy was announced to her; Elizabeth's birth was equally *'miraculous'*, as she was an older lady and post-menopausal. The cult

of John of the Baptist was widespread in the Middle East and never really went away, despite persecutions by the Church, and survives today as the Mandaean faith. It has centres throughout the world, but is particularly strong in Iraq and Iran. They call Jesus *'the deceiver'* and believe that the reason John originally refused to baptise Jesus was not, as the Bible tells us, because John felt unworthy, but because he distrusted Jesus. John was known as, *'The Fisher of Souls'* and *'The Good Shepherd'*, titles which the Mandaeans believe were usurped by Jesus, his one-time disciple.

That aside, John the Baptist was beheaded on the orders of King Herod **(bottom)**, and the Bible tells us that his disciples were allowed to take away his body. Tradition says that John's skull was later in the care of the Knights Templar at Amiens Cathedral, France, where it was known as the Baphomet, and bestowed Grail-like attributes of healing and wisdom when it was drank from. It was the veneration of the goddess Sophia and Mary Magdalene, and drinking from the skull of John the Baptist, that branded the Knights Templar heretics by the Church, and which cost many of them their lives. But it was more than this; what also annoyed the Church was the Templars' continued practice of Gnosticism, by which they sought *direct* contact with the Divine. The great irony of this sad state of affairs is that Jesus himself was probably a Gnostic, and that he sought to demonstrate, by example, that we all possess divinity within.

John the Baptist is often depicted in Church art as somewhat unkempt and disheveled figure, skinny from lack of food, and dressed in rags or animal furs, all of which are deliberate defamations of John by the Church

And yet, this is exactly how I imagine Jesus the shaman, Jesus the wildman, may have looked, especially during his sojourns through the wilderness. Perhaps in images of John the Baptist, such as this one at Lacock Abbey, Wiltshire **(right)**, we may get glimpses of the real Jesus.

Jesus – Man or Myth?

It must be remembered that Jesus was not a Christian by definition, as none existed during his lifetime! He was a Jew, of an ancient Hebrew royal bloodline, and was probably raised in a learned and enlightened household. His formative years, from the age of 12 until 30, are totally missing from the Bible, probably because he was visiting mystery schools, and Gnostic communities, many of which would have been viewed as *'Pagan'*. This would have been unpalatable for the early Christian fathers and writers, which is why we hear nothing of his travels during these years. Some writers have also used this gap in his biography as proof that Jesus never lived (Picknett and Prince 1997). As early as 1903, scholar J M Robertson wrote, *'No one seriously claims that Adonis, Attis and Osiris were historical characters... why, then, is an exception made of the alleged founder of Christianity'.* If Jesus did exist, and I am personally still undecided, perhaps his parallels with ancient, once-mighty gods need not be looked down on by Christians, but taken as a compliment.

To me, it seems that four possibilities exist as to why Jesus' attributes and life events are so similar to several ancient gods and heroes who preceded him:

1) The story of Jesus is entirely fictitious, created by visionary Jewish Gnostics who collected ancient esoteric mystery teachings as signposts to help people tread their spiritual path, and to attain Gnosis, to experience the oneness of all things.

2) Jesus was an historical figure, a reincarnating soul, who purposefully re-enacted myths and legends that he would have been well aware of, so as to reinstate old values that had been lost, choosing well-known stories that people could relate to. He is sometimes shown in scenes with Moses and Elijah (the *Transfiguration*), as shown here at Kelly, Devon **(above & p. 183)**, whom the Church clearly wanted Jesus to be associated with. But were these characters actually previous incarnations of Jesus?

3) Jesus was an incarnation, a physical manifestation, of the same energetic archetype as the gods he so closely resembled. Although the gods of old could be seen as mere fictitious inventions of the imagination, it has been argued on many occasions that, on a metaphysical level, when we *'create'* and imagine gods and goddesses, elves and fairies, nature spirits and demons, we bring them into existence on certain dimensions, potentially bringing them into physical reality. In other words, the physical manifestation of Jesus on the physical plane we call planet Earth was a result of the actualisation of a universal archetype, one that Carl Jung said was present in the greater subconscious of Mankind.

4) Or, lastly, the similarities between Jesus' life circumstances and so many ancient Sun gods are entirely coincidental.

213

I think that we can discount option 4 from the outset. Option 1 has been championed by Tim Freke and Peter Gandy in two noteworthy and well-researched books on the subject (Freke and Gandy, 1999 and 2002). Options 3 and 4 both involve Jesus as a historical person, who lived and died around 2000 years ago in the Middle East. Speaking as an eclectic Gnostic/Pagan, I am still undecided. Perhaps I am viewing Jesus through rose-coloured glasses, with a large dollop of wishful thinking, for it would be inspiring to think that there really existed a wise shaman who preached peace and wisdom as thousands of people gathered around **(left)**, like Apollonius and the Greek philosophers before him. And that this wise soul went on to sacrifice everything, including his life, in order to get the true meaning of his message across to the masses, just like the gods of old. That message was one of pure, unconditional love, like so many gods, prophets and sages before him. Surely this is what is needed right now on planet Earth, regardless of whether he lived or not.

This image **(left)** is of a male figure holding a Sun disc, which I spotted on the font in the church at Spreyton, Devon. This is the ancient solar god no less, still there after all these centuries; sometimes I think we have simply come full circle.

In conclusion, whilst I do not seek to deny anyone their faith, anyone believing that Jesus lived and breathed around 2000 years ago has to do so *despite* the evidence, not because of it.

In Chapter 40, I shall look at the role played by Mary Magdalene in the life of Jesus, and how their story may be but a thinly veiled retelling of the ancient myths and practices concerning *'Sacred Marriage'* and *'Sacred Sexuality'*. But for now, let us look at the archetypal Christian symbol – the cross.

Left: The rays of the Atum (God) raining down on the Egyptian pharaoh Akhenaten.
Right: The light of God illuminating Jesus in the Garden of Gethsemane.

39. The Cross

The cross is a spiritual symbol found as far back as the Palaeolithic, and therefore well predates Christianity. In the Tata Cave, Hungary, a stone disc was found on which was inscribed a cross, dated around 100,000 years old. Crosses carved on a mammoth statuette at Vogelherd, Germany, are around 30,000 years old.

The word *cross* comes, ultimately, from the Latin *crux,* the Roman device used for crucifixion, via the Old Irish word *cros.* To pre-Christians, the cross symbolised totality, the intersection of the two lines representing the uniting of the yin and yang elements. Ancient crosses were often enclosed within a circle and represented wholeness, the 'here and now', a centre point from which all else radiates, the four cardinal compass directions, and the four chambers of the heart, our metaphorical emotional centre (French 2012). The Rosicrucian Cross **(image p. 145)**, has a golden heart in the centre and ten petals representing the perfect Pythagorean number.

When a circle is divided up into eight, the resultant spokes are the rays of the Sun, the Wheel of Life, and represent the eight divisions of the turning year; Karen French considers that, *'Since the cross is integral to the square and the circle, it highlights the way in which every choice, in every moment, is linked to the Universal Plan'* (French 2012, p. 31).

Symmetrical prehistoric crosses represented the Sun, eternal life and the productive powers of Nature, and are seen in the early religious art of Hindus, Buddhists and Jainism. In 336AD, the Syrian philosopher Iamblichus wrote, *'crosses are signs of productive energy and provocation to a continuation of the world'.*

The cross was the emblem of the Assyrian god Shamash, as is shown in this example from the 9th century BC, now in the British Museum **(top)**. I have previously shown an ancient Sumerian frieze on which Tammuz is shown with bunches of grapes and vines in the shape of the cross **(image p. 205)**. A collection of pendants with crosses, dated 2nd millennium BC, was found at Zurich, Switzerland **(centre),** and there are cross glyphs on the Gunderstrup Cauldron **(image p. 185)**. A collection of tombs, known as the *Persian Crosses,* at Naqsh-e Rustam, Iran, were made in the 5th century BC, and are carved into a cliff face in the shape of a cross.

The ankh is a type of cross, and was the most valued and sacred symbol of the Egyptians **(right and images p. 33 & 99)**. It is often depicted in the hands of Sekhmet, Horus, Isis and Anubis.

The ankh combines the tau cross with the vulva/yoni of eternity, the sacred opening from which all issues; the phallus points upwards to the vulva of the Goddess. Egyptians wore the ankh for longevity, and were then buried with the symbol to ensure immortality in the Otherworld. Its shape is relevant, as it is the key that will unlock the gates to eternal life - the ankh was known as the *'Key of the Nile'*. Sometimes a god or goddess is shown placing the ankh at the mouth of the deceased, to engender rebirth, in this case that of Seti I **(left)**. The ankh was even adopted by Coptic Christians as an emblem of life after death.

More solar crosses are shown here, this time from two Bronze Age burials in Sweden. The first **(centre)** is from a *'king's tomb'* at Kivik; the second is from Tossene, and is accompanied by a ithyphallic figure, probably showing its association with a solar god **(third image)**; some early Christian pillar crosses may also have had phallic significance (Bryce 1989).

Australian Aborigines use crosses to control and aid the design of much of their sacred art, and Native American medicine wheels are often laid out incorporating a cross design. To the Vikings, the solar cross was also known as *Woden's Cross*.

Cygnus and Crux are prominent constellations, known as the Northern Cross and Southern Cross respectively. Researchers have found Creation and Otherworld myths associated with Cygnus; the Great Rift, which it houses, was an entrance to the Otherworld, a place of the ancestors. Cygnus is aligned with many sacred sites (Collins 2006, Mann 2011, Biltcliffe and Hoare 2012); in two of my previous works I showed alignments of Cygnus with West Kennet Long Barrow (Knight 2011) and the Cerne Giant (Knight 2013). In Christian times, at least as far back as 592AD, Cygnus was turned into an icon of the Crucifixion, the *'Christi Crux'*. In some depictions, St Helena, mother of Constantine the Great, is shown with this re-mythologised *Northern Cross* **(image p. 115)**. Adrian Gilbert has shown that Cygnus was at the zenith (the highest point in the sky) at the time he calculates that the Resurrection of Jesus took place (Gilbert 2000, p. 231-2).

The Neolithic sites of Callanish, Newgrange and Loughcrew **(below left)**, as well as other passage tombs, have a cruciform plan, a design that was to be emulated thousands of years later in churches and cathedrals across Christendom **(below right)**.

W Ellwood Post illustrates over 60 different designs of Christian crosses (Ellwood Post 1964), as well as various crosses that are the symbols of saints. The cross was a sigil of the Sun god

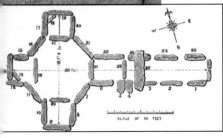

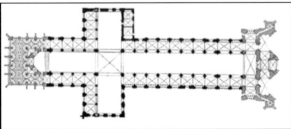

Apollo, and some early Christians even forbade its use because it was such an overtly Pagan symbol, preferring instead the fish or Chi Rho cross, with its angled lines **(right & image p. 16)**. This cross was one of the early symbols used by early Christians in Rome, and is formed by superimposing the first two letters, Chi (X) and Rho (P), of the Greek name for *Christ*. Constantine himself had the symbol put on the shields of his soldiers. Early versions of the cross show the lines crossing at acute angles, like the saltire cross (see below) that represents the path of the Sun, or ecliptic. Later versions show these lines crossing at 90°.

The Church soon realised the pulling power of the Latin cross, with its high crossbar, and it became synonymous with the Crucifixion **(images p. 17 & 56)**; however, it was merely the latest version of the Axis Mundi, the Tree of Life. Crosses with arms of equal length are also common Christian icons. It may, therefore, be surprising to many that the magnificent marble cross shown here **(right)** is not Christian at all, but was unearthed during excavations at Knossos, Crete, and is dated 1600BC!

The saltire cross is in the shape of an X, which is also the Roman numeral for ten. On an Olmec altar at La Venta, Mexico, a saltire cross features just above the mouth of a jaguar, as well as on a Mayan jade axe (Collins 2014, p. 91). The Phoenicians also had an X-shaped motif called the *'taw',* which meant *'mark/'sign'.* All this may have connections with the directions of the sunrise and sunset azimuths of the summer and winter solstices, which form a saltire cross. The cross appears on many national flags across the world, and is also the emblem of St Andrew **(below)**, St Alban, St Patrick and St Osmund. Crossed keys and swords are common in heraldry, and these are also saltire crosses; St Peter's saltire of crossed keys is on the Vatican coat of arms. The well-known emblem of death, the skull and cross-bones, is usually shown as a saltire cross; this image **(right)**, which I saw in Edinburgh, shows both the saltire cross and the cross-bones.

Recent research has suggested that the saltire cross was employed to determine the location of certain sacred sites, which are aligned to form this cross on the landscape, one of which has London at its centre (Thorley ed. 2012). It has also been demonstrated how the Roman roads of Watling Street and the Fosse Way form a saltire cross on the map of England (Heath and Michell 2004), and how this cross defines solstice alignments of Avebury (Mann 2011). It has also been suggested that the crossed keys symbol of St Peter represents two *'Gates of Heaven',* ancient mythical star gates at the two intersections of the ecliptic (the path of the Sun) and the galactic equator (saltire literally means, *'leap into*

Heaven'): 'Perhaps when Jesus entrusted the keys of Heaven to St Peter, it was the saltire star gates he had in mind' (Thorley ed. 2012).

The Celtic or wheel-headed cross incorporates a circle around a centre orb, the Sun, which came to represent God, around which everything revolves. This intricate modern example **(bottom right, previous page)** is one I found at Grittleton, Wiltshire **(also images p. 72 & 82)**. Arguably the finest original Celtic cross is Muiredach's Cross in Ireland, which has Biblical scenes on its faces. Around this time, many old megaliths were remodelled into crosses, or else had crosses carved on them, as in Brittany **(image p. 20)**.

The swastika is a cross that was once used across the ancient world without any negative stigma. It is essentially a spinning cross and appears on numerous pottery from the Neolithic and Bronze Age, such as one 3000BC example from Anatolia in Turkey. The swastika is found on Greek pottery, shown here in Birmingham Museum **(top)**, dated c. 350BC. The swastika can also be found on Celtic and Viking objects, on Sumerian art dating to 3000BC, Cretan coins, Roman mosaics, artifacts found at Troy, Japanese art, and on Navajo blankets. *Swastika* comes from the Sanskrit word for *'well-being - lucky'* and is used as a sacred sigil in Buddhism **(left)**, Sikhism, Jainism and Hinduism, where it is an auspicious symbol, representing wisdom, light, fire, and energy in motion; as a symbol of the fecundity of vegetation, it is sacred to the goddess Maia. The counter-clockwise swastika, or *sauvastika*, was used by the Nazis, and mirrors its use in India as a symbol for Kali, who symbolises death and destruction. It is interesting that the Roman mosaic floor shown here **(left)**, from Saldana in Spain, has swastikas rotating in both directions, reflecting both a spiritual acknowledgement and the Imperialist mindset. The symbol appears quite frequently in early Christian art and monuments, particularly in Rome. The Book of Kells, c. 800AD, contains swastika-shaped decoration, and the motif can be found in many medieval churches.

The cross pattée is one in which the arms narrow towards the centre. A red cross on a white background is associated with the Knights Templar, whilst the black/grey Maltese Cross is the emblem of the Knights of St John (the Hospitallers), both of which are shown here **(left)**; the latter is similar to the Iron Cross awarded to German military personnel.

John the Baptist often holds a staff mounted by a small cross **(image p. 26, 211 & 212)**. At Imbolc, Brighid's crosses **(image p. 23)** are made from dried stems of wheat or barley from the previous year's harvest. The tau cross is in shape of a letter T, and is associated with Moses **(image p. 181)**, and yet the Egyptians used the same cross to signify fertility and life. The name and shape of this cross invites comparison with the T-shaped megaliths of Minorca, which are known as taulas.

At Rosslyn Chapel, there are examples of the engrailed cross of the St Clair family, also known as the Sinclair Cross. Its arms are lined with rugged, concave curves, which can be viewed as the arcs of circles, or indeed trace the form of the centre of the vesica piscis. The cross is said to protect the *'true cross'* of which the Sinclair family were guardians. The wavy lines also represent the *Four Rivers of Paradise* of the Book of Genesis. The engrailed cross is incorporated into the arches at Rosslyn, as well as on shields held by carved angels **(right)**.

The cross is the main symbol of Christianity from its association with the Crucifixion. But Jesus was not the first figure to meet his end in this manner. Crucifixion was used by the Persians, Carthaginians, Macedonians, Greeks and, of course, the Romans (who famously crucified 6000 slaves who had revolted under Spartacus). In Japan, crucifixion was still being carried out in the 19th century, and some early Christian missionaries met their fate in this manner. This method of punishment is still carried out today in Arabia and the United Arab Emirates.

In terms of comparing Jesus to the old solar gods, the classical god Orpheus/Bacchus is shown here on a 1920's drawing of an hematite amulet **(right)**, dated 2-3rd century BC, which bears the inscription, *'Orpheos Bakkikos'.* It was formerly housed in the Kaiser Friedrich Museum in Berlin until it was lost after the collection was dispersed after WWII. As far back as 1926, some scholars had hinted that the object might be a fake; however, I found out that this skepticism was based mainly on the grounds that no images of a Crucifixion scene on a Latin cross had been found as early as that date (they had previously been on a T-shaped cross). But, in my mind, there has to be a 'first' for everything, and perhaps the reason some scholars branded it as a forgery was because it hit a nerve in terms of what it implied. As the object has now been lost to science, it will remain a mystery. But we do know that when the Roman emperor Hadrian visited Alexandria in the early 2nd century AD, he found Christians practicing local pagan-orientated mysteries. It was also recorded by Hippolytus that the Naassenes equated Christ with Pagan *'sacred marriage'* rites performed at Eleusis. This drawing of the lost Berlin object is interesting, in that above Jesus is the Moon (the divine feminine) and below him is a chalice/vulva shape, also symbolic of the feminine principle; the phallus of the cross shaft is literally entering the sacred opening.

Crucifixion by means of a 'T-shaped cross was actually uncommon, as crosses were usually X-shaped, and in many cases people were just suspended from trees and left to die a slow death. In 337AD, Constantine the Great, the first Christian emperor, abolished crucifixion across the Roman Empire out of veneration for Jesus.

One last connection between Jesus and the old solar gods is his halo, which often incorporates a red cross **(bottom and image p. 24)**, which had been the symbol of the Sun for thousands of years; this vivid example is at Ashton, Devon. Jesus is the only Christian character I have found to have this red cross insert; it would seem that the Sun god really did set, only to later rise again.

219

40. The Sacred Marriage

In the natural world, most animals mate and plants pollinate to ensure the furtherance of their species. There once was a time when all ancient cultures saw the union of the divine masculine and the divine feminine as essential for the continuance of all life. This act brought together opposite polarities, the energies of yin and the yang, a mergence seen as vital for the equilibrium of Nature. In emulating the gods, ancient cultures saw the act of sexual union as a natural extension, a confirmation no less, of natural laws. One way of understanding Man's gradual replacement of the goddess with the god is that the last 2000 years have coincided with a progressive withdrawal of our intimacy, both physical and spiritual, with Nature.

In Chapters 16 and 37, I looked at the concepts and sacred symbolism of both the male and female genitalia. But the real divine spark occurred with sexual union. I have already noted how ancient sacred sites often comprise male/yang and female/yin megaliths, such as at Avebury and at Men-an-Tol, Cornwall **(image p. 199)**. This union of the divine feminine with the masculine is also dramatically seen at Silbury Hill around midsummer, as the solar god *'rolls'* down the body of the Earth Mother **(images p. 32)**.

In ancient cultures, most gods and goddesses had consorts or, at the very least, lovers. This was seen as obligatory if the earth was to remain fertile, and with it mankind. A statuette from Romania known as *The Gumelnita Lovers* is dated as Neolithic, c. 4500BC, and may be a representation of a god and goddess **(top)**. In Egyptian mythology, Osiris and Isis were both relatives and lovers **(images p. 15, 33 & 207)**; to Egyptians the world was created by the union of Geb, the earth god, and Nut, the sky goddess **(centre)**. Also illustrated here are two classic A-list divine couples from the Roman pantheon, namely Jupiter with his consort Juno **(left)**, and Mars and Venus **(top, next page)**, the latter of which is a 16th century painting. A phallus and a yoni are carved adjacent to each other on a stone from the Roman fort of Maryport, Cumbria (Bord and Bord 1982, p. 80).

Sacred Prostitution, or Temple Prostitution, was an institution consisting of sexual intercourse or other sexual activity performed in the context of religious worship, such as the fertility rite known as *hieros gamos*. Ancient Near Eastern cultures along the Tigris and Euphrates featured many shrines and temples known as, *'houses of heaven'* at which, according to the 5th-century BC historian Herodotus, rites included sexual intercourse. One Babylonian custom compelled every woman to sit in the temple of Aphrodite and have intercourse with a stranger at least once in her lifetime. To the ancient Greeks, sacred prostitution was recorded in the city of Corinth, where the Temple of Aphrodite employed a significant number of female servants, known as *hetairai*. The Roman emperor Constantine closed down a number of temples

dedicated to Venus in the 4th century AD due to sexual practices, as the Christian historian Eusebius proudly recorded. According to the same writer, the Phoenician cities of Aphaca and Heliopolis also carried out *'temple prostitution'*.

The 'Greek' ruler of Jerusalem (King Antiochus IV Epiphanes) was accused of desecrating the Temple of Jerusalem by rededicating it to Zeus and bringing *'prostitutes'*, the *hetairai*, into the temple to partake in ritual coitus: *'The Gentiles filled the temple with debauchery and revelry; they amused themselves with prostitutes and had intercourse with women even in the sacred court'* (2 Maccabees 6:1-4).

The pivotal sexual act carried out at these temples was hieros gamos. Scholars generally believe that this was a form of the *'sacred marriage'* ritual, such as was staged between the Sumerian king and the High Priestess of Inanna, the goddess of sexual love, fertility, and warfare, shown here on a Sumerian seal **(centre)**. The hieros gamos is said to manifest pure and untarnished love, and is in itself an act that had potency to permeated the world with love and fecundity - for everyone and everything; it is far more profound and wide reaching than the mere act of sex, for there is a sense of perfect openness, intuitive reciprocal love and humility, naked to one another's thoughts and divine intent.

Tantra is the eastern tradition that is often referred to as a technique for the attainment of ecstasy; it comes from the Sanskrit word meaning, *'weaving/web'*, and carvings depicting

this practice adorn many Indian temples **(bottom)**. Tantra refers not only to the merging of male and female energies, but also implies that the very fabric, or web, of life owes its continuation to sexual fusion. These male and female polarities are represented by the lingam and the yoni **(image p. 200)**. Many religious practices and dogma dictate that sex is an anathema to the attainment of a connection with the divine, whereas tantra sees intimate union as a valid *means* to enlightenment. Sexual energy is sometimes symbolised by a coiled serpent, or kundalini, which rises from the base chakra and can be refined into ever more subtle levels through sexual union. The sexual conjoining that follows is that of god and goddess, a blending of souls, where there is neither one without the other - a couple becomes divine, she being Shakti and he Shakta. The Vedic scriptures warn, however, that unless this spiritual transformation takes place, the act of sex is carnal and sinful.

In Sumerian and Hebrew mythology, the sexually dynamic Lilith is shown as a female winged figure **(image p. 37)**. She derived from a Babylonian goddess called Lilitu, which means *'spirit'*. Known as the *Lady of the Night,* Lilith is often depicted naked. Adam and Eve were tempted by the serpent in the Garden of Eden, and yet Eve was merely a reinvention of Lilith, who is shown in this 1892 painting by John Collier **(left)**.

The twinned Nägas of India are often shown as serpents who coil around the other in divine sexual union **(centre)**. This is reminiscent of the Twinned Serpent of the Aztecs, which symbolised the conjoined, balanced polarities of the cosmos **(image p. 121)**, and continued in the form of Gnostic/alchemical dragons **(image p. 132)**. The caduceus is an ancient sigil which comprises two serpents entwined around a central staff **(images p. 123)**; this configuration has been related to landscape alignments such as the St Michael Line (Miller and Broadhurst, 1989), Apollo/Athena Line (Broadhurst and Miller, 2000), and the Belinus Line (Biltcliffe and Hoare, 2012).

In Arthurian myth, King Arthur and Guinevere must wed in order for the land to be fruitful, and when the status quo is upset, Arthur must drink from the Grail in order that he, and the land, are healed; the chalice cup is a classic symbol of the womb – Arthur (male) and the chalice (female) must fuse so the land may be restored. The most familiar icon of this unity of opposites is the Taoist symbol of yin and yang **(image p. 72)** whereby the light also contains the dark, and vice versa.

The multi-headed Hindu god Murugan had many wives **(image p. 117)**, whilst the divine couple of Krishna and Radha are often depicted in scenes full of flowers and natural abundance, symbolising their amorous sentiments. Vishnu and his consort Shri are often seen riding on the back of Garuda, a celestial bird, as they soar through the skies in a state of union. The god Ardhanarishvara is a deity who is both Shiva and Parvati, Shiva's female nature, conjoined down the centre. This example takes the concept of the reconciliation of opposites to its extreme **(bottom)**; note how the figure has but one breast, on the female side. This is mirrored in Greek mythology by Hermaphroditus, the son of Hermes and his consort Aphrodite, who became fused with a female water nymph, and gave his name to the word *hermaphrodite*.

This coming together of polarities is again seen in the vesica piscis symbol, which I dealt with in Chapter 19; the two yin and yang circles overlap to form the vulva of rebirth **(images p. 75)**. In similar vein, the Orphic Egg combines the male principle of the serpent entwined around the egg of life **(image p. 68)**. Incredibly, images of the union of male and female energies continued in medieval Christian architecture, although they were by then seen as representing the *'sins of the flesh'* **(images p. 66)**. The concept of obscenity and sin was of course born of religious piety, and phallic worship became something to be hidden, a taboo subject, and one that was subject to many clerical condemnations. Sex became sinful, and with it countless rites and ceremonies that had been carried out for thousands of years. The story of Adam and Eve and their act of *'Original Sin'* was adopted by literalist Church fathers and forged into a licence to degrade, even outlaw, the act of sexual union, especially outside marriage. Women have never recovered from the ramifications that this disastrous dogma birthed - and neither have men.

Jesus and Mary Magdalene

From Sumeria and Egypt, right through to the early Christian era, the sacred marriage rite between the Virgin/Mother Goddess and her Sun/son-lover god had given mankind its representation of wholeness and fruitfulness, a unifying relationship between Spirit and Nature. So it could be argued that if Jesus was installed as a replacement for the old Pagan solar gods, he too would be expected to have been married, or at least to have had a lover, like the gods of old. Jesus the man would certainly have encountered contemporary Middle Eastern mystery schools, where sexual union was not scorned upon, but embraced. The Gnostic Christian sects, such as the Knights Templar, saw sexual union as a celebration of the union of God and the Goddess (Freke and Gandy 2001), as shown here in this 15th century German painting **(top)**. The Templars practiced the sacred sacrament of ritual intercourse, or *hieros gamos,* causing one early Church writer, Epiphanius, to write how Gnostic sects, *'must ceasingly apply themselves to the mystery of sexual union'.* Many Gnostics believed, as many do today, that Jesus also practiced hieros gamos, or *Sacred Marriage,* and, more than that, may have even taken himself a wife. That wife, of course, is thought by many to have been Mary Magdalene. Research reveals that both Jesus and Mary Magdalene were from high-status families, and both were probably well versed in Gnostic belief systems.

Nowhere in the Bible does it say that Mary Magdalene was a prostitute; if any sexual connotations can be placed on Mary it may be in the context of her role as a priestess in temples where hieros gamos, sacred sex, was practiced. Mary was clearly a high status woman of means for we are told that she sponsored, along with other women, the mission of Jesus. More than this, I believe she was his spiritual equal, an articulate woman well versed in metaphysics. Most scholars now believe that Mary Magdalene and Mary of Bethany was the same person. St Bernard (185-254AD), a Christian theologian in Alexandria, believed this to be the case, and eight centuries later St Bernard of Clairvaux (1090-1153) agreed with him.

It is highly significant that Mary Magdalene was present at some key moments in the life of Jesus, which gives us some glimpses of how important she may have actually been in the unfolding life of Jesus the man. Mary accompanies Jesus throughout his ministry after he had healed her of *'seven demons'* (Luke 8:2, Mark 16:9), which can be interpreted as him balancing/aligning her seven chakras. She is the Mary, sister of

Lazarus, who listened to his teachings, which was exceptional for a woman at that time, and she was rebuked by her sister Martha for it. She famously washes Jesus' feet, as shown here at Winterborne Monkton, Wiltshire **(centre, previous page)**, after which Jesus does likewise to his disciples. It was against the law at that time for a woman to even touch a man in public, let alone wash and dry his feet, *unless they were married*. The archetypal bridegroom of ancient myths could not be complete and whole without his 'mirror' image – his *'other half'*. At the Last Supper, Jesus tells his disciples why they

are not fasting: *'When the Bridegroom is taken away from them, on that day they will fast'* (Mark 2:19-20). Was the wedding in Cana, where Jesus turned water to wine, actually his own, to his bride Mary Magdalene?

Mary Magdalene anoints Jesus' head **(bottom, previous page)** with precious spikenard oil, poured from an alabaster jar, which is her symbol **(image p. 5)**. The pouring of the oil over his head was significant, as it was the traditional practice to anoint a new king in this way. According to Hebrew/Jewish custom, the anointing of the heads of the kings in Sumeria, Babylon and Canaan was carried out by a royal bride or priestess, who represented the Goddess; the king then became the *'anointed one'* or *'Messiah'*. The anointing with spikenard was a charged experience, a divestment of any barriers or separateness, the creation of a complete knowing and understanding and honouring of the other – Jesus and Mary were sharing a sacred and intimate rite. The ancient *Song of Songs* of the Old Testament is believed to have been written by King Solomon around 100BC, and although it refers to Solomon and Sheba, it clearly is analogous to a sacrificed bridegroom. It parallels the anointing by Mary Magdalene of Jesus during their own sacred marriage rite. The *Song of Songs* even makes reference to spikenard!

In scenes of the Crucifixion, although several people are present, I have only ever seen Mary Magdalene depicted at the foot of the cross, often wrapped around it, consumed in her inconsolable grief, some scenes of which have moved me **(top)**. It is she who stays with Jesus as he hangs on the cross when all the others flee (as told in Mark, Matthew and John). In many ancient cultures when a solar/fertility god is slain (such as Osiris, Dumuzi and Adonis), it is the bereaved widow, such as Isis, Inanna, Aphrodite, who grieves, prior to his resurrection; Mary now played out that role.

Mary Magdalene and Joseph of Arimathea took the body of Jesus to a rock-cut tomb that was donated by Joseph, scene tenderly rendered in here at Tavistock, Devon **(centre)**. Later, Mary comes to the tomb with Mary the Mother **(image p. 172)** to anoint the body, but finds it is not there. It is interesting that in John's Gospel (John 20) Mary Magdalene comes to the tomb *by herself*. An angel proclaims that Jesus has risen, in what is known as the Ascension, illustrated here **(left)** in St John's, Glastonbury. Later, she returns and Jesus appears to her and only her the garden, which I think is very telling in regard to her spiritual, and perhaps marital, status. She calls him *'Rabboni'* and reaches out to touch Jesus; in previous translations he says, *'Do not touch me';* However, this has recently been reinterpreted as meaning, *'Do not cling to me',* which has a different meaning, as he tells her that she must emotionally let him go. Mary addresses Jesus by the title of rabbi/priest, and it is perhaps relevant that in the Holy Land at that time a rabbi was compelled to marry, for to refrain from procreation was viewed as an insult to God, and still is amongst Orthodox Jews (Picknett 2003, p. 67). This beautiful window of the scene is in Christchurch Priory, and in it Mary wears *'Magdalene Blue'* **(right)**.

Many books have been written about Mary Magdalene and her relationship with Jesus, as well as what happened after she fled from Jerusalem (McDonald 2006, Picknett 2003, and Starbird 1993 are recommended). Was Mary pregnant? Had she already given birth to a child by Jesus, and did the bloodline of Jesus continue? (Brown 2000). Is it Mary that sits next to Jesus in *The Last Supper* by Da Vinci? **(image p. 203)**, and does the landscape of Rennes-le-Château hold hidden secrets concerning the Magdalene? (Baigent, Leigh and Lincoln 1982); Mary Magdalene is shown here in the church at Rennes-le-Château **(right)**.

From a personal point of view, I have been studying the subject for many years and in the process have come across some Christian depictions that may have been encoded with secrets, visible for those who have eyes to see. At Kilmore, on the Isle of Mull, is the renowned window by Thomas Eversfield, dated 1905, showing Jesus and Mary Magdalene hand in hand, and clearly depicting Mary as pregnant. She is dressed in her *'Magdalene Blue',* mirroring the lapis lazuli and chrysocolla stones of the Magdalene Rosary (McDonald 2006). No one can deny the intimacy of the scene, as the couple hold hands **(right & back cover)**. The inscription beneath the window quotes Jesus when he says, *'Mary hath chosen that good part which shall not be taken away from her'.* Also in the church is a plaque to the memory of Eversfield, which bears the Knights Templar cross.

I have found other images in churches of Mary in which she appears to have a swollen, pregnant-like midriff, a notable one being at Child Okeford, Dorset, where the church guidebook gives her identity of Mary of Bethany; she looks lovingly into the eyes of Jesus, who returns her gaze **(top image, next page)**. Her stomach is swollen and on it she rests her jar of anointing oil.

But the image that both surprised and moved me was a window I came across at the church at St Neot's, Cornwall **(centre, next page)**. Three adjacent windows depict the Crucifixion, and shows Jesus on the cross in the centre, St

225

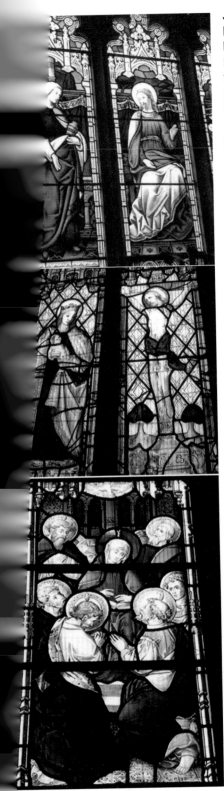

John the Divine on the right, and to the left Mary Magdalene (blond hair and red clothes); in her arms she holds an infant, whom she is holding up to Jesus! I have not read of anyone else who has spotted the relevance in this scene – to me it speaks volumes, and perhaps goes some way to righting a great wrong. The truth is out there if one has eyes to see.

The additional gospels found in recent years have shed new light on Mary and suggest that she was a profoundly wise and spiritual woman, who certainly never was a prostitute, the title that she was undeservedly given. In fact, Mary carried high status amongst some Christian sects, and became the patron saint of the Knights Templar. In some of the new texts, Mary is described as comforting the disciples after the Crucifixion, as well as trying to get them to comprehend Jesus' deeper teachings **(bottom)**. And yet, even today, she is often depicted with long red or blond hair, head uncovered, garbed in red garments – the *'scarlet woman'* no less **(image p. 69)**. In many ways she resembles Jezebel, the Biblical priestess of Baal, daughter of the Phoenician king Sidon; even today the term *'Jezebel'* has negative, sexual connotations. Yet Mary Magdalene represents the free-thinking, feisty, sensuous, sexual essence of women, Venus and Aphrodite incarnate, all qualities that did not sit well with the founding Church fathers. At the Council of Nicaea, in 325AD, Jesus was declared divine, a god no less, and yet, unlike the gods of previous civilisations, he was denied union with the divine feminine; this god was to be, to all intents and purposes, a eunuch, a god to whom women were not seen worthy. But, in Book of Revelations (19:7) we read: *'The marriage of the Lamb is come, and his wife has made herself ready for him'.* It does appear, after all, that Jesus will be allowed to take a wife on his return!

Let's hope that at some time in the future, the balance of yin and yang, man and woman, god and goddess can be returned to world. Perhaps the reason why this has been denied to followers of Jesus for so long is that sacred coitus in a loving relationship can in fact open the door to the process of ascension, the evolution of the individual soul. For me, the great tragedy, and lost opportunity, of Christianity is that it was St Peter who was to drive the fledgling religion forward down its patriarchal road, and not Mary Magdalene as Jesus may have intended.

As she was a priestess, and possibly his wife, it was to Mary Magdalene that Jesus gave the deeper wisdom and spiritual knowledge of Gnosis, teachings that we know went way over the heads of most of the other disciples; she was in fact called, *'The Apostle of the Apostles'.* Her name in full was Mary the Magdalene, a title which comes from *Magdala,* meaning *'tower',* and she was certainly a tower of strength to Jesus whilst he lived, and, I believe, can be an inspiration to us today. She may have been, arguably, the most important woman in history (Picknett 2003), and a reappraisal of her life and her gospel may go a long way to repairing an unbalanced Christianity, in which God was made in the image of men, not women.

I have been amazed how, in so many supposed images of the Virgin and child, Mary is wearing not blue and white, but red and sporting red or blond hair **(image p. 137)**; equally, I have seen many images named as being Mary Magdalene, but which she is shown wearing blue and white. This has made me wonder how many of the latter are really images of Mary Magdalene with *her* child. The example shown here **(right)** is in St Cross church, Winchester, which is a Knights Hospitaller foundation. It is described as an image of the Virgin and child; with an uncovered head, red clothes and long red hair, I think not! In her left hand, the lady in question takes grapes from a tray – the symbol of Jesus; is this imagery telling us that the baby is Jesus, or is it his child?

Jesus made it clear that he was into monogamy, but his liberal views towards women were not represented in the sexually oppressive religion founded in his name.

Lastly, here is a window showing Mary Magdalene in the church at Georgeham, Devon **(right)**. She is shown as a sensuous, feisty woman, with flaming hair and strength of character; the window even depicts the form of her breasts under her garment, which is unusual in Christian stained glass. This independent, purposeful woman is the *real* Mary the Magdalene.

> *'She walks upon our meadows green*
> *The Lamb of God walks by her side*
> *And in every child is seen*
> *Children of Jesus and His Bride'*

William Blake, from *'Song of Jerusalem'*.

Mythology and Symbolism Today

I believe that ancient myths can be just as valid today as they were thousands of years ago. Myths were always intended to be allegories, aids to attaining enlightenment – Gnosis, and there is as much need for this today as ever. The primal urge to *'Know Thyself'* is never far below the surface, in the depths of our consciousness, waiting to be coaxed to break those surface waters, like a majestic whale. Myths and symbols are multi-layered and entwined with hidden meanings and multiple interpretations, and some see this as a detracting attribute, the fact that there is no single answer, no magic bullet. But for me the truth is exactly the opposite, for myths and symbols may trigger

vastly different archetypal imprints to different people, leading us to places we never dreamed of, understandings that were previously beyond our grasp. Myths possess the power to engage not only the mind, but also the heart.

As I have said previously, perhaps we should not enquire as to whether a myth is historically accurate, but rather whether it is spiritually valid – *to us individually*. I believe they can be. The Grail of Arthurian myths had to be recovered in order for Arthur and the land to be healed, and surely it is timely for us to reconnect with that which has been lost, and indeed that which we have been denied. For we are all on our personal Grail Quest, whether we know it or not, and that journey is not one that looks back to the past, but one that creates our future. For we are all simultaneously both the God and the Goddess, and we all possess both the lock and the key to live our lives consciously.

Perhaps only as sacred symbols reveal their true inner meaning and wisdom will pictures really begin to speak a thousand words.

Above: *Anno Domini*, by Edwin Langsden Long (1829-1891). Mary and Joseph with the infant Jesus arrive in Egypt, unnoticed and unannounced. With great irony, there is a grand procession celebrating Isis and Horus (held high in the centre); they are mirrored by the Virgin and the child, on whom would be founded Christianity, which would ultimately replace them.

"Much of the Bible is creative writing, this is true, and old Pagan myths were retold and reinvented with good intention to give the new religion substance. But if we take the Bible as literal fact, we must then ask ourselves if the words contained within the Mabinogion, Le Morte D'Arthur, the Gnostic Gospels, the Bhagavad Gita, the Tao Te Ching, the Qur'an, the Adi Granth, the Vedas, or the Torah are 100% factual records. Myths have been used to get messages across to the masses since time immemorial. The organised religions have merely retold established and ancient creation myths, miracle stories, heroic quests and the like to forward their own agendas. All religions have done it - because the strategy works! .... As to whether a myth is historically true or not - does it really matter?"

Peter Knight, from *'Thirteen Moons - Conversations with the Goddess'.*

Amen Awen - May your god or goddess go with you.

References and Further Reading

Albrecht, Klaus (2001), *Malta's Temples*, self-published.

Allegro, John M (1970), *The Sacred Mushroom and the Cross*, Hodder and Stoughton.

Ashe, Geoffrey (1990). *Mythology of the British Isles*, Guild Publishing.

Bahn, Paul G, and Vertut, Jean (1997), *Journey Through the Ice Age*, Weidenfeld and Nicolson.

Baigent, M, Leigh R, Lincoln H (1982), *The Holy Blood and The Holy Grail*, Jonathan Cape.

Baring, Anne, and Cashford, Jules (1991). *The Myth of the Goddess*. Viking Arkana.

Bauval, Robert, and Hancock, Graham (1996), *Keeper of the Genesis*, Heinemann.

Beamon, Sylvia P (2009), *Royston Cave – Used by Saints or Sinners?* The Temple Publications.

Bédoyère, Guy de la (2002), *Gods and Thunderbolts – Religion in Roman Britain*, Tempus.

Biltcliffe, Gary (2009), *The Spirit of Portland – Revelations of a Sacred Isle*, Roving Press.

Biltcliffe, Gary, and Hoare, Caroline (2012), *The Spine of Albion*, Sacred Lands Publishing.

Bord, Janet and Colin (1982), *Earth Rites*, Granada.

Bord, Janet and Colin (1986), *Sacred Waters*, Paladin.

Brennan, Martin (1994), *The Stones of Time: Calendars, Sundials and Stone Chambers of Ancient Ireland*, Inner Traditions International.

Brighton, Simon, and Welbourn, Terry (2010), *Echoes of the Goddess*, Ian Allan.

Broadhurst, Paul (1992), *Tintagel and the Arthurian Mythos*, Pendragon Press.

Broadhurst, Paul (2006), *The Green Man and the Dragon*, Mythos.

Brown, Dan (2000), *The Da Vinci Code*, Bantam.

Bryce, Derek (1994), *Symbolism of the Celtic Cross*, Llanerch Publishers.

Burke, John, and Halberg, Kaj (2005), *Seed of Knowledge, Stone of Plenty*, Council Oak.

Cater, Karen (2010), *Spirit of the Hare*, Hedingham Fair.

Collins, Andrew (2006), *The Cygnus Mystery*, Watkins.

Collins, Andrew (2014), *Göbekli Tepe – Genesis of the Gods*, Bear & Co.

Critchlow, Keith (2007), *Time Stands Still*, Floris.

Devereux, Paul (2000), *The Sacred Place*, Cassell & Co.

Dhanjal, Beryl (2008), *Signs and Symbols*, Chartwell.

Doel, Fran and Geoff (2001), *The Green Man in Britain*, Tempus.

Ehrman, Bart D (2012), *Did Jesus Exist?* Harper Collins.

Ellwood Post, W (1964), *Saints, Signs and Symbols*, SPCK.

Foley John (1993), *The Guinness Encyclopedia of Signs and Symbols*, Guinness.

Freke, Tim, and Gandy, Peter (1999), *The Jesus Mysteries*, Thorsons.

Freke, Tim, and Gandy, Peter (2002), *Jesus and the Goddess*, Thorsons.

French, Karen L (2012), *The Hidden Geometry of Life*, Watkins.

Furlong, David (1997), *The Keys to the Temple*, Piatkus.

Gardiner, Philip, and Osborn, Gary (2005). *The Serpent Grail*, Watkins.

Gibson-Forty, John (2012), *The Interconnectedness of All Things*, Quicksilver.

Gilbert, Adrian (2000), *The Signs in the Sky*, A R E Press.

Green, Miranda (1989), *Symbol and Image in Celtic Religious Art*, Routledge.

Hannat, Sara (2011), *Mummers, Maypoles and Milkmaids*, Merrell.

Harding, Mike (1998), *A Little Book of the Green Man*, Aurum Press.

Harwood, Jeremy (2006), *The Freemasons*, Hermes House.

Heath, Robin, and Michell, John (2004), *The Measure of Albion*, Bluestone Press.

Hicks, Clive (2000), *The Green Man – A Field Guide*, Compass Books.

Hinkley Allen, R (1899), *Star Names and Their Meanings*, The Lost Library.

Hodges, Michael (1998). *Helis, the Cerne Giant and his Links with Christchurch*. Self-published.

Hodges, Michael (2008), *Here Be Dragons*, Natula.

Husain, Shahrukh (1997), *The Goddess*, Duncan Baird.

Hutton, R (1996), *The Stations of the Sun*, Oxford University Press.

Jones, Kathy (1994), *Spinning the Wheel of Ana*, Ariadne.

Jung, Carl (1964), *Man and His Symbols*, Aldus.

Kelly, Eamonn P (1996), *Sheela na Gigs – Origins and Functions,* Country House.

Knight, Peter (1996), *Ancient Stones of Dorset,* Power Publications.

Knight, Peter (1998), *Sacred Dorset – on the Path of the Dragon,* Capall Bann.

Knight, Peter, and Power, Mike (2000), *Dorset Pilgrimages: A Millennium Handbook,* Power Publications.

Knight, Peter (2001), *The Grey Mare and Her Colts – The Goddess, the Sun God and Sirius,* Journal No. 2, Dorset Earth Mysteries Group.

Knight, Peter (2007 and 2010), *Thirteen Moons – Conversations with the Goddess,* Stone Seeker Publishing.

Knight, Peter, and Perrott, Toni (2008), *The Wessex Astrum – Sacred Geometry in a Mystical Landscape,* Stone Seeker Publishing.

Knight, Peter (2011), *West Kennet Long Barrow – Landscape, Shamans and the Cosmos,* Stone Seeker Publishing.

Knight, Peter (2013), *The Cerne Giant – Landscape, Gods and the Stargate,* Stone Seeker Publishing.

Knight, Peter, and Wallace, Sue (2014), *Calne – Gateway to Ancient Wiltshire,* Stone Seeker.

Krönig, Jürgen (2001), *The Secret Face of Nature,* Gothic Image.

Larousse (1974), *The New Larousse Encyclopedia of Mythology,* Hamlyn.

Leith, Yuri – ed. (2013), *Signs and Secrets of the Glastonbury Zodiac,* Avalonian Aeon.

Lincoln, Henry (1991), *The Holy Place – Decoding the Mystery of Rennes-le-Château,* Jonathan Cape.

Mann A T (1993), *Sacred Architecture,* Element.

Mann, Nicholas R (2002), *Reclaiming the Gods,* Green Magic.

Mann, Nicholas R (2011), *Avebury Cosmos,* O Books.

Mann, Nicholas R, and Glasson, Philippa (2007), *The Star Temple of Glastonbury,* Temple Publications.

Matthews, John (2002), *The Summer Solstice,* Godsfield Press.

McDonald, Jan (2006), *Mary Magdalene – Lost Goddess, Lost Gospels,* Capall Bann.

Meaden, Terence (1991), *The Goddess of the Stones,* Souvenir Press.

Meaden, Terence (1999), *The Secrets of the Avebury Stones,* Souvenir Press.

Michell, John (1983), *The New View Over Atlantis,* Thames and Hudson.

Millar, Ronald (1997), *The Green Man – Companion and Gazetteer,* SB Publications.

Miller, Hamish, and Broadhurst, Paul (1989), *The Sun and the Serpent,* Pendragon.

Miller, Hamish, and Broadhurst, Paul (2000), *The Dance of the Dragon,* Pendragon.

Neasham, Mary (2004), *The Spirit of the Green Man,* Green Magic.

Neumann, Erich (1972), *The Great Mother: An Analysis of the Archetype,* Princetown.

Newman, Paul (1987), *Gods and Graven Images,* Robert Hale.

North, John (1996), *Stonehenge – Neolithic Man and the Cosmos,* Harper Collins.

O'Donnell, Mark, and Airey, Raje (2005), *The Complete Encyclopedia of Signs and Symbols,* Anness Publishing.

Oxford University Press (1967), *The Bible,* Oxford University Press.

Pakenham, Thomas (1996), *Meetings with Remarkable Trees,* Cassell.

Phillips, Graham (2002), *The Moses Legacy,* Sidgwick and Jackson.

Picknett, Lynn (2003), *Mary Magdalene – Christianity's Hidden Goddess,* Robinson.

Picknett, Lynn, and Prince, Clive (1997), *The Templar Revelation,* Bantam.

Pitts, Mike (2000), *Hengeworld,* Century.

Queally, Jackie (2007), *The Spiritual Meaning of Rosslyn's Carvings,* self-published.

Raine, Kathleen (1970), *William Blake,* Thames and Hudson.

Rosslyn, Earl of (2012), *Rosslyn Chapel,* Rosslyn Chapel Trust.

Scott, George Ryley (1966), *Phallic Worship - a History of Sex and Sexual Rites,* Senate.

Starbird, Margaret (1993), *The Woman with the Alabaster Jar,* Bear and Co.

Stewart, Malcolm (2011), *Symbols of Eternity,* Floris Books.

Street, Chris (1990), *Earthstars,* Earthstars Publishing.

Taylor, Richard (2003), *How to Read a Church,* Rider.

Thom, Alexander (1967), *Megalithic Sites In Britain,* Oxford.

Thorley, Anthony, ed (2012), *Legendary London and the Spirit of Place,* Archive Publishing.

Tilly, Chris (1994), *A Phenomenology of Landscape,* Berg.

Tresidder, Jack (2000), *Symbols and Their Meanings,* Duncan Baird.

Trubshaw, Bob (2011), *Singing up the Country,* Heart of Albion.

Wallace-Murphy, Tim (2005), *Cracking the Symbol Code,* Watkins.

Wallace-Murphy, Tim, and Hopkins, Marilyn (1999), *Rosslyn – Guardian of the Secrets of the Holy Grail,* Element.

Ward, Geoff (2006), *Spirals – The Pattern of Existence,* Green Magic.

Weir, Anthony, and Jerman, James (1999), *Images of Lust,* Routledge.

Westropp, H, and Wake, C (1875), *Ancient Symbol Worship,* The Book Tree (1999 ed.).

Whitlock, Ralph (1979), *In Search of Lost Gods,* Phaidon Press.

Whitlock, Ralph (1983), *Here be Dragons,* George Allen and Unwin.

Williams, Mike (2010), *Prehistoric Belief – Shamans, Trance and the Afterlife,* The History Press.

Willis, Roy, et al (1993), *World Mythology – the Illustrated Guide,* Duncan Baird.

Acknowledgements

Although I took a large percentage of images in this book myself, I must thank the following for the use of their images or their resources: Sue Wallace, Pete Harlow, Google Art Project, Devizes Museum, Wikipedia. I also thank the great painters from the past, whose works I have used, some of whom left coded messages in their brush strokes.

The following people (sometimes identified only by their online pseudonym) are credited for donating their work for free use under the Wikipedia Common License:

Carl Bloch, J. Miall, G. Dallorto, Guiseppe Angelleli, Jean Clottes, Edning, Idobi, Anne Burgess, Glyn Baker, Otter, Johanne McInnis, Zafram, S J Reed, Rufus46, Renata, Sureshcnair, Optimist on the Run, Studio 31, Jason Pratt, Tourism NT, The Yorck Project, Andrew Bossi, David Liam Moran, de Benutzerverwustung, Andreas Praefcke, Tahc, Hispalois, Austin Henry Layard, Anagoria, Suseno, James Tissot, Anagoria, Joe Rabel, De Molai, Kober, Golden Meadows, PD-Art, London Dodd, Bibi Saint-Pol, M.E. Winge, Demeester, Mark Zamoyski, Frieda, Agtfjott, Edal Anton Lefterov, Guido Reni, T Wright, El Commandante, Judy Smidt, Orlovic, Dnaloroi, Hawobo, Prithvi Man Chitrakari, Prasiliades, Jean-noel Lafargue, Seeros123, Akoliasnikoff, Johanne McInnis, Saya M, Sergey Serous, Iokath, Jacob Bryant, Antonio De Lorenzo, Public Works Dept., Matthias Süben, Robin Leicester, British Museum, William Blake, Maria Reiche, Tuxrader, Daderot, Al Mare, Klaus Peter Simon, Gerard Ducher, Alchemist-hp, Gryffindor, Ssolbergj, G Dall, Orto, Roman Museo Barraco, Lewis-Williams Clottes, Young Bohemian, R J Gibb, Steven G Johnson, Radomil, Jonoikobangali, Pietro Lorenzetti, Marie Lan Nguyen, Siga, Jastrow, Man Vji, Karen Rose, Ingo Zwank, Carole Raddato, Bibi Saint-Pol, Rosemania, Jeff Dahl, Ravi Valma, Adrian Pingstone, Michael Gunther, Geni, ATSZ56, Michael F Mehnert, Jack Ma, Sovery, Little Honey Bee, Etan J Tal, Joe Mabel, Laiki ac, Ardfern, Kev747, Andreas F Borchet, Motacilla, Janet Richardson, Jaqian, Ramanarayanadatta astri, Mariano, Olaf Tausch, Monfie, Ameins, Raymond Spekking, Si Garb, Subramaniam KV, Ricardo Liberato, AW 58, Benh Lieu Song, The BIH Lover, Tony Grist, Urban, Rosmaria, Locutus Borg, Jastrow, Ad Meskens, Lloyd Baltazar, Ross Berteig, Chris Nas, Sailko, Henry Walters, Paul Barlow, Cristian Chirita, Shiv Shankar, Roi Dagobert, Claire H, Gryffindor, A Parrot, Louvre Museum, Jastrow, Israel Government Press Office, Pvasilladis, Bjoertvedt, Nachbarnebanan, Uwe Glaubach, Marshall Astor, Bazara Art, Hawobo, and Wootton Courtenay.

I would also like to thank Sue Wallace, for help compiling the index, taking several of the images, for mercilessly carrying out the proof-reading, and her unwavering support, which included many gallons of tea. And finally, thanks once again to the excellently efficient staff at the Chippenham branch of my printers, CPI Antony Rowe.

About the Author

Peter Knight is well known for his inspirational PowerPoint presentations, workshops, and field trips on topics relating to sacred sites, ancient wisdom and dowsing. He has been leading tours to sacred sites since 1995 and has spoken at several international conventions in the USA, Malta, and around the UK. He is co-founder of the Dorset Earth Mysteries Group and has been awarded honorary membership of both the Dorset Dowsers and the Antiquarian Society. He is also a member of the Wyvern Dowsers and the Society of Leyhunters.

This is the author's 10th book, and he has also contributed to several magazines and journals. He has appeared on BBC local radio, and on TV, such as on Channel 4's *Don Roamin''* with Monty Don, and ITV's *Weekend Escapes with Warwick Davis*. Peter is the founder and organiser of the *Convention of Alternative Archaeology and Earth Mysteries*, held annually in Wiltshire, which gives a platform to both new and leading researchers. In 2004, he established Stone Seeker Publishing, and in 2005 launched Stone Seeker Tours, which promotes holistic tours of sacred sites across the UK. He also conceived and hosts the *Ancient Ambient Chill-Out*, combining world music with large-screen images of sacred sites, planet Earth, and tribal cultures.

His PowerPoint presentations are informative and inspiring. The subjects include the Sacred Symbolism, the Cerne Giant, West Kennet Long Barrow, Avebury, Stonehenge, Ireland, Malta, Dorset, Glastonbury, Brittany, dowsing and earth energies, and stone circles (see website for details).

Peter lives near Avebury and his interests include walking, drumming, world music, dowsing, prehistoric art, astronomy, shamanism, and nature photography. He is a grandfather, a vegetarian, and follows a goddess-orientated spirituality, whilst honouring all spiritualities and religions. He is co-founder of the Calne Environmental Network, which endeavours to make his town more sustainable and wildlife friendly.

His 'mission' is to help people connect with sacred sites and sacred landscapes, as a means of enhancing the lives of individuals, and to actively promote planetary healing.

Peter is available to do inspiring full-colour presentations about this book to local groups and societies, as well as to lead field trips.

Contact Peter:
stoneseeker@waitrose.com

Web site: www.stoneseeker.net
Peter also has a Facebook page

Index

235

Hedgehog; detail of St Fr
window, Islington, Dev